Praise for Regina Leeds' *One Year to an Organized Work Life*

"Use this guide to organize your office—and mind."
—*Shape*

"Streamline one domain a month to prune clutter and spur productivity."
—*Self*

"Readers should find plenty of smart, straightforward and rewarding ways
to eliminate chaos from their work lives."
—*Publishers Weekly*

Praise for Regina Leeds' *One Year to an Organized Life*

"Making your New Year's resolutions? If your goal is to finally clear the clutter,
One Year to an Organized Life will break the task down week by week."
—*Parade*

"This 12-month guide offers the chronically messy a genuine sense of serenity."
—*USA Today*

"Not only shows us the importance of organization, [but] takes us week-by-week
through the chaos of our lives and tells us how to get it together, from schedules
to scrapbooks to celebrating holidays."
—*Minneapolis Star Tribune*

"If this week-by-week guide to getting yourself organized
won't do the trick, give up."
—*Newsday*

"This easy-to-use … domicile detox program will help you
tackle every inch of your life."
—*Women's Health*

"The perfect book for anyone wanting to find important papers instantly
or have a navigable closet. Full of useful information for everyone,
from the person who needs simply to clean a messy desk to the person
requiring a whole new approach to life; highly recommended."
—*Library Journal*

ONE YEAR TO AN
ORGANIZED FINANCIAL LIFE

ALSO BY REGINA LEEDS

One Year to an Organized Work Life

One Year to an Organized Life

The Complete Idiot's Guide to Decluttering

Sharing a Place without Losing Your Space:
A Couples Guide to Blending Homes, Lives, and Clutter

The Zen of Organizing: Creating Order and Peace
in Your Home, Career, and Life

ONE YEAR TO AN
ORGANIZED
FINANCIAL LIFE

From Your Bills to Your Bank Account,
Your Home to Your Retirement,
the Week-by-Week Guide to Achieving
Financial Peace of Mind

REGINA LEEDS
WITH RUSSELL WILD

Da Capo

LIFE
LONG

A Member of the Perseus Books Group

Editorial production by *Marra*thon Production Services. www.marrathon.net

DESIGN BY JANE RAESE
Set in 12-point Bulmer

Cataloging-in-Publication Data for this book is available from the Library of Congress.

First Da Capo Press edition 2010
ISBN 978-0-7382-1367-5

Published by Da Capo Press
A Member of the Perseus Books Group
www.dacapopress.com

Da Capo Press books are available at special discounts for bulk purchases in the U.S. by corporations, institutions, and other organizations. For more information, please contact the Special Markets Department at the Perseus Books Group, 2300 Chestnut Street, Suite 200, Philadelphia, PA 19103, or call (800) 810-4145, ext. 5000, or e-mail special.markets@perseusbooks.com.

10 9 8 7 6 5 4 3 2 1

This book is dedicated to Jamie Ann De Stefano . . .

. . . cousin, mentor, and friend.

CONTENTS

ONE YEAR TO AN
ORGANIZED FINANCIAL LIFE

Introduction

Reflect upon your present blessings, of which every man has plenty;
not on your past misfortunes, of which all men have some.

—CHARLES DICKENS

CERTAIN FOUR-LETTER WORDS CAUSE a stir when uttered in polite society. But a simple five-letter word seems to trump them all: money. You would think it was the Devil's own invention the way some respond. We treat money as if it had a magical power all its own. We say it "slips through our fingers" or, worse, "burns a hole in our pocket." Some believe it's "the root of all evil." Gordon Gekko, in the movie *Wall Street,* felt that "greed is good," while saints of all religions have exhorted us to give it all away and live simply. What's a person to do?

GETTING A FRESH PERSPECTIVE

Money itself is neither good nor bad. If it's managed with wisdom and care, however, it can bring much good into our lives. The goal of *One Year to an Organized Financial Life* is to bring clarity, simplicity, and order to your finances—helping you feel secure for the future, no matter what life throws at you (or your bank account).

Really, money is nothing more than a tool. A hammer can help you build a home, or you can drop it on your toe and yelp in pain. The power lies not in the hammer but with you and the decisions you make about how to use it. Just so, money can help you keep a roof over your head, educate your kids, secure your retirement, and travel the world. A lack of a financial plan, or an obsession with it, can turn an otherwise good life into one of constant struggle and sweat. Are you the friend who always picks up the tab at dinner? Are you driven to buy the trendiest clothes? Nothing is inherently wrong with being generous with your money or fashionable. However, if these traits are, over time, leaving you without emergency funds, a retirement portfolio, or adequate medical insurance, you might want to adjust your priorities.

As the world economy has tumbled and seemed to reinvent itself, it has become evident that everyone must take responsibility for his or her own financial well being. For example, do you know how much cash you have in the bank? Are you aware of the total you owe on credit cards and what interest rate you are paying? Is your family adequately covered by insurance? Could you be paying less for your mortgage? Do you follow the progress of your investments? Are you on track for retirement? How might you find qualified professionals to guide you, if you need assistance? The average person runs the engine of his or her personal economy as if it were controlled by a runaway train. We close our mental and emotional eyes and hope for the best.

Often, beyond not knowing what we owe, we have no idea how the money we earn is spent. "'Budget?' I don't have the time." A 2008 National Foundation for Credit Counseling survey of Americans' spending habits found that just 42 percent use monthly budgets and that 64 percent had not ordered their credit report in the past year. And MSN Money reports that nearly 30 percent don't know the interest rates on their credit cards.

As a professional organizer, I don't make stock picks for my clients. I can, however, show you how to keep each aspect of your finances organized in a simple, easy-to-retrieve fashion so that the decisions you make are informed. And with the help of my coauthor, expert financial planner Russell Wild, we'll open the door of understanding to some areas that may have confused or mystified you in the past. If your eyes glaze over at the mere

Russell Wild and I decided to present a united front by using the pronoun *I* throughout the book, with the occasional *we* tossed in for good measure. You can probably guess who knows more about creating a great file system and who wrote the passages about mortgages. We've taught each other a lot this past year. And now you'll benefit from our collaboration.

mention of a Roth IRA, you're holding the right book. After all, knowledge is power.

Taking care of business when it comes to finance can be a daunting task, and surely one the average person puts on hold for a variety of reasons. Perhaps you haven't known where to begin or who to go to for guidance. Maybe you were so afraid of making a bad move in investing that you decided not to get involved. The stock market can wait, you thought. It all boils down to fear. In this book, Russell Wild and I give you a basic financial education. And you have a year to complete your studies and implement as much of the program as you are comfortable embracing. Rome, after all, wasn't built in a day.

HARRY AND SALLY'S STORY

Several years ago I organized the home of a wonderful man I'll call Harry. He lived in a large house outside a major metropolitan area. He was married to a great lady and they had three children. It was clear that

Harry's career as a top attorney afforded a luxurious lifestyle. Every nook and cranny of the house, however, was filled with unnecessary and space-robbing stuff. How had they accumulated it all? This is the story Harry shared with me.

Harry met Sally when he was in college. They fell madly in love and decided to get married while he was in graduate school. Neither came from a wealthy family, so the frugal life of a law student and his wife was simply a continuation of their childhood experience with money. When Harry graduated at the top of his class, he was hired by a prestigious law firm; for the first time, they had a large income.

Neither Harry nor Sally had ever created a budget. Nor did they have a clue how to invest or manage the sudden influx of funds. With their newfound wealth, they denied themselves nothing. High-end furniture, top-of-the-line-kitchen equipment, and expensive linens began to fill their small apartment. Then they decided to buy a big house, which they promptly filled before their first baby arrived. Soon, instead of watching their money grow, they were watching their credit card bills soar. One day they realized that they had a problem and decided to get financially sober.

Harry and Sally worked with a financial planner and made a commitment to stop their out-of-control spending. They put into place a budget, a savings plan, and an investment plan, and the first order of business was to pay off those credit cards.

Years later, however they were still weighed down by all those purchases they had made. They had so much clutter, it was not only overflowing their home but also filling several rented storage units! (An expense they hadn't shared with their financial planner because they were ashamed.) I was called in to restore order to the home and release them from the bondage of those units. Now financially solvent, it was time to put the last piece of the financial-order puzzle in place. In every case, clutter represents some type of issue. In Harry's and Sally's case, clutter was a relic from their days of profligate spending.

THE TWELVE-MONTH PLAN

Each of us is buffered by the winds of economic change in unique ways. Has your home lost considerable value? Did your sister just lose her job and with it her medical insurance? Or perhaps your 401(k) did a bigger vanishing act than Houdini at the height of his powers? There is an old saying: It isn't what happens to you in life that matters. It's how you handle it. If your financial world is spinning out of control, you might make the unconscious decision to ignore yourself. Suddenly you aren't eating well, you're swilling caffeinated beverage, and you aren't getting enough sleep. Stress may tempt you to live solely in your head where worry festers.

Too often, we seek to make sweeping changes overnight but then get overwhelmed by the amount of work to do or frustrated that everything can't be accomplished at once. I firmly believe that given the manageable timeframe of a year, anyone can change his or her life for the better. In this book, each month covers a different aspect of our financial lives. Here are a few highlights of what you'll find throughout the book:

- Organize your files (plus your wallet and purse)
- Assess your current financial situation
- Get your bills paid on time
- Save on your taxes
- Cut costs while saving time and personal energy
- Stick to a budget
- Get out of credit card debt
- Maximize your retirement savings
- Hire a financial planner
- Clear the clutter
- Teach your kids about money
- Find the insurance you need—and don't need
- Curb your holiday spending
- End-of-the-year decisions to save on taxes

This is *not* a book about "beating the stock market," speculating on real-estate foreclosures, setting up offshore tax havens, or getting rich quick. Rather, it is a holistic resource about getting a firm handle on your finances and understanding the basics of managing your money effectively so that you can live a life that is calmer, richer, and organized.

You'll be able to reference the months out of sequence if you want with one caveat: Peruse the material in the first two months before you create your own journey. The work you do at the start lays a firm foundation for everything that follows. You need a realistic picture of your current financial life before you can change it for the better. In addition, a functioning work space and file system will help maintain your relationship with the newly organized aspects of your financial life.

All the books in the *One Year to . . .* series have a four-weeks-to-the-month schedule. But every quarter has thirteen weeks, so use the free week to get caught up and stay on schedule. Finally, remember that this book can be started at any time of the year. The right time to begin is now.

ZEN FINANCIAL ORGANIZING

The philosophy we use throughout this book is Zen Organizing. When I was growing up, I had no idea my mother was organized. I thought everyone lived in a home that was free of piles and followed the mantra: "There is a place for everything and everything must be in its place so that the next time you need or want it you'll be able to find it." There was a feeling in our home of peace and calm. After I became a professional organizer, I noticed that newly organized areas in my clients' homes quite literally felt different than they had before we began our work of transforming the space. The spaces no longer felt angry, stressed, and chaotic. They felt like my childhood home.

I wanted to write a book about this so I could reach a wider audience. But how would I describe this transformation? What would be the word or words that would give my readers instant recognition? One day a client said to me: "Oh! You mean it's Zen-like!" For the average Westerner, the word *Zen* conjures an image of a peaceful, clean, calm environment decorated with minimal objects. At that moment I knew I had the word.

I became the Zen Organizer. My first book was called *The Zen of Organizing,* and I have used the concept in my subsequent *One Year to an Organized Life* books. You don't have to reduce your possessions until you feel as though you are living in a prison cell. Nor is it necessary to become a Zen practitioner or twist your body into complex yoga poses. Zen Organizing is about creating *systems* that will provide a place for everything in your life. When life brings chaos and upset, as it inevitably will, you will not have to begin at square one. You'll have a system in place that simply needs to be restored.

But Zen Organizing is about more than systems. It's about you. My goal is to help you create environments that inspire, sustain, and nurture you. I want to free you from ones that inhibit, limit, and drain you emotionally, physically, spiritually, and financially. The environments I speak of are those in the physical world around you as well as the one you create in your head. If your inner dialogue is fixated on clutter and lack, no amount of Zen Organizing can free you. In many respects my function in these pages is that of a life coach.

But to apply Zen Organizing to the world of money and investing, you also need a hands-on financial guru. And that's where my wonderful coauthor, Russell Wild, comes in. Russell Wild knows money. A Registered Investment Advisor licensed by the Pennsylvania Securities Commission, he is also a NAPFA-certified, fee-only financial planner. Russell has worked with hundreds of clients over the years to help them manage their finances. He holds an MBA in international management and finance from the Thunderbird School of Global Management, in Glendale, Arizona. He is also the author of numerous other books on personal finance. After reading this book, you might want to read his *Index Investing for Dummies, Bond Investing for Dummies,* or *Exchange-Traded Funds for Dummies.*

Together, Russ and I have created a week-by-week organizing system to transform your financial life.

THE MAGIC FORMULA

I started my organizing career more than twenty years ago. It didn't take very long to see a pattern emerge with all my clients. The garage, the clothes closet, the kitchen cupboards, even the file cabinet all came to order following the same three steps. What varied was the item I had in my hands, not the approach.

Later I discovered that the steps could be applied not only to areas of a home or an office but also to processes: completing a project for work or school, planning a party, even packing a suitcase. These three steps—eliminate, categorize, and organize—struck me as nothing short of magical, hence the name the Magic Formula. During the writing of this book, I applied these steps to organizing your personal finances. Let's take a look at the power of Eliminate, Categorize, and Organize.

Eliminate

The whole of any project is overwhelming until you eliminate what you no longer want, need, or use. In the world of organizing, elimination is actually a creative step because you have a multitude of options. You might donate an item to a charity, return something to a store for credit or exchange, or simply return the item to the area of your home or office where it belongs.

When it comes to organizing your finances, however, tossing and shredding become your new best friends. You'll find that once the elimination phase is complete, the area you are working in looks and feels less daunting. You'll find yourself eliminating in other creative ways. Perhaps you won't renew those magazine subscriptions you never have time to read. Or maybe you'll bring your morning coffee to work in a thermos rather than stopping at the local designer coffee house. You might pocket enough in a year to save for something you really do need.

Categorize

The second step in the Magic Formula, categorize, happens *while* you are working the elimination phase. You don't have to go back and handle again all the items you have chosen to keep. As you go along, you simply put them in designated areas and, voila!, you have categories.

Categories make you powerful. Keeping related items together allows you to have inventory control. You won't be buying multiples of items and exclaiming: "Why didn't I know I already had five boxes of pens?" You'll be saving money! In addition, creating categories means that all your insurance policies, income tax deductions, and mortgage or rent payment receipts (to name but a few possibilities) will be together rather than scattered in piles around your home.

Organize

During the last phase of the Magic Formula—organize—you make use of the tips, tricks, and guidelines set forth in this book. You can also employ wonderful products designed to help even the most inexperienced organizer function like a pro. Imagine the sweet smell of success when a family member, mortgage broker, or tax preparer asks you for a specific document regarding your finances and you can put your finger on that information in seconds. That's the power of the Magic Formula in a nutshell.

PAVE THE WAY FOR (POSITIVE) CHANGE

When I lecture across the country, some of my students tell me they want to get organized but feel overwhelmed. How can they jump-start the process? The best way is to create positive new habits. Psychologists have found that it takes twenty-one consecutive days of repeating an action before it becomes a habit. *Consecutive* and *action* are the key words. The intention of this book is to help you organize your finances, but you have a residence and most likely a job or career outside the home. Life is a balance, and *everything* needs to work in concert to keep you productive and positive.

Take a look around. Is your home tidy or do you see stuff scattered everywhere? Are dirty dishes stacked in the kitchen sink? Did you wake up this morning without a thought about making your bed? Is every horizontal surface covered with papers, magazines, mail, and newspapers? This kind of environment will add to your stress and create depression.

Why am I asking these questions in a book about getting your financial life in order? What does making your bed have to do with your portfolio? The simple answer is "everything." A wonderful Zen proverb says: "The way a man does one thing is how he does everything." You don't have to believe it now. Suspend judgment for the moment and go along for the ride. In a year I predict your face will have a big smile of recognition!

To help you create the positive energy you need to get your life and your finances in order, I recommend the following:

- Make your bed every morning.
- Never leave dirty dishes in the sink.
- Don't allow clean dishes to languish on the drainboard.

- Put your keys in the same place the minute you come home.
- Create a set place for items that are forever getting lost (such as reading glasses or the remote control).

Master just two of these tasks at a time. This is a deceptively simple list, but you'll be amazed what a challenge it can be to repeat these actions for twenty-one consecutive days. You'll be equally amazed by the transformation they make in your environment. If you are feeling overwhelmed, success with the tasks in this list will build your self-esteem. Your home will feel and look more in keeping with the organized way you want to live. Chaos spreads like a fungus throughout the home and into your finances. It breeds exhaustion and depression. Order has energy as well and spreads peace and calm. Everything starts to feel possible—even a balanced budget and an early retirement.

You'll find that the habits you cultivate at home will have counterparts when it comes to organizing your financial life. Remember that nicely made bed? A clear desk at the end of your work day will bring the same sense of ending one aspect of your day as another begins. After you start putting away items such as dishes, keys, and glasses, it's only a matter of time before you file all your financial papers in the correct folders. In the world of Zen Organizing, the organizing principles stay the same; the objects shift and change.

Each month begins with a new financial habit for you to cultivate. You'll find that you embrace some instantly while others elude you. Give it your best shot. Along with the new habit, you will find a tool. Topics such as drinking plenty of water, getting enough sleep, and meditation may not seem like they belong in a book about financial organization. The reality, however, is that these are universal tools that help you do your best work in every area of your life. Give each one the old college try. You have nothing to lose and everything to gain.

THE JOURNEY BEGINS

During our year together, you'll be reading about many nuts-and-bolts issues of finance, such as budgeting, taxes, and investments. But I'll also be encouraging you to take care of yourself and your environment, to monitor your thoughts, and to never lose sight of your dreams. These are the seeds of your future experience. And now it's time to turn the page and allow that experience to begin to unfold. As Lao-Tzu said:

> The journey of a thousand miles
> begins with a single step.

1. JANUARY

Take Control

To undertake is to achieve.

—EMILY DICKINSON

This entire year is about organizing the details of your financial life. No more papers scattered everywhere. No more dramas over lost documents. No more wondering whether you can afford a new house, a car, or a college education for your child. You're going to know what's really going on in your life in black and white—and make a plan to get out of the red.

First, though, I go through some exercises to help you understand your experiences with money and how the past affects you now. Then you deal with the mundane but necessary world of items that support you daily, such as keeping purses and briefcases organized, and move on to organizing your workspace. We finish this month with the creation of a working file system, so you will have a logical place to keep all your financial receipts. As we move through the first quarter of the year, I think you will be amazed to see how your physical space mirrors your financial state.

When one is in crisis, it's almost assured the other will be as well.

In addition, each month introduces a habit and a tool to help bring order to all aspects of your world.

HABIT OF THE MONTH: DRINK WATER

If you are a coffee or soda addict, it's time to break that habit and start drinking pure, fresh, calorie- and caffeine-free water. Set your goal to drink an additional 16 ounces (two glasses) of water a day. It's okay if it takes the entire day to consume it. Keep a glass on your desk at work. Pop a reusable water bottle in your car's cup holder if you spend most of your time driving. We're starting with two glasses, but the ultimate goal is to drink eight 8-ounce glasses a day. You'll find that being well hydrated relieves stress and improves your ability to think clearly.

With the switch to drinking water, you'll save money and save in other ways. Soft drinks are usually also high in caffeine, calories, and sugar. If you give these up, in just a few months you'll be in better health.

TOOL OF THE MONTH: A FINANCIAL NOTEBOOK

I'll be asking you to make some notes and do a little soul-searching when it comes to finances. It's best if you keep this information in one place rather than on miscellaneous slips of paper that can so easily get lost. Feel free to make notes on the computer or get a composition book from one of your kids. Or you might want to splurge and buy a fancy leather-bound book. The key is that your notebook needs to be something you will enjoy using. I've used all three types over the years. Choose the one that's right for you.

WEEK ONE

Uncover the Origins of Your Relationship with Money

This week, you can

- Set financial goals
- Examine the past for clues to your current economic situation
- Move beyond the past to a successful financial future

PENNY MARRIED RANDY RIGHT AFTER she graduated high school. He was in his late twenties and established in his career. Randy hadn't wanted a wife who worked outside the home.

In the beginning it looked as if hers would indeed be a storybook life. In quick succession she had three healthy, handsome sons. Her husband prospered. Penny took care of their large home and the children. And then one day everything changed. Randy came home and announced he was leaving her for another woman.

When he requested the divorce, Randy promised to support Penny in the lifestyle she had grown accustomed to. He promised to pay her child support. He assured her she would stay in the house. There was just one problem. Randy never kept his promises.

Penny did some soul-searching when Randy left. At first she was terrified that she wouldn't be able to support herself or her children because she thought Randy held the key to her financial security. As she peeled back the layers of her belief system, she discovered that from the time she was a child, the messages she got from her family and the society in which she lived fed the notion that women aren't capable of handling money. "It's a man's job."

Have you ever taken the time to examine the financial messages you received as a child and young adult? Very often it isn't just what adults say that influences us; it's what they do. I'd be willing to bet that you will uncover something from your childhood that drives your current experience with money. And with any luck, it will be positive! If it isn't, you are free to let it go and replace it with a more realistic value system. Penny left behind the belief that women can't handle money. Moreover, she went back to school and discovered something about herself: She loved working with numbers. Penny had always been able to do complex math computations in her head. She went on to become a top real-estate agent in Los Angeles.

ESTABLISHING YOUR FINANCIAL GOALS

This week is not about looking for blame. Instead, it's about simply understanding the reality of the past so we can move on and create something better. Knowledge really is power, especially where money is concerned.

Change is never easy. Equal measures of commitment and courage are required to weather the storm that change inevitably creates. When it's thrust upon us, change is particularly thorny to navigate. But when the going gets tough this year, you can be grateful that you have *chosen* to make improvements in your financial life. You are the architect of the change, not its victim.

We—and our financial circumstances—also are the result of our experiences. Grab your financial notebook and let's do some digging into the past.

Set your timer for thirty minutes. (Your cell phone has a handy alarm.) Here are the questions I'd like you to answer. Record the first thoughts that come to mind. Later in the week you can add more notes if you feel you have opened the door to something you need to explore.

Are you ready? Let's begin with a series of questions that will help you focus on specific goals for the year that we're going to spend together. After each question, take a minute to reflect or have a sip of water.

1. What are your three biggest challenges in terms of finance? (Common ones include: "I never pay my bills on time." "I run up huge bills." "I have no savings.")
2. What are your top three goals for the year? (For example: "I'd like to save for a down payment on a home." "I need to learn how to budget money." "I want to be able to pay for the extras in life rather than charge them on a credit card." "I want to have a secure retirement.")
3. What are your top three financial strengths? It's important to give yourself credit for what you do handle successfully! (For example, "I always pay my bills on time." "I have life insurance in place to protect my family." "I have a will.")

EXAMINING YOUR PAST

Now let's shift our focus to the past and see whether, like Penny, you can uncover the origins of the negative beliefs that hinder you today in your quest to understand finances.

If you discover that you can't remember many details of your childhood, don't worry. You have lots of company. If you have siblings or your parents are still alive, give someone a call. See what he or she remembers. If no one is around, look at a few family photos to jog your memory. See if you can find the person or object that can help open your memory bank. Reconnect with your past. What you learn can help you heal today and forge a more secure future tomorrow.

Keep your financial notebook handy and answer these questions:

1. How did you learn about money? Was it through formal lessons with one of your parents or from their offhand comments? Or did a family member, friend, or teacher act as your mentor?
2. Was this training adequate? Do you think it serves you to this day, and if so, how?
3. If you now regard these lessons as woefully inadequate, when did you first wake up to this reality?
4. Was your home life stable in terms of money? Did both of your parents work outside the home? Do you remember having a feeling of financial security?
5. Can you remember your parents having money or did they have arguments about it? Did they have similar values when it came to finances? Who are you most like in terms of how you relate to money?
6. What would you say are your major issues with money today? Did the same problems crop up while you were growing up?
7. Did you get an allowance? Were you required to do chores to earn this money or did it come with no strings attached? Was the amount adequate?
8. Were your friends in basically the same economic boat as you were? Or do you remember feeling privileged or living in a state of lack in comparison?
9. How did your childhood experiences make you feel about money? Were you eager to earn your own? Did you resent money?
10. Do you feel that anyone ever used money to try to control you? Who? In what way?
11. Finally, were you taught to save on a regular basis?

Right about now you may be feeling like your head is going to explode. You probably haven't thought about these things in years, if ever. Let me tell you about my first money lesson. See how it compares to yours.

THE ORACLE OF BROOKLYN

It was a hot August afternoon in Brooklyn and I was five years old. My mother came to me and said in a tone I hadn't heard before: "Tomorrow your father is going to teach you about *money*. You'll need to understand money when you start school in a few weeks." The next day, as promised, my father called me to him. My mother sat on the side watching with what seemed a mixture of pride and apprehension. Suddenly I wondered if this money thing was a lot more complicated than I had imagined.

My father laid out one quarter, two dimes and a nickel on the kitchen table and identified each one. He told me how two dimes and a nickel were equal in value to a quarter. So far so good: This money thing was pretty easy, I thought. Next my father explained how money should be used. One dime represented the percentage of the money you earned that would pay for the necessities of life like a mortgage, insurance, or food. The other dime represented the percentage that would be salted away in a savings account for a rainy day. And the lowly nickel represented the money one needed to have fun. My father paused. He seemed to be searching my face for recognition. "So now you understand money, right?" I was too young and inarticulate to say something pithy like, "Uh . . . not so much." I was stunned and the lesson was over.

After this lesson my father did something destructive that ironically came from a loving place. It crippled my understanding of money for many years. My father said, "But don't worry. You save your money and I will take care of you. Just tell me what you need." And he did. I was raised as a privileged only child. My description of my childhood is that I was given everything I asked for except a horse. (It's hard to keep one in a Brooklyn brownstone; otherwise I'm sure I would have been given one.) I traveled the world. I had pretty clothes. I never had a job. This pampering led to my "magical thinking" that money somehow just appears when you need it. It's not an uncommon problem for people with money issues.

When my father and mother died, I had a small inheritance. It took twelve years

but one day it was gone. And then credit cards became the magical source of extra money for all those things I was certain I needed. I was an actress at the time with the volatile income typical of any artist. One month you're raking in the dough and the next six you're subsisting on rice and beans. It's a hard life even if you are financially savvy. Well, more than a decade ago, I went through bankruptcy proceedings. Much like Randy leaving Penny, it was my wake-up call.

It takes ten years for a bankruptcy to vanish from your credit report. During those years I worked diligently to rebuild my credit. I learned that earning money raises your self-esteem, as does learning how to manage it well. The most humiliating experience of my life ultimately empowered me.

As you examine the past, you will likely find that you received mixed messages about finances. My father wasn't the greatest teacher when it came to sharing lessons with me. He was, however, an amazing example of a responsible adult. He purchased the home I grew up in with cash. He had one credit card and paid the balance monthly. Every insurance policy you can imagine a family might need, he purchased for us. Had he died suddenly, his will was in place. He tended to the tiniest detail: My mother and I were both signatories to the family safety deposit box. And we knew what was inside and where the key was.

If you have difficulty getting your financial act together, I understand your struggle. But understanding the connection between the past and the present is the first step to taking control of your financial life.

MOVING FORWARD

Previous questions were about understanding how you were first taught about money. Many of you are decades past your childhood. Here are four final questions to answer in your financial notebook. These questions will help you understand the evolving nature of your relationship with money. These bring you forward in time and allow you to see how you managed when on your own. I'd like you to make a connection between what you learned and how it affected you.

1. When you first left home to live on your own, did you know how to manage your money? Were your bills paid on time, for example, or were you always calling home for a loan?
2. If you are married or living with someone, who is in charge of the finances? Does this arrangement suit you? If you have relinquished financial management to your partner or spouse, would you be able to take over control if necessary?
3. Are you a dreamer who trusts the future will take care of itself, or are you a planner who manages every detail of your financial life?
4. What's your biggest financial regret? Are student loans weighing you down?

Did your house lose a great deal of equity in the recent downturn? Do you overextend on your credit cards?

DRAWING CONCLUSIONS

As the week comes to a close, you now have more insight into the reality that brought you to your current situation. We all come away from our past with things we're grateful for and things that make us shake our heads in wonder. Whatever the situation, there's no blame to be laid at the feet of anyone—especially ourselves. It really is true that we're doing the best we can at any given moment. With the understanding you acquired this week, you've leveled the playing field. You are no longer driven by elements from the past: unconscious forces, wounds, or inadequate instruction.

My father was trying to give me the childhood he was denied. He didn't intend to cripple my understanding of money. Ultimately I acknowledged the source of my money issues and disengaged. Today I understand something my father knew only too well: Making and managing money is incredibly empowering. I have embraced the example he set and found other teachers and mentors to give me the instruction he didn't know how to impart. Just so, your future is bound to be better.

WEEK TWO

Clean Out What You Carry

This week, you can

- Clear out the debris from everyday items such as your purse or wallet
- Organize your laptop bag or briefcase
- Clean out those conference goodie bags
- Deal with a multiuse space

As I said in the introduction, one of my favorite zen proverbs is: "The way a man does one thing is how he does everything." You probably want to jump right into examining your stock portfolio statements or organizing the papers stacked around your office. You may be thinking, "What does it matter if my computer bag is a mess, or my purse weighs a ton, or my wallet is crammed with receipts?" Trust me. It's all the same. By keeping these portable "money zones" organized, you're building a foundation. Start small and it will lead to big accomplishments down the road. Gentlemen, please read the following section. Some of the tips have broad application even if you don't carry a "man bag"!

ORGANIZING YOUR WALLET, PURSE, AND TOTE

Many of my clients carry large purses in addition to lugging around a gigantic tote. They wonder why their backs hurt and they lean to the side like a sinking ship. "Never mind!" they shout with glee." I can save the day by pulling out the most esoteric item anyone might need!" Does that sound like you? Let's turn over a new leaf. From now on, other people are responsible for having their own supplies. You carry only what you need.

Empty your purse, and that tote bag if you habitually carry one, onto a clean, wide surface such as your bed or the dining room table. Have a trash can handy.

The first thing I want you to do is a speed elimination. Set a timer for ten minutes. Toss whatever you can. This will probably include stale candy and gum and business cards from people you don't remember.

After this first pass, create some categories by grouping related items in separate areas. These categories generally include make-up and hair supplies, miscellaneous business and personal receipts, and any number of fairly esoteric things such as an umbrella or a few novels you hope to read. (Kindle, anyone?)

Take a good look at each category and ask yourself whether you really need to have these items with you. Let's consider makeup. I think one lipstick and some powder are adequate to the task. Leave the full makeup kit at home.

The basic thing to remember is to keep related items together. If your purse doesn't have sections, use multiple small containers. You can purchase small, sturdy, lightweight containers that close with a zipper, Velcro or a snap at a beauty supply store or The Container Store. Pare every category to the minimum. If you get stuck, ask yourself: "When was the last time I used this item?"

Grab your umbrella when the weather report predicts rain. Otherwise leave it at home. Perhaps you can keep an extra one at the office for emergencies? And be sure your umbrella is a travel-size one if you are going to toss it into your tote. (I work at home but I keep one in the trunk of my car.)

Dealing with Money and Credit Cards

When it comes to your money, are coins rattling around the bottom of the bag in search of a home? Do you stuff bills wherever you can? Being organized about money includes treating it with respect.

Keep your paper money arranged in denominational order facing in one direction, right side up. (I thought my dad was the only person who did this until I saw Suze Orman talk about it on *Oprah*.) It makes it easier to grab a particular denomination when you need it. And it's another sign of respecting your money. Are you prone to stuffing bills in the back pocket of your jeans and then, weeks later, finding a $20 that's been run through the wash? Make it a habit to keep your cash only in your wallet, and make sure the wallet you do use is small.

What about credit cards? Do you carry every department store card with you so you can shop at a moment's notice? Do you have multiple major credit cards "just in case" one or two are denied? We'll be dealing with credit in May. For now, minimize a credit-financed lifestyle. Have one major card exclusively for business entertaining. Keep a personal card with you for emergencies. Only take a department store card with you if you plan a trip to that store.

Receipts

As you're cleaning out your wallet and bags, grab some envelopes. Set aside any receipts that can be used for tax deductions or that you're saving for expense account reimbursement, medical reimbursement, rebates, or other reimbursement. Keep these in separate envelopes. We'll be designating a home for these receipts at the end of the month, when we create the financial file system. Toss extraneous receipts. Shred them if they show an account number or other personal information.

As for "receipt maintenance," you'll want to tuck them into one location only. This in effect creates a habit. You wouldn't exit the house, drive down the street, and suddenly remember you hadn't brushed your teeth. We have ingrained habits that make life easier because we do them almost by rote. Having a system for dealing with receipts and other important papers is simply another example of an ingrained habit. A visit to your local office supply store will show you a world of wonderful products that are fun to use. Here are some of my favorites:

- To catch receipts throughout the day, try a product called a Document Envelope, available in an inexpensive but durable poly material or fine leather. Empty this at the end of each week or each day (my choice).
- Do you love expanding file holders? You can purchase a scaled-down version with six compartments to hold receipts. It will fit into your purse or the glove box in your car. The everwonderful See Jane Work Web site (www.seejanework.com) even has one with a mileage log (Receipt Catcher-Car from Buttoned Up).

The basic thing to remember is to keep related items together. If your purse doesn't have sections, use multiple small containers. Pare every category to the minimum. Your back and neck will be grateful. If you get stuck, ask yourself, "When was the last time I used this item?"

ORGANIZING YOUR BRIEFCASE OR LAPTOP BAG

When you're traveling outside the home or office, you can carry the business papers and tools you need in many creative ways. The traditional briefcase is still in vogue with high-level execs. More and more, however, the briefcase of choice is a laptop case that holds all your traveling office needs. I travel with a mini PC that weighs 2.6 pounds and slips easily into any large purse. No matter the form, you want to be as lean in this arena as we were in organizing a purse.

An overstuffed briefcase, which is the business equivalent of the gigantic purse or tote, can be an expression of many things but most are related to fear. Do you want to be able to save the business day by being able to produce any type of document or gizmo? Are you unsure how to make good decisions in this area? Why do you regularly transport too much?

It helps to identify the source dictating your behavior. You'll be less tempted in the future if you can unhook yourself from the pattern that urges you to hold onto things. If you clutter your briefcase, I bet your office is filled with unnecessary debris as well. I would go further and bet there's debris waiting to be tossed in every corner of your life.

Clear a space so you can empty the contents of your briefcase. (If you carry a laptop, please set it aside.) Do a ten-minute speed elimination to get the ball rolling. Toss anything that is old, stale, broken, or outdated. Set aside important papers. We'll deal with them at the end of the month when we set up our files. Let's take a look at the common culprits:

- Do you carry a full-size office tool such as a stapler or tape? How often do you need it? What about purchasing a mini kit?

- Do you carry items you need but in too-large quantities? A few paper clips are good to have, but boxes of binder clips in every size are overkill.

- Do items free-float in your briefcase? You can find plastic storage bags in different sizes at an arts and crafts supply store such as Michaels. Don't want to be seen with plastic storage bags? Use mesh bags made for makeup. They come in an array of colors and are inexpensive. The goal is to corral related items.

- Was your briefcase a gift when you graduated law school twenty years ago? Needs have changed over the past few years, and it may be time to purchase something more utilitarian. Please don't stuff the old one in the back of a closet for sentimental reasons—toss it.

- Never underestimate the power of a lightweight flash or thumb drive to keep you feeling secure when it comes to document transport. My computer technician carries his flash drive on his key chain. Where will you keep yours?

- If you lose your flash drive while traveling, you'll be all set if you've kept documents backed up in a cyber location, which can be accessed from anywhere in the world. The original documents should be on file where you work; then a colleague could e-mail the files to you if necessary.

- When you take files with you in your briefcase, a manila file folder can get a bit dog-eared. Enter the world of Pendaflex PileSmart QuickView jackets. These poly folders are sturdy and waterproof. Keep two or three in your briefcase when you travel so that any material you acquire can be immediately popped into a folder for safe transport back to the office.

TOSSING IT: THE GOODIE BAG

When traveling to conferences or seminars, we frequently come home with a tote bag of goodies. For some reason these traditionally wind up on the office floor or shoved in the back of a closet. Clients tell me they want to be able to prove to Uncle Sam that they were in attendance. I can assure you that Uncle Sam is far more interested in your hotel, meal, and conference registration receipts than in your canvas bag collection. Take a few minutes now to clean these bags out. File anything pertinent. Toss whatever is obsolete or stale!

CONTINUING TO CLEAN OUT

After you do these clean-out exercises, you may discover over the next month that you left something out of your bag that you do use. Return that item if you see that the need for it will recur. But avoid the temptation to return everything you left at home. However, I am sure that instead of adding items, you will find more to toss or leave at home. Why? Because clutter suffocates you. Space and order free the mind. If you want to make sound financial decisions, create an atmosphere that promotes clear thinking. Russell and I both work with well-to-do clients. Can you guess what they all have in common? Order in their environment. It's as if they are unconsciously putting out the welcome mat for more order. That's what you are doing this month.

WEEK THREE

Streamline Your Home Office Space

This week, you can

- Look at your workspace with fresh eyes
- Prepare your work space to support your financial organization
- Manage a work space that has dual purposes

JACK NEEDED TO ORGANIZE HIS HOME office. He rarely paid the family bills on time, and the interest rates, penalties, and amounts due were skyrocketing out of control. Jack also had a secret: He never told his wife, Susan, that the bill-paying "system" he set up when they got married was inadequate and broken. Now he was riddled with a combination of fear and shame. What would happen if she found out?

As Jack and I cleared out the debris and set up files that would support him, it became clear that he appreciated the new setup but was unlikely to use it. He had been raised to believe that men pay the bills and women run the home. The problem with this kind of stereotype is that it doesn't allow for natural abilities. Jack's wife was like Penny, who you met previously this month. She loved all things to

do with numbers. What if Susan, like Penny, could take over the bill-paying duties?

As you might imagine, Susan had a minor meltdown when she discovered the situation with the credit cards. But she happily took over paying the bills and maintaining the office organization. It takes time to eliminate the damage to one's credit, but this couple persevered. About a year after we worked together, Jack called to tell me he had discovered that he had a skill set he was previously ignorant of: He was adept at changing diapers.

Personal finance is more than a series of tasks we need to perform. It becomes part and parcel of how we judge ourselves. We allow it to affect our self-esteem. When you can't pay a bill, provide health insurance for your children, or meet your mortgage, you don't feel great about yourself. When your workspace is full to the rafters with stuff, you aren't as likely to be as productive as you would be in a space that promotes order and clear thinking. This week we take a step to make planning easier by organizing the space where you do the bulk of your financial management.

ASSESSING YOUR WORK SPACE

First, make an honest assessment of your work space. Most people manage their finances from their home office, so I'll be coaching you based on that scenario. However, you can use the same guidelines to organize any space. If you work in a tiny apartment with one file box, you can still pick up some useful tips. Wherever you work, take a minute in that space and pretend you have never been here before. Ask yourself these questions, which are geared to having you look at your office with what I call "fresh eyes."

- What do you know about the occupant(s)? In general, are they tidy or is the room chaotic?
- Does the desk appear to be the right size? Or is it too big for the space or too small to be useful? Are there desk drawers for small supplies? Is there at least one drawer for files?
- Is the lighting adequate? Would a lamp on the desk be a good idea? Or is there one there now that takes up too much space?
- Is there glare on the computer screen from artificial lighting or the sun?
- Is the chair comfortable? Does it sit on a chair mat so you can slide around?
- Where is the phone? What side is it on? Most people have it on the right side, which is fine if you're right-handed. If you're a lefty like me, you'll be dragging a cord across your desk. A portable phone eliminates this issue.
- Is there a file cabinet? How full is it?
- If there is a bookcase, is it underused or so crowded that the shelves are bowed? Do you see any bookends?
- What is the condition of the office? Could the walls use a coat of paint?
- Are there signs of life in the room, such as plants or pets? Do they add to the ambiance or make it difficult to think or use the space?
- Finally, is this room dedicated to doing work or is it also a guest room, a gym, or a storage place?

Are you happy with the state of this room? If you feel you need to do some work, first decide how much you can accomplish right now. This week we dedicate time to getting the room free of clutter and ready to support you. Schedule time in the future for a fresh coat of paint, new carpeting or rugs, and perhaps a shopping trip for ergonomically correct furniture.

CLEANING YOUR WORK SPACE: PHASE ONE

This week we aren't concerned with the stacks of wayward papers. We'll handle those next week. Instead, set a timer for thirty minutes and let's do another speed elimination. Be sure you have some sturdy garbage bags or boxes on hand. Does music get you moving? Crank up that rock 'n' roll, country western, or hip hop! Here's what we're looking for.

Invitations to past social engagements. There will be other opportunities. If you need to include a new address, set the invitation aside and label it with a Post-it that says "Address Book Updates." Do the input later in the day or week. We're on the move now!

Newspapers older than yesterday's or magazines older than last month's should be tossed into the recycling bin. Let's be realistic: If you haven't read them by now, what are the odds you will in the near future? More issues are coming! The most current information in any category is on the Internet and updated all the time—you can always Google the article later. If you feel you must keep something from one of these paper sources, set aside the article from the newspaper or magazine. Put a Post-it on it that says "Read." Toss the extraneous paper, and keep moving!

If you come across personal items you want to save, make another pile. This Post-it will say "Memorabilia." Do not stop to enjoy a love letter, a piece of children's art, or a note from your late mother. There will be time do to this in the future. These thirty minutes are sacred to the task of creating order by eliminating debris.

Go through your bookcase. Do you have duplicate books you won't read again? Donate them to the library; check out www.PaperBackSwap.com, an online service for swapping books with others; call a used bookstore in town; or if you have a specific category of books, contact a school. A friend who is a retired judge had saved hundreds of law books during his career, starting in law school. He recently donated the collection to a law school library. When I gave up acting, I donated my play collection to the theater department of a performing arts high school. What solution works best for you?

What's on your office floor? Did several pairs of shoes migrate here? In a box in the hallway, put items that you know live elsewhere in your home. Return these items when your thirty minutes are up in this room.

Take a look at your office tools. Do you have old hard drives, used toner cartridges, multiple staplers, and too many pens? (After the timer goes off, spend a few minutes checking those pens, Sharpies, and markers to see which have dried up waiting for you to use them.) Make a pile of items that can be recycled or donated. I'm going to bet that someone at Goodwill can fix that broken inkjet printer and you'd have a tax deduction. Most computer companies and large office supply stores have programs to help you recycle old equipment and products. Consult your local yellow pages for recycling programs. Nothing has to collect dust and occupy space in your office.

You get the idea. Attack every nook and cranny even if I didn't mention the item here. We want a clear, organized, tidy space that immediately invites you in to do your best work in peace.

When you're finished, distribute items around the home and take out the trash. Immediately box up anything earmarked for donation. Call for a pickup if you can't transport it. If you have a car, put the donated items in your vehicle now. Take out your calendar and schedule the time for drop off. Or if you know you're never going to get around to donating the items, throw them away. You don't want that clutter languishing in your trunk for the next six months. When this phase of our operation is complete, you may need a break. I suggest some fruit, cheese, and an extra bottle of water, and a walk around the block. When you are ready, please return refreshed for round two.

CLEANING YOUR WORK SPACE: PHASE TWO

When you look at your office now, I hope you can breathe more easily. Absence of clutter does that to a space. It opens it up literally and energetically. If you aren't used to it, you may feel uncomfortable when you look around and see open space in your office. People often nervously ask me, "What goes there?" Maybe nothing! Let's keep working and let the office come to life slowly. You are more than a Zen Organizer at this moment; you are a designer. Let's see what we can create.

Here are some questions about the space to help you keep moving for the next thirty-minute period. Don't concern yourself so much with speed now as with progress. This is a time for creation. Are you ready?

I want you to feel powerful in this space. When you sit at your desk, is your back to the door? I'd like you to move your desk, if you can. You want to avoid being in direct line with the door or sitting with your back to it. I'd like you to be able to look up and see everyone who enters. Yes, this applies even if you live alone.

Sit in your chair in its current position. How do you feel? Now move your chair to the new location. (Pretend your desk is already in place.) I bet you feel better. These are basic Feng Shui tips. Just try it. What have you got to lose? Are you concerned that you will have wires cascading down the front of your desk? Start a shopping list. You can get plastic tubes in white or black that will grab these wires and keep them contained. You can also reduce the number by going wireless.

Do you have lots of technological gadgets in your office? Let's see: printer, scanner, fax, photo printer, computer housing, laptop . . . the list is endless, isn't it? I have two concerns: Do you use all these gadgets, or did they make you feel good when you purchased them? Keep the ones out that you use. Store the others so they are easy to grab when you need them. Feel free to donate or recycle any that are just technology trophies at this point.

When you look at the gadgets you do use, are they conveniently placed in reference to your desk? Most of my clients don't realize that they have to get up every time they press Print on their computer to get the paper out of the printer. Do you have a return on your desk? Keep the most frequently used gadgets there, if possible. No return? How about a rolling cart? Steps saved equal time saved. And you know the old bromide: Time is money.

What about your office supplies? I'm going to bet you shop at a store such as Costco or Sam's Club from time to time and stock up. This is a great idea but it can backfire. If I buy enough staples to fill the staplers for fifty people for a year, guess what? I haven't been prudent. I've wasted space. Pare your supplies to a realistic number. If by chance you are running short, please add those items to your shopping list.

Where will you store your backup office supplies? If you can clear a closet in your home office, that's ideal. Perhaps you can use a shelf on your bookcase or purchase an inexpensive file tote box to be your own private Office Depot.

I have to share a pet peeve. Everyone needs paper stored near the printer and the fax,

but many people leave the package torn open. If ever a visual makes me tired, it's this one. The thought is that leaving the paper partially exposed will keep it in one location. Try this: Purchase a simple, inexpensive paper tray. Voila! Your paper supply is tidy, contained, and ready to serve.

Look at your desk. Do family photos, plants, and several containers with writing tools take up space? Eliminate the first one. You have the rest of your home to honor your family. Move the plant where it has better light and won't be disturbed. You need space to place your papers while you work.

Desk liner and drawer organizers make your desk drawers more efficient. I've seen offices that looked tidy and organized until I opened the drawers. Are the drawers in your desk scary? Clean them out! You can find basic drawer organizers at any office supply store and the kitchen section of a store such as Bed Bath & Beyond or The Container Store.

DEALING WITH A DUAL SPACE

If your home office has multiple functions, it's important to organize all aspects of the room. What is the point of a tiny organized corner office in a room that otherwise looks like a cyclone hit it? The most common shared functions are home office and gym, guest room, or storage area. Here are some guidelines to help you make the entire room work with all its objectives:

Use rugs to mark areas for specific activities. If the room has a wood floor, an area rug in the section for the home office can visually mark the change in energy (work versus guest area versus gym).

You want your guests to be comfortable but you don't have to indulge them to your own detriment. If they have half or less of the closet space, they should be thrilled. You can pop a simple, inexpensive bookcase on the other side of the closet for office product storage (and a place for business and reference books).

Is the room crowded with guest amenities? Sometimes toiletries in a guest room are better donated or tossed. You need the space, so be ruthless when it comes to items set aside for guest comfort.

Is your office space also a gym? Who uses the equipment? Keep what is used, and donate the rest. I want you to exercise, but if you bought a piece of equipment and no longer use it, lose it. You can't afford to waste space.

Whether other family members are going to work out or you have frequent guests, you need to establish set times that you have access to the office space. You don't want to be thrown off your newly organized financial schedule because Aunt Tilly is in town or your teenage son and his cohorts want to bulk up. Boundaries are a beautiful thing to establish in life.

If you share the space with your spouse, life partner, or roommate, are you going to share the same desk? If you have different styles, this can be dicey. The three keys to making this work are commitment, communication, and compassion. You want to be committed to achieving your shared financial goals. If the space is shared but the goals are not, you want a commitment to honor the hard work you have put into organizing and transforming the space. You'll need to communicate how you feel about the use of the space and what is fair. Compassion allows you to view another person's way of doing things with respect. Sometimes it pays to give in just so the other person feels appreciated.

ADDING THE FINAL TOUCHES

I think you have enough material now to make a difference in your work zone. Consider everything in the space even if I didn't mention it. For example, as you gaze at your finished masterpiece, do you notice that the window is dirty? You might have to put that on your calendar as a to-do item when the weather gets warmer. Or perhaps you need to run the vacuum here before you exit? Train yourself to consider the whole of any project. This global outlook will not only enrich your physical experience but also help you be much more organized when we tackle paper next week.

WEEK FOUR

Set Up a Financial File System

This week, you can

- Buy the necessary tools for creating a file system
- Create a simple yet effective file system to keep track of your important business and financial papers
- Organize information in a way that suits you
- Create a group of action files
- Make a binder for frequently accessed instructions and a list of your files

THIS WEEK WE MOVE ON TO THE creation of a financial file system. You need to know what to keep, what to toss, and what to shred. You also need to be able to put your hands on key papers at a moment's notice. And so you shall by week's end.

When I teach my organizing class, I begin by announcing that I have good news and bad news. The good news is that everybody is already organized. Not only are they organized, they have a system in place. And they work their system with the zeal of a religious fanatic. Most of my audience will stare at me in disbelief. I can feel them thinking, "Not me, Regina!" That's when I tell them the bad news: Your system may not be a nurturing one that sets

you up to win. It may sabotage your best efforts at every turn.

I have been a professional organizer for more than twenty years. I can tell you that finding a client with a well-crafted, functioning file system is a rarity. Usually the file cabinet, which should be a storehouse of present-day material, is a cemetery honoring past accomplishments. Other times it's used as a place to store office supplies or, worse, junk! Your financial papers deserve to be treated with respect, which means they have a designated spot. You need to clean them out periodically and archive, toss, or shred material. And you should be able to put your hands on any document in a matter of seconds. This is our goal for this week. The work is intense, but the rewards you reap over time make it more than worthwhile.

BUYING THE BASICS

Let's take a look at the supplies you'll need to create your file system:

- Rails for the file drawer if they are not currently present
- Hanging file folders
- One box of two-inch-wide box-bottom hanging file folders
- Long tabs for the hanging file folders
- One box of one-third or straight-cut manila folders
- A label maker with extra tapes
- Binders or project boxes (optional for most)

If you aren't a devotee of office supply stores like I am, you may not know what some of these items are. Let me offer some explanations.

Rails are metal rods that run on the sides of your file cabinet. They are often built into the file drawer or as part of a frame that was placed in the drawer. Frame sets come in different sizes, so measure the drawer before you purchase your frame.

Hanging file folders have hooks on the ends. You put the material you want to save into a manila file folder and that folder gets placed into a hanging file folder.

A box-bottom hanging file folder is handy when you have several manila files that relate to one topic because the folder allows you to keep everything in one place. This saves not only space in your drawer but also time. A box-bottom hanging folder is wide at the bottom, with a cardboard strip you insert in the bottom. Use a folder no wider than two inches because if the folder gets too heavy, it will tear.

Note: Most people need a combination of regular hanging file folders and the box-bottom variety. I like to keep a box of each type handy in my personal supply area.

Long tabs are plastic and attach to the hanging file folder. Inside the tab you place a piece of supplied cardboard, where you indicate the material enclosed in the folder. When you buy regular hanging file folders, they come with short tabs, which I find too short to be useful. Instead, it's worthwhile to pick up a bag of long tabs.

Manila folders are utilitarian and house the everyday business of life. If you feel that colored financial folders will make the business of financial management more fun, by all means get a box of your favorite color files. Some people don't use a manila folder and instead place their information directly inside the hanging file folders. However, if you take the information out for review, it's now loose on your desk. Papers can get separated or misplaced, and in the end you have created more work for yourself.

Third-cut folders have a nice amount of space on which to attach a label for your file folder. The hanging file folder label (on the plastic tab) often announces a category and the manila folders make up the category as a whole. The fifth-cut variety has an area that is too small to be useful. Straight-cut folders give you the length of the file folder for writing the title.

Label maker: What can I say? This is a tool you can use in many places. I prefer the Brother P-touch models, but purchase whatever brand you like. The low-end of the Brother P-touch product line costs around $30.00; however, watch for sales and you can snag one for about $15.00. You will need batteries and additional tape. I prefer black ink on a white background because color is often difficult to read. If your prefer color, use that version consistently in your files for a uniform and therefore calming appearance.

Binders with tabs to separate various aspects of a project or topic are similar to box-bottom hanging file folders with several manila folders inside. One sits on a shelf and the other pops into a drawer. What you choose to use depends on your physical setup and the way you relate to materials. Please read through the text for this week before you go shopping so that you can make the best choice.

GETTING STARTED

To create files, group related expenses. In this way, you are creating a category. You will have master categories and subcategories. A master category groups the many parts of a multifaceted topic. For example, the master category "Insurance" might have the following subcategories: "Automobile," "Homeowner's," and "Medical." You could have the subcategories in alpha-

> Only current financial materials need to be in the file drawer and at your fingertips. If it's a receipt for personal items, such as purchases at your local Target, save the receipt until you reconcile your monthly statement and then shred the receipt.

betical order in a file cabinet, but then they would be spread out and possibly located in different drawers. With the master category called "Insurance," all your policies would be in one place.

When you look at the following list, pretend each entry is a file in your file drawer. The master categories (in bold) are the names on the long tab attached to the hanging file folder. Place all these tabs on the far left.

Automobiles
Lease or purchase payments
Maintenance

Banking
Business account
Personal checking

Business-related expenses
Charitable donations
Continuing ed. classes
Entertaining clients
Gifts for clients

Children
Child care
Legal documents

Medical expense
Medical records
Tuition

Credit cards
Bloomingdales
Capital One
Neiman Marcus
Providian

Household expenses
Gardener
Mortgage or rent
Phones
Utilities

Income record
Freelance income
Money from eBay sales
Salary

Insurance
Automobile
Health
Homeowners
Long-term care
Renter's insurance

Investments
Brokerage accounts
College savings plan
401(k)
IRAs
Savings bank

Legal
Alimony
Child support payments
School loan payments
Wills and estate plan

Medical
Bills
Claim forms
Power-of-attorney
Records

Miscellaneous
Pets

If a master category has several parts, you could easily use a box-bottom hanging file folder. Sometimes these folders come in handy even if there is only one folder but it's large (such as a real estate transaction or a complicated medical history). If you have a thick file, however, do your best to break it down. For example, with a real estate purchase, you might have the following:

Appraisal
Deed
Inspections
Real estate agent contract
Misc.

This way, if you need a piece of information from a particular category, you don't have to hunt through every piece of related paper to find it. You can go to the individual folder where it would most logically have been filed.

GROUPING INFORMATION YOUR WAY

As mentioned, in the preceding lists, the name in bold is the name on the long tab attached to the hanging file folder. The names below appear on the individual manila folders. Please note that both my master categories and the individual files are in alphabetical order. Getting organized, however, allows for creativity. You might group the information in a slightly different way. For example, you might keep your automobile insurance with your automobile expenses rather than with all the other insurance policies. Your automobile section might look like this:

Automobiles
    Insurance
    Lease or purchase payments
    Maintenance

What happens if your family has several cars? Now you have insurance policies, lease or purchase payments, and maintenance for each one. How will you keep track? Here's how it might look:

Automobiles
Camry
    Insurance
    Lease or purchase payments
    Maintenance

Mercedes
    Insurance
    Lease or purchase payments
    Maintenance

Toyota truck
    Insurance
    Lease or purchase payments
    Maintenance

"Automobiles" is still your master category. That tab appears on the left side of your hanging file folder. All master category tabs follow in alphabetical order. You'll see them at a glance when you're looking for a particular category. "Camry," "Mercedes," and "Toyota truck" are long tabs on the right side of hanging file folders. When I see tabs on the right, I know instantly that a master category is complex and has been broken down further to enable me to find what I need quickly. If I want to check a repair bill for the truck, for example, I don't have to wade through a bulging folder with repair receipts for three vehicles.

Take a few minutes to play with your budget. Do you need to add other folders? After you have divided your items, it will be a snap to create your new file system.

You can use these guidelines to create your entire file system. You might have a master category for "Recipes" or "Travel Articles." Under the former you might have file folders for appetizers, breads, desserts, main dishes, and soups. Or if you like ethnic cooking, perhaps you have the folders organized by "Indian," "Mexican," and "Thai." You could divide your travel articles by area: "Africa," "Asia," "Europe," and "South America." Or if your travel plans are closer to home, you might have folders for local places you want to visit. Feel free to be creative and honor the way you think about the material you are organizing.

CREATING ACTION FILES

I have a series of files in the file drawer in my desk that are in a master category called "Action files." I create these same files for all my clients. The "Action files" category holds the work we have to do. In general, I use red folders for this group. In most cases, they contain the following folders:

> Bills (not yet paid)
> To-do ASAP
> To-do low priority
> To file (includes paid bills)
> To read

If you run a business from your home or work outside it, you might want to have a version like this:

> To-do business
> To-do personal

Some of my clients find that although most items on a to-do list require action, some are phone call–only related. You can put these in a "To-call" folder.

For some people, dividing items into "To-do" categories helps make their work less overwhelming. You can add another file to your "Action files" group to reduce stress even further. Let's say you are disputing a charge on a credit card bill. You've made the requisite call, sent a follow up e-mail, and even written a letter. Now you're waiting for a response. You don't need to look at that piece of paper every time you open your "To-do" folder, but you can't lose track of it. Create a "Pending" folder. Here I place all items that are in the process of being handled. I check this folder at the end of each week to see whether I need to reconnect with anyone the following week.

KEEPING A REFERENCE BINDER

Do you already have extensive files for your business or hobbies? Write a list of your existing files and then look for the connections, as demonstrated in the examples provided previously. From this initial list, you can create your categories. If you have several file drawers, you might want to take the time to put the list on your computer. Print a copy and keep it in a slender binder on your desk. On the spine of the binder, create a label that says "Reference."

Place in the binder any material that you reference regularly. I like to keep this information in sheet protectors so that the paper doesn't get dirty and dog-eared. Remember to update the computer list as you create or delete files, and then make a fresh printout for your binder. This may sound like a lot of work, but you will find that after you create a master list, your file system will be fairly static. Files will periodically come and go rather than be in a constant state of flux.

KEEPING DOCUMENTS FOREVER

Now that you have created a file system, be sure that you file the material that you need to keep forever. Material in this category includes the following:

- Birth and death certificates.
- Passports and immunization records.
- Marriage and divorce papers.
- A will and health care proxy.
- Insurance policies. (Take photos of expensive items and store the memory card in your safety deposit box, if you have one.)
- A list of all bank and brokerage accounts, along with the beneficiary designation forms.
- If you own your home, keep a record of all capital improvements. This record is invaluable if you decide to sell the property. Digitized photographs are a wonderful addition.

Shred obsolete copies of the preceding. Use a cross-cut shredder for safety.

REWARDING YOURSELF

We've come to the end of a week that required a lot of mental focus. Next month we'll be dealing with the complex issue of taxes, and it will be much easier to navigate those waters because of the work you did this week. Why not plan a reward for the weekend? Have you been meaning to visit the local museum? Has it been ages since you and your best friend met at the local coffee shop to chat? If a mild weekend is predicted, could you visit the zoo or a park? This is hard work, so be kind to yourself. You deserve it.

JANUARY SUMMARY

WEEK ONE

Uncover your financial upbringing.

WEEK TWO

Clean out the tools that should support you, not drag you down: purse, wallet, and briefcase.

WEEK THREE

Streamline your designated home office area.

WEEK FOUR

Create a working file system so you can put your hands on any document in seconds.

2. FEBRUARY

Assess Your Finances

I am breathing in and making my whole body calm and at peace.

I am breathing out and making my whole body calm and at peace.

This is how one practices.

—THE SUTRA ON FULL AWARENESS OF BREATHING

MY BEST FRIEND COLLECTS BUTTONS. She has one that I really like: "Reality! What a concept!" Most of us put our head in the sand and avoid the reality of our finances. We know we make money and we're certainly aware we have bills to pay, but we're not sure of the totals in either case. We have no clue exactly how much we spend on miscellaneous items.

Everyone has a personal weakness when it comes to unconscious shopping. Perhaps you have a mountain of shoes in your closet? If I were to ask you about it, you might say you can't resist a good sale. Or maybe you have a hobby such as scrapbooking, tinkering on cars, or cooking. You make purchases for these endeavors and never add up the damages. If push came to shove you couldn't find that important receipt. This month all that changes. We get into the reality of our money situation and how to track it. Are you ready?

HABIT OF THE MONTH: DECLUTTER

You cleaned out debris last month, so it's only logical you'll want to prevent its return. Keep the momentum of change going. To this end, you need to dedicate ten minutes a day to decluttering. Each night when you get home, spend a few minutes maintaining the order you have created. Don't let receipts sit stuffed in corners. Pull out the scraps of paper on which you wrote important phone numbers and appointments and transfer them to your phone book and calendar.

TOOL OF THE MONTH: MEDITATION

Many people feel inadequate when it comes to getting organized. The discomfort level rises when you layer on tackling finances. If your chest tightens, your breath becomes shallow, and you want to run away and do something more fun, stop and watch your breath.

One of the classic meditation practices for the beginner is to observe the breath. Try it now. Sit with your back straight, your feet firmly planted on the ground, and your hands relaxed in your lap, palms up but not touching. Close your eyes. Take a few deep breaths. Feel the breath as it enters your nose. Feel it as you exhale.

How many breaths before you start thinking, "Oh boy, is this a waste of time"? Or maybe, "I'm never going to organize anything, much less my finances"? You'll be amazed where your mind takes you. Be patient with yourself. Stop or release the thought and return your awareness to your breath. You may find that this simple breathing technique becomes one of your favorites that you stay with all year. But for now, I want you to be able to meditate for a few brief minutes each day as a way to calm your fears.

WEEK ONE

Pay Your Bills on Time

This week, you can

- Handle mail daily
- Devise a simple system to stay current on your bills and protect your credit in the process

IF YOU HAVEN'T BEEN PAYING YOUR bills on time, you need to understand why. For some the problem is cash flow: a lost job, no more savings, or overspending. However, many people don't pay their bills on time simply because they forget. They have no system in place for bill paying or are bored by the process. This week we put solutions in place. Paying your bills on time, every time, helps boost your FICO score—the powerful number that directly affects your access to credit and the interest rate you pay on credit cards, loans, mortgages, and so on.

DEALING WITH MAIL

Let's start with the moment you pick up your mail in the evening. Chances are you're exhausted from a day at work. For many of you, the work day isn't over yet because you have a family waiting to be fed, homework to be checked, and lunches for tomorrow to be planned. Laundry is probably piling up. And of course you brought a little work home from the office, didn't you?

The key to dealing with your mail is to ritualize the steps outlined in this section. You brush your teeth. You change your underwear. You open your mail and set a time to pay your bills. Quite a combo, isn't it? Who said financial matters can't make you smile?

Step One: Deposit
Rather than toss your mail in any old place, I want you to have a single container and a designated spot for depositing mail as soon as you walk through the front door. Later in the evening, you can carry this container to the place where you deal with home finances. The container should hold no more than two day's mail, and ideally it gets emptied daily. You don't want

one that is the size of a bathtub! My clients try this one from time to time thinking I won't notice.

Why does size matter? If you use a huge container, you are just delaying making decisions. I want you to become an assured, speedy decision maker. This skill will benefit every part of your life.

Mail frequently includes newspapers and magazines. You can buy stylish matching containers for each at places such as The Container Store. My holders are near the couch, which is where I sit to read. If you keep large items in the mail container, it will quickly overflow. The minute something isn't easy or fun to use, it's no longer a solution. It's now part of the problem.

Step Two: Eliminate

I check my mail on the elevator en route back to my apartment. I stop and dump any junk mail (that doesn't need to be shredded) before I even set foot inside so it never enters my home. See how much you can throw in the trash or recycling bin immediately.

Take the remaining mail to your designated container. Now you must decide if you'll deal with it immediately or at the end of the day. The key is to make sure you go through and open your mail every day. Keep a letter opener in your basket.

Bills today come with an astonishing array of junk, don't they? Toss newsletters you're not interested in reading and ads for items you don't want as well as the envelope the bill arrived in. If you are paying online (I talk about this later), you can also toss the return envelope. As a result of a

few simple actions, you're left with one piece of paper.

Step Three: Schedule

Decide how you will pay your bills each month—throughout the month as they come in or all together on a particular day—and stick with your choice every month.

Whether you use a calendar on your computer or PDA or a paper version you carry with you, note the day a bill is to be paid.

When a bill is noted for payment later, put the coupon and if necessary the return envelope in the "Bills" folder of your "Action files" master category. (Refer to January.) On the day you designate for payment, you'll know exactly where to look for your bills.

PAYING YOUR BILLS IN DIFFERENT WAYS

When it comes to bill paying, you have several choices. You can pay bills the old-fashioned way, by writing a check and mailing it. You can go the other extreme and turn the task over to someone else and simply look over a monthly statement. Other options are to pay some or all bills online or use automatic bill payment.

Whichever method or methods you choose, after you pay a bill, mark on the slip the date the bill was paid before you file it. It takes about two seconds to toss a receipt on your desk and have it get lost in a sea of paper. It takes about the same time to toss it into a designated folder.

TRIAGE

If you can't pay all your bills this month, which ones come first and which do you put on the back burner? When you finish this book, I hope choosing which bills to pay won't be an issue, but it may be right now. Here are some guidelines:

- Pay Uncle Sam first. Trust me on this; the IRS can make your life miserable like few other creditors can. But do know that installment options for paying your taxes are often available. More on that in March.
- Ask yourself who can repossess. Your mortgage company and the auto dealer come next in order of importance. You obviously don't want to come home to find your furniture on the street or your vehicle towed.

- Seek the lowest cost. If you have two credit cards (what American doesn't?) compare the interest rates you'll be paying for holding off full payment, and pay off the interest card with the higher rate first. Make sure that you make at least the minimum payment on each card to avoid what often can be ridiculous late fees.
- Tap your conscience. This last consideration isn't strictly financial, but if you can pay only one creditor this month, and it's a question of whether it's, say, a large department store or a Mom-and-Pop down the road, consider that the smaller creditor might be waiting for you to pay your bills before he can pay his.

Paying by mail. The time-honored, age-old method of bill paying is to use the United States mail, otherwise known as snail mail. If you choose this method, be sure that you allow for travel time—pay at least seven business days before the due date. Grace periods are getting shorter.

Now, don't fret and think less of yourself if you prefer this method. Using a computer doesn't bestow financial acumen on anyone. The person saving receipts in a shoebox and paying bills by hand is head and shoulders above everyone else if that system keeps things on track. There isn't any one person we all fall in love with nor any dessert that is universally enjoyed. It's the same with bill-paying options. Choose the method or methods that suit your needs and personality.

Online bill payment. Paying bills electronically saves time and money. You can pay some vendors directly on their Web site. For others, you may find that online bill paying is available as a free service through your bank.

Whether you use the bank or go directly to the vendor's Web site, setting up online bill paying takes only a few minutes. There will be clear online instructions, and just about every vendor has a help line you can call for assistance. After the first time, you'll be a champ. You need a password that is easy to remember, but avoid all the clichés: date of birth, names of children, or names of pets. And if you want to use different passwords for each account, record them in an unusual place, not in the folder for that vendor!

Most credit card companies allow you to go to their site and specify what you want to pay and when the transaction should take place. Suppose you have a credit card due on the fifteenth of the month. You could go online the day you receive your statement, specify the amount to pay (I hope it's the entire balance), and set the payment to be "sent" on the fourteenth. No more worries about a check getting there on time. Just be sure you note the payments in your checkbook.

You usually have the option of continuing to receive a paper statement in the mail or having one sent by link through e-mail. Watch out: Some companies are beginning to charge for paper copies of bills.

Automatic bill payment. This method is a great timesaving choice. Consider how many static bill amounts you have, such as an automobile lease payment or an insurance payment. Then check to see whether the company offers automatic bill payment, sometimes referred to as EFT (electronic fund transfer).

Use this option with care because you don't want to overdraw your back account. Your responsibilities are to note the amount being deducted and to make sure you have enough money in the bank to cover the amount. Set up overdraft protection, just in case.

The trick with automatic payments is remembering to deduct them from your checkbook. Use your calendar and your checkbook in concert. On your calendar, note the amount due the day it's to be paid. For example, suppose you have an automatic car payment of $365 due on the seventeenth. When you look at your calendar on that day, you see the reminder "$365 car payment." Subtract that amount from your checkbook, and copy the calendar note to the next month. Do this each month.

Another method, if you have enough in reserve, is to simply record these payments when you receive your bank statement each month. For example, if you know that $1,300 is automatically deducted each month for various bills, always make sure you have that much set aside.

Other regular payments vary each month, and you want to be in control of the amount your creditor receives, whether it's the electric company or your credit card. To that end, you can make the payment online but don't give permission for it to be automatic. You also want to review the statements for these payments to be sure the amount is in keeping with the actual usage. We all know the story of someone who got an astronomical bill and had to contact the media because the utility company wouldn't adjust the total due.

Bill-paying services. If you have the means, consider hiring someone to pay your bills for you. Accounting firms can take this burden off your shoulders. Your accountant will not only pay your bills but also track your tax deductions. You'll have one-stop shopping! At the end of the month, you receive a statement; carefully monitor the monies that went out that month and catch anything you think might be out of line.

WEEK TWO

Determine Your Income and Fixed Expenses

This week, you can

- Figure out your income
- Calculate your fixed, or discretionary, costs
- Assess your job security

THIS WEEK, WE BEGIN OUR LOOK AT the money you have coming in (*income*) and going out (*expenses*). In other words, we're taking an aerial shot of your financial landscape. I've allotted two weeks for this task so you won't feel rushed. This week you determine your income and fixed expenses, and next week you do the same for your variable expenses.

You're free to go through the material for each week in one sitting. It's equally effective to divide your time into several work sessions. You probably won't know most of this information off the top of your head, so you will have to do some research. Now that you have a crackerjack file system, this research will be a breeze. Having to sift through piles of papers would find you wanting to tear your hair out. There is method to my Zen Organizing madness after all!

CALCULATING YOUR INCOME

Do you know *exactly* how much money you have coming in each week? Each month? Each year? You probably do if you have a salary, own no rental properties, and have no sizeable interest- or dividend-bearing investments. If you work freelance, are a consultant, or are in sales, or you have sources of income aside from a regular paycheck, your income may fluctuate. If you're in the latter category, use the figure you used to calculate your Federal income tax last year—and maybe (if business is good) add a few percentage points—to give yourself an income estimate to help work through the rest of this exercise. You want to use the *net monthly income,* that is, how much you bring home after taxes and other deductions from your paycheck. If the amount varies, note the

If you regularly exercise, be sure you keep up your regime. If you have become a couch potato, I want you to move your body five minutes a day. Take the stairs instead of the elevator to your office. Get off the bus or train a few blocks before your regular stop and walk to work. Give Fido the thrill of his life and give him an extra walk around the block. Pop in your favorite exercise video and follow along for a few minutes. Move that body! Along with exercise, continue to eat well and drink water. These three tools are part of your daily experience for the rest of the year and, I hope, well beyond.

average. Write the number on a page in your financial workbook.

Cash flow refers not only to what is coming in each month but also the monies that flow out. You have two types of expenditures. *Nondiscretionary costs,* or *fixed costs,* are regular monthly expenses such as the mortgage and cable. *Discretionary costs,* or *variable costs,* are things such as movies, gas, and magazines you grab at the newsstand.

CALCULATING YOUR FIXED COSTS

This week, you determine your fixed costs. Determining your variable costs is

more work, so we save that as the sole task for next week.

To find your fixed costs, look at your bank statement as well as your credit or debit card statements for recurring expenses. You can also check the files you created last month. Your receipts should be filed away by this point, making the information easy to retrieve. Following are some examples of fixed costs to get you started:

Cable, TV, and Internet
Car loans
Child care expenses
Groceries
Health insurance
Home insurance
Life insurance
Magazine and newspaper subscriptions
Mortgage or rent
Phone
Property taxes
Student loans
Tax preparation
Transportation expenses
Utilities

DETERMINING YOUR JOB SECURITY

Some jobs that were once secure can no longer be depended on to be there tomorrow. Auto workers, for example, who once had secure jobs and enviable retirement plans, have been laid off in droves by the former giants of Detroit. Many lawyers are struggling to make a living, as are realtors and stockbrokers. Firefighters, police officers, and mail deliverers are just about the only people in your neighborhood who still have both secure jobs and fixed pensions.

Let's take a look at your career and current job security. Are you secure or are you in a shifting industry? You can respond to the following in your financial notebook. Here are some questions to help you decide:

1. Are you happy in your current position?
2. Is your boss happy with you?
3. Has your company or industry had recent layoffs, or has there been buzz in the hallways about impending layoffs?
4. Has there been talk of new management or new ownership of your company, or possibly a merger with another firm? (Mergers and acquisitions often lead to staff turnover.)
5. How healthy is the job market in your field? (A good indicator is the number of employment ads you see. Are there many or few?)
6. If you lost your job tomorrow, what would you do? How long would your savings sustain your living expenses? And how long might it take you to get another job? (Generally, higher paid jobs take longer to find.) The answer will help determine how much you need to save for an emergency fund.
7. Are you grateful you are in your profession? Or is it time to get into a more lucrative or secure field? What steps would you have to take to make the shift a reality?

Former President Bill Clinton once said that in the twenty-first century, the average person would have several professions in his or her lifetime. I have had three. Don't consider changing careers as a betrayal of your original goals—embrace it. A career change may be your best bet for financial salvation.

WEEK THREE

Determine Your Variable Expenses

This week, you can

- See the folly in false assumptions about your spending
- Calculate your variable, or nondiscretionary, costs

THE SNAPSHOT OF YOUR FINANCIAL life is coming into focus. This week we examine discretionary expenses. But don't panic! I'm not going to ask you to forgo all the expenses that bring you pleasure.

Did you know, for instance, that food—at least the kind you buy on-the-run, rather than supermarket groceries—is classified as a discretionary expense? Maybe you could eliminate that pretzel you buy in the subway on the way home or that large fancy coffee you get at lunch? We're going to brush away the mask of unconscious spending and see what's really happening in your life. *Unconscious* is the key word in that sentence. We so often spend money without thinking, and little purchases snowball into giant losses.

KNOWING THE HAZARDS OF ESTIMATING

Do you know how much you spend on your variable, or discretionary, costs? Just about everyone can come up with a figure, but few are ever on the mark. Russell reports that many of his new clients, when asked to give a quick estimate of where the money goes, are shocked when they've performed some tracking and found that their original estimates were off by a huge margin, sometimes 300 or 400 percent! One couple in their early thirties—he has a very successful dental practice—said during their first meeting with Russell that they estimated "maybe 3 to 4 percent" of their income went to food. But after adding their receipts from (elegant) restaurants for a month, they discovered that nearly 20 percent of their budget was being covered in cream sauce and eaten!

CALCULATING YOUR
VARIABLE COSTS

There is only one way to know exactly what you are spending: You need to crunch the numbers.

Every day for a week, get a receipt for absolutely every penny you spend, from the morning latte to that pack of gum you occasionally grab at the corner newsstand.

Carry an index card with you so you can write down the name and amount of items for which you can't get a receipt, such as parking meters, hot dog vendors, and the newsstand periodical.

Look at credit card statements and bank statements.

You might find it easier to record your variable expenses if you simply decide to go an entire month and put everything on your debit or credit card. That way, Visa or MasterCard does the adding for you. Just make sure that you pay off the full balance by the due date. I do not want you paying any interest.

At the end of the week (or month, if you are doing this exercise using your debit or credit card), add everything you spent. Are you surprised by the total?

Realize that variable expenses give you only a snapshot of a particular month. For example, your expenses in June won't reflect the school clothes you buy in August. You also need to account for, say, the family vacation in June as well as presents for holidays, birthdays, and graduations.

The keystone of financial strength is a good solid cash flow, which means that the money coming in is enough to cover all your expenses, savings for a rainy day (such as the Friday when you might get a pink slip), and savings for retirement. Later, we'll talk more about how much you should be saving, but Russell and most financial experts agree that most folks should save at least 15 percent of their income.

Most people are unconsciously bleeding money from relatively small purchases. I remember one housewife who appeared on *Oprah* and spoke of how her family wasn't able to make their mortgage. It turned out that this woman was spending more than $300 a month at Starbucks. A little self-control could easily save at least $1,000 a year without denying her an occasional treat.

WEEK FOUR

Take a Fresh Look at Your Expenses

This week, you can

- Begin to create a budget
- Create a safety net
- Work toward your saving goals

THE WORLD SEEMS TO BE DIVIDED into two groups when it comes to a budget: those who can't live without one and those for whom it's one more item on their to-do list. Math was never my favorite subject in school, but I have discovered something wonderful about numbers as an adult: They don't lie. You always know where you stand. This week, we embark on creating a preliminary budget, the culmination of the financial groundwork we've been laying this month. I think you'll find it gives you a sense of security.

Budgets, like everything in life, shouldn't be rigid. If they are, they tend to be ignored. In April, when we wrap up the budget process, you'll be reviewing ways to reduce expenses and finding ways to make more money. If you are having trouble gathering your budget data, you have a little breathing room to do your research. But don't put it off until the last minute!

After you have all the information you need, you'll be guided by a realistic personal budget. And you'll understand how to tweak it as your circumstances change.

Budgeting is a way to look at both current and future household cash flows. The goal of a budget may vary, but it is most commonly used to improve cash flow by spotting areas where cash inflow might be increased or, more frequently, where cash outflow can be decreased. It isn't enough to "think" that you know where your money is going! Having a formal budget, written on paper (or an Excel spreadsheet or other software), is essential. Keep in mind that budgets aren't set in stone.

At a minimum, budget your expenses for one month to three months. Six months to a year is even better. If at the end of that time, you feel you have a strong handle on your cash flow, you may decide to end the exercise. However, some people find that keeping a budget in writing is something they want to do—or must do—over the long haul. And other people even find maintaining a budget fun!

PUTTING YOUR BUDGET ON PAPER

To begin, open your financial notebook to a blank page. You can also perform this exercise using Excel or an online software program. (The free budgeting program on Mint.com works well.)

Now, start with a column on the far left side of the page and list your net monthly income. If the amount varies, note the average. Below that, list your expenses, dividing them into nondiscretionary (fixed) and discretionary (variable). Note, however, that even fixed costs can be changed. *Fixed* really means automatic—the cost is incurred unless you make a decision to change the cost. For example, your cable TV expenses are fixed, but you can always shop for another, perhaps more economical, plan. Your transportation costs are fixed but can obviously be changed quite a bit, depending on whether you decide to drive a flashy car, drive a clunker, or take the bus. Variable costs, such as whether to see a movie Friday night or go bowling, fluctuate from month to month and are often made as daily decisions. You tallied these costs in weeks two and three this month.

Note that Judy and Juan Navarro's budget (see at right) shows things how

JANUARY HOUSEHOLD BUDGET FOR JUDY AND JUAN NAVARRO

Income	Actual	Goal
Juan's Income	3300	3300
Judy's Income	3200	3600
Total Income	6500	6900
Expenses—Nondiscretionary		
Mortgage	1800	1800
Property tax	350	350
Home insurance	250	250
Utilities	120	110
Health insurance	600	600
Groceries	500	450
Child care	500	500
Clothing	50	50
Health care co-pays	100	100
Auto expenses	400	350
Tolls	50	50
Cable	60	60
Accounting services	30	30
Credit card interest	100	0
Total nondiscretionary expenses	4910	4700
Expenses—Discretionary		
Movies, concerts, shows	100	80
Vacation	100	80
Dining out	400	300
Health club	60	60
Lawn cutting/snow shoveling	150	100
Day spa	200	150
Charity	200	250
Total discretionary expenses	1210	1020
All expenses	6120	5720
Savings	380	1180

they are and how the couple would like them to be. I want you to do the same. You have actual costs in the left column, and now I want you to create a second column titled "Goal," which is what you *want* to spend. During this week, and throughout the next month, revisit this budget to see where you'd like to trim costs. In April, I talk about specific ways to reduce expenses as well as how to increase income. For now, you—and any family members— should think about reasonable ways to cut costs.

This month isn't meant to scare you. We want you to have an all-encompassing snapshot of your financial picture rather than a version that doesn't include key items. But don't worry if you don't have immediate solutions to the issues raised this month. Now that you know what you need, you can be on the lookout for solutions and calmly consider your options. And during the next ten months, you'll investigate ways to increase your financial security.

BUILDING AN EMERGENCY FUND

It's important to have a financial cushion to cover your basic living expenses for at least three to six months in case you lose or decide to change your job. Don't count on government unemployment payments to carry you. You won't get unemployment if you quit or are fired with cause, and the benefits don't always kick in when you need them or in the amount that you need. (Amounts vary depending on the circumstances of your unemployment and the state where you live.)

In addition to building an emergency cushion, you might also consider a Plan B in case of sudden unemployment. Can you borrow from a family member? Find a temp job? Relocate to find new employment? What kind of credit do you have? (It might be dangerous to live on credit— you could find yourself in a deep hole of debt—but credit can sometimes be a lifesaver). If you're thinking of having a baby or going to grad school, would it be more prudent to build this safety net before you increase your financial drain?

Everyone should have at least three to six months of living expenses in an emergency fund. This money needs to be *liquid.* That means that you don't want the money in a retirement account, such as an IRA or your 401(k), which ideally shouldn't be tapped until retirement. You don't want it in any volatile investments, such as stocks or long-term bonds. You certainly don't want it tied up in real estate! And you don't want it in anything that penalizes early withdrawal, such as an eighteen-month CD. You want your emergency fund in a savings or checking account (look into online options, such as ING Direct or Emigrant, for the highest rates) or a money-market fund (Vanguard and Fidelity tend to have good rates). The Web site Bankrate.com can be helpful in shopping for good rates for your liquid money.

In June, I'll talk a lot more about investments and where to keep both your liquid money and long-term savings.

MAKING GOOD DECISIONS

After you can see the imbalance in your budget, it will be easy to understand why you have high personal or credit card debt. You need to know the amount you are short so you can figure out a specific strategy to earn more or reduce your expenses. Do you need a higher paying job or a second job? Can you sell some assets and eliminate the debt that's causing the discrepancy? Or can you simply carve away at the fluctuating items until you have your expenses in line with your income? This is the creative part of crafting and using a budget.

If you're amazed to see that you have a surplus each month, commit to putting this money into that three- to six-month emergency fund mentioned previously. Put any remaining money into your retirement nest egg. In the past you may have frittered this money away because you weren't keeping track. Now that you are keeping track—and making changes— you'll watch your debt shrink and your wealth grow steadily over time. It's always better to understand the reality of your situation than to keep your head under the proverbial rock.

REWARDING YOURSELF

If this is a particularly tough week for you, be especially careful to monitor your self-care. This isn't the time for a gallon of Rocky Road ice cream and a spoon. It's time for a few extra minutes of exercise, maybe another bottle of water, and some nurturing food. Remember that these actions will help you think more clearly. And there is no more critical time for good decision-making than "budget week"!

Congratulate yourself for all your hard work this month. Rewards are a big part of Zen Organizing. What treat can you afford this week? Not sure? Check your budget!

FEBRUARY SUMMARY

WEEK ONE

Set up a system for paying your bills on time, and watch your credit score rise.

WEEK TWO

Record your income as well as your fixed, or discretionary, costs.

WEEK THREE

Record your variable, or discretionary, costs.

WEEK FOUR

Create a preliminary budget and begin thinking about ways to save.

3. MARCH

Get Ready for Taxes

I have no tax planning.

I don't have an accountant.

I don't have tax shelters.

I just follow what the U.S. Congress tells me to do.

—WARREN BUFFETT

IF YOU HAVEN'T BEEN ORGANIZED UP to now, I'm going to bet getting ready for tax time puts a big strain on you and possibly on your relationships. Surveys show that the average American spends nearly thirty hours tracking down, figuring out, filling out, and mailing off tax forms. (This does not include time spent cursing those forms.) One Associated Press poll indicates that two-thirds of all Americans agree that the Federal tax system has become too complicated. This month, I'll reduce at least some of your anxiety. Being organized will make the process easier.

HABIT OF THE MONTH: FILE PAPERS

Spend five minutes a day putting papers in their appropriate file folders (or the shredder). If you don't have the necessary file folder, create it. These five minutes will make a big change in the way you deal with paper. If you hit a particularly busy day, gather the items to be filed and pop them into the "To-file" folder in your "Action files" master category.

TOOL OF THE MONTH: MUSIC

Music can create an atmosphere of peace and calm or it can make you move to the beat and work faster and harder. Whatever type of music you like, enjoy it while you work if that will help take the edge off dealing with your finances.

WEEK ONE

Decide Which Documents to Save

This week, you can

- Know which documents need to be kept and for how long
- Find ways to store files

I HAD A CLIENT WHO BECAME A DEAR friend. Long before I met her, she had been emotionally traumatized by an IRS audit. As a result, she saved *everything*—every billing statement, every letter, every receipt. I couldn't get her to part with a single piece of paper. She had boxes of obsolete receipts going back decades—a mountain of space-robbing eyesores. Would anyone need to be this cautious? If you are in a cash business (a laundromat owner?), take huge deductions (trying to write off the new BMW?), or are a big-gun lawyer who deals in securities issues, perhaps yes. But not the average taxpayer.

KNOWING WHAT TO KEEP

Are you like my friend? Do you say you're going to keep every document just in case? This is a thorny issue but the bottom line is straightforward: Some documents you

do need to keep for life, some you need to keep three or more years for the IRS, and others you can feel safe tossing or shredding. (Be sure and add file folders for any materials you missed in January).

Tax backup material that should be saved. This material supports the most common tax deductions and must therefore be saved. It includes:

- Investment papers that confirm the purchase, sale, or transfer of your holdings.
- Pay stubs.
- Finance-related statements, including those from your broker, mutual funds, 401(k), and all other retirement plans as well as your children's college savings plan.
- Bank statements. The IRS can check these for income you may have forgotten to declare.
- Credit card statements (if they in-

clude deductible purchases for which you have no other receipts).

- Utility and phone bills, if they are deductible (which they could be if you run a home business).

Shred monthly or quarterly statements after you have received your year-end statements.

Documents that are safe to shred. Thank goodness for this category. Otherwise we'd need to rent space just to store all the legal docs in our lives.

- Credit card statements if the purchases are solely personal and not deductible. Shred them after your payment has been credited. If there is a purchase dispute, hold onto the statement until the dispute is resolved. And remember that most statements are available online for up to a year or more with most financial institutions.
- Utility and phone bills if these are not deductible. Shred them after a month when you see that your payment has been credited.
- ATM receipts and deposit slips can be shredded after you reconcile your bank statement.
- Any paperwork that duplicates files you have safely stored online. You can always generate a printout if you need one.

Old tax forms and backup materials. Uncle Sam may want you but not all your backup paperwork. At least not forever, thank goodness. Here are the current guidelines.

- Save the Federal and state tax returns you file forever. Copies are always helpful as guides for future returns or amending previously filed ones. And in case the IRS claims you failed to file, you can easily prove them wrong.
- Hold onto backup material for at least three years beyond the date you file your taxes. Most audits happen within three years. Keeping backup files for up to six years is better because the IRS can audit you beyond three years if fraud is suspected. (No state requires record retention beyond six years, so you are covered on this front.)
- As for state returns, every state has a different time frame for how long you need to hold onto state-tax related receipts. In California, for example, this time period is four years. Check with your tax preparer, who will be current on any tax law amendments. Your state representative's office can also fill you in on any tax laws pertinent to your state or locality. If you care to get the information online, do a search for "tax office" and put in the name of your state.
- Regardless of your state laws, in certain situations it is advisable to keep tax-related documents until they can no longer affect future returns. And that, in some cases, can be far longer

than three years, says Julian Block, a tax attorney based in Larchmont, New York. Examples of papers to keep for the long haul, says Block, include records that show what you paid for stocks, mutual funds, real estate, and other investments. Those records are vital, not only because you may need them for an IRS audit, but because you need them to figure your profits or losses on sales that may not take place until many years later.

STORING OLD TAX FILES

Keep copies of every year's tax returns in a fireproof metal box or at least a metal filing cabinet. (Most metal file cabinets won't be fireproof, but it's still a step up from a cardboard or plastic box.) You can store tax return backup material in two plastic bins with locking lids. Put every category of deduction in a clearly marked large envelope. For example, "Medical Receipts," "Utility Bills," and "Mortgage Payments" might be some of your tax-deductible expenses stored in individual envelopes. If you need to check a particular category, you want retrieval to be a snap. Being organized means you are always saving time.

Are you running out of storage space for your returns? After a decade or two it starts to get overwhelming, doesn't it? Starting this year, why not scan them onto your computer? Or ask your tax preparer to provide your copy on a disc. I've seen clients store their old tax materials in metal file cabinets in the garage. This is a great solution provided you can lock the cabinet. (You don't want a nosy neighbor or day worker combing through your most private papers one day when the garage door is open!) And please remember that safe place you've chosen to keep the key.

You don't need to store every piece of paper forever. I hope you'll feel free to shred and toss the obvious excess or unimportant papers you may be hoarding. That said, when it comes to the tax code, information is subject to change at a minute's notice. Be sure to check with your personal tax preparer for up-to-the-minute advice.

WEEK TWO

Stop the Paper Stacks

This week, you can

- Gather your tax-support materials and receipts
- Sort and categorize your tax papers

YOU KNOW THE FAMILIAR PICTURE: A man or woman walks into the accountant's office in early April with a shoe box filled with receipts. This is not only a cartoonish view of how taxes are paid in America—it often reflects the reality! Taxes, even in this electronic age, mean paperwork. Lots and lots of paperwork.

GATHERING THE STRAYS

For our purposes, the *strays* are not the neighborhood dogs without a home but those papers I know you didn't get to in January, when we were concerned with simply developing a system for your current workspace. Pretty much every unorganized person has years of paperwork gathering dust and taking up space. This week you'll gather everything and sort through it all. This may take more than two hours if you never did anything like

this in previous years. Take heart. You won't be faced with this task again because I know you aren't going to fall off the organizing bandwagon. How do I know? When someone makes a commitment of time, expends energy, and reads a book like this, he or she is truly ready for change. Let's begin.

For this project, you'll need some Post-it notes. Use the medium size rather than the itty-bitty ones, which may get lost in the process. You'll also need a heavy-duty garbage bag and a paper shredder at the ready. At the end of January you created your basic file system. Last week you identified additional financial categories, such as retirement and real estate. If you're like most readers, creating the files was easy but gathering the stacks of papers from around your home was daunting, so you decided to wait and deal with them later. Am I right? I have some good news for you. The majority of the papers you see scattered about your home and office will fall nicely into these very same categories. Up until now you haven't known what to do with them. This week we're creating a home for them. By week's end, you will have identified all current categories and individual files in your personal system.

Now, I want you to collect your papers from every corner of your home and office. Put them in a pile (or piles) in one spot. Keep the stacks neat, so that visually things look under control. If you're working on a stack and look over and see an enormous paper bomb, you're going to be discouraged and overwhelmed before you make a single decision. Never underestimate the power of the visual to help or hinder your progress.

SORTING YOUR PAPERS

Clear a space, perhaps on the floor or your desk, wherever you feel most comfortable. (My dogs used to love to come in and walk on my sorted piles. Maybe the door should be closed to Fido and Fifi the cat for this process?) Keep a water bottle handy and maybe a few slices of fruit and cheese. Your blood sugar may plummet at the very prospect of dealing with all this stuff!

Step One: Eliminate
Pick up a small stack of paper no more than two inches thick. Take one piece of paper at a time and identify it. Remember the Magic Formula: first, eliminate. Can it be tossed? Does this piece of paper need

to be shredded? If your stash of papers is large, I suggest you not shred as you go along but rather have a box handy to catch it all and shred it later. Or use a professional service that will come and shred your papers for you. This works well if you think you'll fill a box or two. Or deliver the material to the service and save a bundle.

Step Two: Categorize
The second part of the Magic Formula is to categorize. You will be creating three overall categories: papers from the current year, papers pertaining to last year, and papers from before last year. But don't worry, there is less detailed organization to do as we delve into the past. It isn't likely you will need these papers, but we do want a fighting chance at easy retrieval if you suddenly have to research something for yourself or the IRS.

Papers from the current year. Make Post-it notes for your various categories. (These categories become piles of papers as you begin going through your papers.) If the paper in question relates to the current year, put it in the appropriate category. You will file all this material at the end of the day in the folders you created. Organizing this material will make tax prep *next* year a breeze.

Papers from last year. Material from *last* year should also be identified and set aside in categories. You need this information to prepare *this* year's tax return. (For example, if the current year is 2010, you'll be filing 2009's tax return.) If you are getting ready to file last year's taxes, don't make file folders for the material. Use large envelopes only. You aren't going to keep this material in your file cabinet. You're going to store it, so get it ready for that purpose. Again we want to save time and steps every chance we get.

As early as January you'll start receiving the tax documents you need to use in preparing your April 15 returns. Now, as you go through your paper piles, you're looking for:

- W2 forms, which report your income if you're a salaried employee
- 1099 forms, which you may receive if you're an independent contractor
- Mortgage interest statements
- Receipts for contributions to charities
- Interest, dividend, and capital gain statements from banks and brokerage houses

You don't want to lose these documents, so let's create one place for them to reside. I would use a manila file jacket that expands up to two inches. (Don't use a box-bottom hanging file folder for this purpose, even though it also expands two inches, because it is open on the sides and I don't want you to lose any of these valuable docs.) You can label this folder "Tax Docs/Year End" and keep it in front of your "Action files" master category. How's that for easy?

Papers from two years ago or earlier. Any papers from prior years that you need to hold onto as part of your tax backup material should be saved in large envelopes by year only. Don't bother to sort

and make individual folders for specific categories. If you are audited, you can pull out this material and sort it at that time. No point in making extra work for yourself today.

Step Three: Organize

The final step in the Magic Formula is to organize. Remember the papers from the current year (and last year if you aren't close to filing for taxes)? Now is the time to file them. You've already indicated the different categories with Post-it notes. If you have your file folders and envelopes ready and waiting, filing will be a breeze.

Keep your files in alphabetical order and use a label maker to identify each. You'll be amazed how much easier it is to retrieve material when you can easily read the folder name. If you have a category that has several parts (for example, a real estate transaction) remember to keep all the files that constitute the category in alphabetical order within the box-bottom hanging file folder that houses them.

This phase of the Magic Formula, as you experienced in January, can be a bit tedious. Don't give up! Remember that a functioning, beautiful, and easy-to-maintain file system will save you time during the year. And I just can't say it often enough: Time is money. Time is also a commodity. You get each minute only once. Rather than squander time searching for papers you need, you'll be saving time to devote to your financial planning, or better yet, to enjoying the rewards it will bring.

WEEK THREE

Prepare Your Tax Returns

This week, you can

- Weigh doing taxes yourself, with a software program, or by hiring a professional
- See the pros and cons of tax prep software
- Know what you need to work with a tax professional
- Consider itemizing deductions
- Find where to get free tax help

AN ASSOCIATED PRESS POLL TELLS US that about six in ten Americans pay someone to help do their taxes. The rest of us manage it alone. Either way you go, the process needn't be the numbers equivalent of a root canal.

Generally, you'll have your main tax form—the 1040 or 1040EZ (for very simple filing)—mailed to you. They are also available online at www.irs.gov and at your local tax office and library. If you decide to purchase tax-preparation software, the form is provided as part of the package.

CHOOSING A TAX PREP METHOD

Whether or not you decide to do your taxes yourself—either the old-fashioned way, with paper and pencil, or by using a software package—is up to you. If you're comfortable with numbers, if you're generally well organized, and if your tax situation isn't too complicated, you might want to give it a stab.

If you do decide to do your own taxes, know that entire books have been written on tax preparation, and I would urge you to read at least one! The perennial classic is J. K. Lasser's *Your Income Tax,* published by John Wiley & Sons. The 2009 edition was 816 pages and cost $18.95. (Yes, you can deduct that price from your taxes.) Warning: Discount book dealers will often sell last year's tax books for 80 percent off the cover price, but buying and using last year's tax book—given the substantial changes in the law that can occur year to year—makes about as much sense as buying month-old milk!

If you hate numbers, tend to have poor attention to detail, have numerous sources of income or deductible expenses, or have had a major life change in the past year (such as a divorce), you're probably better off hiring a pro. If you have your own business, operate rental properties, or have a job that offers deferred compensation, I would also recommend working with a professional. If your business is incorporated—whether an LLC or an S Corp—please hire a tax professional.

When searching for a good tax preparer, I suggest that you ask for referrals from friends and colleagues who seem to be savvy about finances. If you have an attorney, an investment advisor, or a realtor, ask who he uses as a tax preparer. You might also call a local college, ask for the accounting department, and get references.

You might at some point also consider the chains: the largest are H&R Block, Jackson Hewitt, and Liberty. Tax-preparation chains may offer bargain-basement prices compared to most independent practitioners, but you may also find that your delegated tax preparer, although adept at using tax preparation software, doesn't qualify as a tax expert. Going to a chain is similar to doing taxes yourself with a good software package. I advise against using a chain unless your tax situation is simple and straightforward.

WORKING WITH TAX PREP SOFTWARE

If you decide to use tax-preparation software, and your total income is below $56,000 (as of [year], filing [single, married, etc.]), you are eligible for the IRS's free software. Go to www.irs.gov/efile. Unfortunately, the IRS software won't help with your state taxes.

If you are paying for software, amateurs and professionals alike give TurboTax high marks. Says Kevin Brosious, MBA, CPA/PFS, CFP, president of Wealth Management, Inc., in Allentown, PA, "I like TurboTax for my personal tax info. It works well, and I can file online to save time and get a quicker refund. I have never had a problem with it, but I have had issues with other tax prep software. (I won't mention the names.) The tax software will also eliminate those pesky math errors!"

Other things Kevin likes about the program? TurboTax:

- Walks you through a tutorial process when preparing your taxes.
- Prompts you if there is an error or omission and provides audit flags.
- Has a state module, so you don't have the tedium of reentering all your personal info.

But even with the best software, tax filing can be tricky and items can be forgotten. We suggest that even if you use TurboTax, you might want to touch base with a tax pro at least once every three to five years to make sure you're not missing something important.

Now if you have lots of investments, own property, and get a slew of 1099's and W2's at the end of the year, you might want to consider the merits of dealing with a professional. Laurie A. Siebert, CPA, CFP, practitioner with Valley National Financial Advisors in Bethlehem, PA, has some perfect examples of clients who used tax software and came to her to see what they missed:

"I have one client who . . . could not differentiate between mortgage interest for his home and his rental property. He wound up with huge deductions on both Schedule A and Schedule D [which] I had to correct."

"One young couple was buying and selling a home. They took money out of a retirement account to float them for a while. They wound up paying taxes and a 10 percent penalty on that money. They didn't know that they could have paid that money back within 60 days and thereby avoid having to pay the tax and the penalty. That's not something the software would pick up."

"Another client said, 'We're going to take money out of our retirement account to redo the kitchen.' They didn't realize that taking that money out would raise their AGI [adjusted gross income] and raise their tax bracket so that they'd be paying much more on Social Security. . . . They would be much better off tapping a home equity loan."

These real-life examples underscore the fact that although a software program can prompt you with relevant questions, users may not understand the implications of the questions or they may go through them so quickly something gets missed. A tax preparer will go through some of these same questions but will know what may or may not apply. This human contact opens the door for an invaluable and often money saving discussion.

What's the moral of the story? Even if you use software, and know what you're doing, it is probably best to see a professional tax advisor once every three to five years for tax-planning and tax strategy purposes.

WORKING WITH A TAX PREPARER

If you're working with a tax pro, he or she has probably sent you some worksheets. Be sure to enter your data today, or over the next few days, using the folders I had you create in January. You will want to bring your completed data sheets and all necessary tax documentation (such as W2's and 1099's) with you to your appointment.

Make sure that you get the most out of the time spent with your tax professional. His or her job should not only be to fill out forms, but to advise you as to how you can save money on taxes. Be sure to ask the following questions:

- Am I maximizing my potential deductions?

- Am I contributing to the right kind of retirement plan?
- Should I consider refinancing my mortgage?
- Are there any investments I might sell to tax-loss harvest? (If you don't know what that means, see December, week two.)

ITEMIZING DEDUCTIONS

It's easiest to take standard deductions, but itemizing your deductions can often save you considerable money.

Charitable Deductions
I'm a big fan of setting up reminders on your computer—in your Outlook calendar, for example—provided you don't overuse them. (I can imagine someone whose computer is dinging all day long with reminders. Pretty soon none of those reminders will mean anything.) One reminder I would schedule is to make charitable contributions in December. If you want to deduct these, remember that the rules have changed. You must have receipts to take the deduction. Each time you make a contribution, be sure you put it on a charge card, write a check, or get a receipt from the charity. No longer can you say, "I put $10 in the basket every Sunday."

Other Deductions
Giving to charity isn't the only thing that can reduce your tax hit. So can these other deductions:

- Mortgage interest payments
- Legitimate expenses for your business
- Capital losses (investments sold for less than you paid for them)
- Medical expenses beyond 7.5 percent of your income
- Contributions to most retirement accounts

Keep deductions in perspective, warns Laurie Siebert. Don't get so carried away looking for deductions that you lose the big picture, which is to save money in the end. "I was once doing taxes for a farmer who wanted to buy a $20,000 tractor to save on income taxes," says Siebert. "Yes, it might have saved him $5,000 in taxes, but I pointed out that he'd still be out $15,000. I asked him if he really needed the tractor, and he said 'no.' Don't spend money just to get a tax deduction." Is there a "tractor" in your past?

FINDING TAX HELP

What happens if you can't afford a professional or the software? Help is at hand. This section describes some resources you can use.

Provided your adjusted gross income is under $56,000, go directly to the IRS Web site and take advantage of the free software they make available to the public. The site is http://www.irs.gov/efile/article/0,,id= 118986,00.html.

VITA (Volunteer Income Tax Assistance Program) provides free assistance to low-income filers. Certified volunteers sponsored by various organizations receive training to help prepare basic tax returns in communities across the country. VITA sites are generally located at community and neighborhood centers, libraries, schools, shopping malls, and other convenient locations. Most locations also offer free electronic filing. Call 1-800-829-1040 to find a center near you.

AARP does free tax returns for modest-income people. You need not be elderly. Find details at https://locator.aarp.org/vmis/sites/tax_aide_locator.jsp.

WEEK FOUR

Signed, Sealed, Delivered

This week, you can

- Double-check your returns
- Decide the fate of your tax refund

YOU CAN TOIL FOR DAYS PULLING together your tax forms, adding, subtracting, multiplying, dividing, sharpening your #2 pencils, and filling in line after line of all those forms. Then you drive to the central post office and get your package in the mail just before midnight, April 15. But driving home, you start to wonder, "Did I remember to put a stamp on the envelope?" If you didn't, all was for naught. Such is part of the madness of taxes. This week takes you through the final steps of tax filing.

CHECKING FOR ERRORS

Yes, it's true. Even the most left-brained among us sometimes make simple mistakes. But you know what they say: forewarned is forearmed. Here are some of the most classic errors or omissions people— even some professionals—make in prepar-

ing taxes, according to expert Kevin Brosious:

Watch for mathematical errors. Double-check your figures.

If you support a parent or other relative, don't forget to list him or her as a dependent.

File as head of household if you are eligible.

List all Social Security or taxpayer ID numbers (including dependents). Be sure they are correct.

Even if your employer did not withhold taxes from your paycheck, you are still liable to pay them. Add this income to your 1040.

In certain states, pension and IRA distributions are not subject to state income tax. What are the rules for your state?

Did you overlook *carry-forward* items (items from last years' taxes that can still affect this year's, and possibly next year's, taxes) from previous returns, including capital losses and passive losses? Losses can be carried forward indefinitely and applied against capital gains, or if you had no gains, you can still deduct $3,000 per year against your ordinary income.

If you worked for more than one employer during the year, your deductions for Social Security may be off the mark, and you could be due a refund.

Take the time to calculate your itemized deductions rather than automatically using the standard deduction.

Some states allow you to deduct contributions to a 529 plan. Check the rules for your state.

Finally, don't forget to

- Sign and date your returns;
- Include all the necessary forms;
- Photocopy your returns;
- Include a stamp and a return address on your envelope;
- Mail your returns before the deadline.

Remember that you can always file for an extension. If you have the time, but not the money, payment plans are possible. And if you ever get an audit notice, that's serious business, and it's time to look at tax pros to help you. In the event of an audit, they will accompany you, not your Zen Organizer!

SOCKING AWAY THAT TAX REFUND

After you've completed your tax forms, you may discover that you owe Uncle Sam money, and you'll need to send a check or allow for the funds to be deducted from an account. (Paying with plastic is a possibility, but there's generally a "convenience fee" of 2.49 percent. Too high a price, in my book.) Or you may discover that the taxes you've been paying either through your employer or directly to the IRS earlier in the year have earned you a refund.

If you do score a refund, well, most people jump for joy. But refunds aren't necessarily great things. Think about it. You paid the IRS too much earlier in the year instead of having that money in the bank working for you. But still, I won't deny that getting a refund check can feel good.

Unfortunately, many people fritter this money away on big-ticket items they could easily live without. I know the Super Bowl would look great on a gigantic screen, but wouldn't you feel more secure beefing up your savings or investment accounts? Balance is the key here. You want to avoid spending all of the refund to make yourself feel good, just as you want to avoid socking it all away and feeling deprived. Find a reasonable reward you can enjoy now.

Here are some ideas for that tax refund that will reward you in due time.

A White House initiative passed in September 2009 will create a little box on next year's tax form. Check the box, and you can get your refund in the form of United

> You are working hard this month, but remember to take the time to look for end-of-winter sales and impossible-to-beat deals on items such as heavy coats, gloves, hats, snow shovels, and skis. (But don't spend your entire tax refund!)

States Savings Bonds—not a bad alternative if you are the kind of person who otherwise would spend your refund money on nonessentials.

Do you have a savings account that will cover at least six months of living expenses in the event of an emergency? Start one or add to it with your refund check.

Are you saving to purchase a house? The refund check can be added to your down payment savings account. In today's economy, with the credit belt tightening, you'll likely need to put down at least 20 percent and perhaps up to 30 percent of the price of a home. This isn't a small consideration. Let your tax refund move you closer to home ownership.

Check the interest rate on your credit cards. Pay down the highest rate card. The interest you're paying each month serves no purpose. It adds to the original purchase price of all items and it isn't a tax deduction.

Add to or establish an IRA or other retirement account. Social Security is not going to fully fund your old age.

Add to or establish a 529 college plan for your children. Encourage them to study hard so that they can earn scholarships. And be sure they learn how good it feels to make money by helping them secure part-time work from a young age. You'll likely need several sources to pay tuition.

FEELING IN CONTROL

I hope this month has helped you feel more in control of your tax dollars. With sage advice from the experts in your life and careful planning, you can find a balance between the support you owe the government for the programs we all rely on and the money you need to govern your personal life and expenses. Now that your papers are in order and you have a long-term system in place for maintaining that order, you'll have more time to investigate and manage your financial life.

MARCH SUMMARY

WEEK ONE

Gather, sort, and file tax-related papers.

WEEK TWO

Tally those sorted receipts.

WEEK THREE

Determine whether to use a tax pro or software or do taxes yourself.

WEEK FOUR

Check for errors on your tax forms. How will you use your tax refund?

4. APRIL

Spend Less, Save More

We must be willing to get rid of the life we've planned,
so as to have the life that is waiting for us.

–JOSEPH CAMPBELL

WE ALL KNOW IT'S EASIER TO spend money than to save it. Spending money often offers us immediate emotional comfort. The ways we spend become habitual and unconscious. Do you stop every morning at the coffee shop even though you have a coffee maker and insulated travel mug at home? Do you pick up magazines every time you grocery shop even though you don't have time to read them? You get the idea. Changing your financial life is, to a great extent, about setting in motion new habits and new expectations. You can "just say no" to impulse shopping. It can be incredibly fulfilling to realize that your actions (or inactions) provide you and your family with long-term financial security, which is a lot more fulfilling than those designer jeans and leather jacket you've been eyeing in the store. The information this month is intended to inspire your creativity.

HABIT OF THE MONTH: LOG YOUR SAVINGS

This month, have saving money on the brain. Every evening, make a note in your financial notebook that shows what you saved that day. (Set aside a few pages for this so that you can keep your log in one section of your notebook.) One day you might enter the amount of change you deposited in your piggy bank. Another day you might note that you saved $3 at the grocery store using coupons. And, if you're really lucky, one day you might log that you set aside several hundred dollars in your savings account to bolster your rainy day funds. No matter the amount, it all adds up.

TOOL OF THE MONTH: SLEEP

Are you getting enough sleep? Western medical experts say the average adult needs between seven and nine hours a night and the average child needs eight to ten hours. Traditional Chinese medicine further suggests that the sleep you get before midnight is the most beneficial. But who among us is getting this kind of quality sleep? Stress, menopause, work, and new babies are just a few of the things that cause us to miss our needed hours of rest. Your body breaks down without adequate time to replenish itself. It's more difficult to think clearly. We're cranky and on edge.

You can't make up lost sleep over a weekend. Nor can an occasional nap replenish your system. Whether you sleep in a bit later each morning, go to bed earlier, or give up those late-night video games, get adequate rest! Add fifteen or twenty minutes to your current sleep regimen. Try this for two consecutive weeks and see how you feel. What have you got to lose this month except those bags under your eyes and that exhausted feeling?

WEEK ONE

Reduce Your Expenses

This week, you can

- Explore many ways to reduce your living expenses
- Understand when a bargain is actually a waste in disguise

SHOULD YOU BE MORE CONCERNED with reducing your mortgage payment or cutting back on those morning lattes? The truth is, you can save big money in both arenas. I was curious what a pro would say about the best place to focus our energy. The answer came from Gregory Karp, writer of the nationally syndicated newspaper column "Spending Smart." Says Karp, "It's really both. The real problem is that most people put their effort into the big expenditures, such as buying homes and cars, while thinking nothing of overspending on groceries and their phone bill. Any kind of repeat spending is insidious because the amounts seem small, but they truly do add up."

REDUCING MONTHLY EXPENSES

This week, consider implementing ways to rein in your monthly costs. Making a few changes in your lifestyle could save you several hundred dollars a month. When we hear about small amounts of money being saved through a cost-cutting measure, it's easy to dismiss the suggestion. "What good is that going to do?" we ask ourselves. Karp broke down some specific savings so you could see how consistently saving a little will add up to a lot. Here are his key examples.

Did you know the average family of four will spend $7,500 on food each year at the grocery store? And that is just the food bill. This figure doesn't include paper products (toilet paper, napkins, paper towels, and so on), personal care products (hair care, soap, and dental products), and miscellaneous items (such as floral bouquets). If you can cut your food spending by 20 percent (start using coupons or buy less-expensive cuts of meat, for example), you can save $1,500 a year!

ONLINE DATING

Match.com and eHarmony.com are popular but are quickly losing out to free sites such as PlentyofFish.com, OkCupid.com, and the brand new RewardingLove.com (which is free for now, but may charge down the road). Why pay to meet your next love when you can get the same service for free? If you find your soul mate, he or she is more likely to be frugal, just like you!

The devil really is in the details. A movie rental service is great provided you're an avid movie watcher. A gym membership can keep you fit, but the benefits are yours only if you actually go! If the fitness center you haven't seen in three months charges you $70 per month, you could pocket $840 at the end of the year if you cancel your membership. And if you shave a reasonable $17 a month off your food bill, you'll have $884 at the end of the year. You can probably get new walking shoes or a used bike for about $100. You'll still have a major boost to your savings account without sacrificing your ability to stay in shape.

Do you feel conflicted when you make a large purchase such as a washing machine or computer and the salesperson really, really wants you to buy the extended warranty? Gregory's tip: Don't bother buying the warranty on low-ticket items. Instead, if you want, put that amount in the bank. If an item goes on the fritz, you have an emergency fund just for this purpose. In addition, I would add that the store and the manufacturer will usually cover the item for at least ninety days (sometimes up to one year), by which time most lemons will have announced themselves.

You know that temporary emotional high you get when you spend money? After this week you're going to experience the same good feeling every time you save money. But there's a catch: Spending money is a temporary high but saving money offers multiple long-term highs. How can this be? First, you're happy because you just saved money. Next, you're happy because you're watching your savings grow. And then you're happy because you can now afford something important that was out of reach before.

None of the tips that follow may seem like much on their own, but multiply the savings over the course of a year, and see how they can add up. We have lots of categories, so choose a few that work for you. Build your "saving muscle" a few dollars at a time.

Turn cost-cutting into a game. How much money can you save? Figure out the exact dollar amount you'll be able to sock away and earmark those funds for your savings account. Do that with as many of these suggestions as you can.

Hearth and Home

Without leaving the house, you can save money. The opportunities are everywhere, but we don't see them. We're glued to the computer or TV screen. Maybe we're busy eating or napping! Let's see what saving opportunities are quite literally under our noses. After you read this section, see how many tips you can add on your own.

Close off the rooms you don't use on a regular basis and use space heaters or portable air conditioners or fans in the rooms you do occupy.

Do you need to reinsulate? You can save a bundle if you've been letting heat or air conditioning escape to the outside. And remember to close your fireplace damper during the summer months.

When you leave for the day, don't forget to set the thermostat to an energy-saving level.

Could you clean out the garage and rent it to someone with a car that needs to be kept safe? Is there a room that's separate from the house on your property (above the garage or a guest house) that you could rent to someone who needs a studio or an office space? (Check zoning laws.)

Have you switched to energy-saving light-bulbs yet? The Environmental Defense Fund has an online guide to help you choose the correct energy-saving bulb for your needs. They also have an online calculator that tells you how much energy you will save. Don't let the extra $8 or so a bulb dissuade you. You'll have the bulb for years!

These lights do have trace amounts of mercury, so you'll have to dispose of them carefully. Stores such as Ikea and Home Depot will take them off your hands for free. Or call 1-800-CLEAN-UP, visit lamprecycle.org or earth911.org, or contact your local government agency in charge of household hazardous waste (start with your sanitation department) for recycling options in your area.

If you really want to save energy, check out the Environmental Defense Fund's online quiz to calculate your personal energy impact and see how else you can save. Go to http://www.fightglobalwarming.com/carboncalculator.cfm.

Speaking of electricity, don't forget to unplug items when they aren't in use. In your office, use a power strip so you can shut off multiple devices with the flick of a single switch.

Phone Service

Gone are the days when a household had a single phone. You had to leave home with pocket change in case you needed to make a call at a public pay phone. Today you'd be hard pressed to find one! Let's see if we can't whittle away at those multiple phone bills: cell, land line, dedicated computer. Which ones do you have?

Examine your cell phone bill to see whether you're paying for more services than you need, such as extra minutes, texting, and Internet. When I bought my new phone, the young salesclerk wanted me to sign up for unlimited texting. I had to explain that it wasn't as important to me as it might be to her. It would have added $15 a month to my bill. That's $360 over the two-year life of the contract.

If you have a cell phone that's for emergencies only, you might save by switching from a long-term contract to a prepaid wireless phone. It could be the difference between paying $60 a month ($720 a year) versus $180 a year. The latter would be for the $15 monthly basic pay-as-you-go plan from a major provider such as Verizon. The industry leader in pay-as-you-go service is Tracphone. Check them out at www.tracphone.com. You can tailor these plans depending on your needs. Teenagers, for example, will surely need some kind of texting plan! Check your current bill to see if you are underutilizing the minutes you're paying. But don't switch in the middle of your contract or you could negate your savings with a hefty fine.

Do you need both a cell phone and a home phone, or just one?

You may be paying for services you don't need on your home phone as well. When I signed up with my new provider, I bought a service package. When the first bill came in the mail, you can imagine my surprise when I saw an extra service giving me lower-cost calling abroad that had been tacked on for my "convenience." The fly in the ointment is that I almost never call abroad! A fee of $5 might seem benign, but that's $60 a year I could be saving.

More and more, we're seeing phone service that runs through the Internet (some-times called broadband telephone), and it tends to be free or close to it. Check out Vonage.com and Skype.com. The quality isn't sterling yet, but it is getting better all the time.

Entertainment

Although I certainly want you to have quality entertainment in your life, it's wise to make honest appraisals and see what can be eliminated or replaced with lower-cost versions. Here are some suggestions to get your creative juices flowing.

Do you really need cable or satellite television? Remember that without cable or satellite, you'll still have the basic channels. In addition, the Web site for the television channel provides many television programs soon after they air. Check out www.hulu.com for even more options.

You can also get caught up on the movies you've missed in the theaters by joining a subscription service such as Netflix.

For even more savings, simply check the films out of your local library. If you and your friends have hundreds of DVDs, why not rent movies from each other?

Finally, check out www.InsideRedbox.com. They have coupons for the DVD kiosks you see in grocery stores, McDonald's, and Wal-Mart.

Food and Dining

Are you a certified foodie or a fast-food junkie? Do you always hit the grocery store when you are starving? Let's see if we can't find a few money-saving alterations to your current regime. We need to eat, but if we aren't careful those empty calories will be emptying our wallets as well!

Is it time to abandon the upscale grocery store with the higher markup and support your local farmer's market? What about getting shares in CSA (community supported agriculture)?

Could you switch from brand names to store brands for some products? And don't forget coupons. Some stores double the value at the register. You can find coupons online and save the cost of the Sunday newspaper. If you have the space, stockpile whenever there's a sale. You'll wonder why you ever paid full price.

How often do you eat out? Try cutting back on the number of nights you dine out, even if it's just once a week. Drop to once a month or every six weeks, for example. We all need a treat from time to time—but how often do you really need it? Jot down the average price of a meal for your family at your favorite restaurant. Multiply that by however many weeks you eat out. The figure will probably astound you. I bet you could pay off one of your credit cards with what you'd save.

Now ask yourself how much it would cost to duplicate those meals at home. Maybe eating at home could be more fun if you added candles or spread a blanket on the floor and ate in front of the TV while getting caught up on some of the programs you missed last week. If you can run your computer through your TV, you're all set!

What about frequenting less-expensive, off-the-beaten-path restaurants as a periodic treat rather than a nightly or weekly ritual?

I have a friend who loves to cook. She formed a cooking circle with a group of like-minded friends. They take turns preparing meals at each other's homes, sharing the expense of the food. And they swap the recipes at the end of the evening. There is no one to tip and they have spent more quality time together than if they had just met in a restaurant. If you live in the same neighborhood, you can leave your cars at home! Would this work for you?

Stores such as Williams Sonoma host free cooking classes. Why not take one as a family and then spend one night a month practicing your new skills? Go to www. williams-sonoma.com and click "Store Events."

If you have a backyard, grow some food. Russell Wild takes this one step further: He grows vegetables and fruit trees and donates the bounty to a local food bank.

Membership Bonus

For several years friends tried to get me to join Costco. As a single woman I had no idea how to handle the large quantities. But then I cleared some space and voila! I had storage for the paper products and office supplies I love to have on hand. I've also learned to share the fresh produce bounty with neighbors and friends.

Membership stores like Costco or Sam's Club can save you a bundle on staples such as paper towels and toilet paper. If you have no space to store a large quantity, split your order with a good friend. In fact, why not split the membership fee? It's especially important to go to these large stores with a shopping list and a realistic eye for a true bargain. For example, I live alone. If I bring home the large economy bag of bananas, they will rot before I can consume them all, so I haven't saved any money. On the other hand, while it can be a challenge to store paper products, I shop for them once a year. Take a look at your weekly shopping list and see which items would be more cost effective to buy in bulk.

A company called Reusablebags offers a special kind of reusable plastic bag that keeps produce fresh much longer than other more common kinds of storage. Go to www.reusablebags.com.

Are you a part of a union? Have you ever checked out the privileges of membership? You'll be amazed at the variety of offers, from low-cost insurance to affordable legal advice. Go to www.unionplus.org for a sample of what is available.

Are you over fifty? AARP (American Association of Retired People, at www.AARP.org) has a laundry list of member benefits. What about the Auto Club? You'd be surprised at the range of benefits the card carries with it. Next time you take the family to a museum or an amusement park, check to see whether you can save on admission. Go to: www.autoclub.com. Enter your zip code to find a local office.

Car

With the cost of gas on an ever-upward spiral, it's important to save every chance you get with your vehicle. Before we check out these tips, let me ask you a key question: could you live without your car? You could put the savings from gas, insurance, and repairs in an account and see a substantial gain in only one year.

Do you commute to your job? Have you considered taking public transportation instead? You'd save on gas and maintenance, and you might even be able to lower your insurance premium. You could end up saving a bundle! Aside from the money you could save, you might also use the commute time to get caught up on your magazine reading and personal phone calls.

To get a rough idea how much it costs to own and operate a car, consider the IRS's business mileage deduction rate of 55 cents a mile. The Feds are assuming, in other words, that if you drive 10,000 miles in a year (not much for the average commuter), that your cost is running about $5,500.

If your workplace isn't too far and you live in a temperate climate, what about using your bike to get to work? Or maybe get a good pair of walking shoes? These choices will slim your waistline and your pocket book at the same time!

Could you carpool? Whether it's going to work or taking the kids to school, a little planning can easily reduce the number of cars on the road and the amount of gas your family has to purchase. Many offices have a carpool bulletin board. If yours doesn't, why not ask your Human Resources department if you can start one?

Remember that tankers deliver the same gas to all retailers. Although some companies have additives that may work well for your vehicle, the markup basically pays for marketing costs. Find a lower-priced gas station and save big. Check out www.gasbuddy.com and www.gaspricewatch.com. Be sure to regularly check tire pressure, eliminate heavy items from your trunk, and keep up with factory-suggested maintenance. These simple steps help you get maximum gas mileage.

On the Job

Large corporations usually offer more cost-saving amenities and benefits than smaller ones simply because their employee pool is so large. See what's available and don't be shy about making some cost-cutting suggestions to the powers that be. In today's economic climate, your financial savvy is bound to be noted.

Have you read your employee handbook or had a talk with the folks in Human Resources lately? There may be perks you aren't aware of that will save you money. For example, does your employer offer education reimbursement? If you can add skills to your resume or an advanced degree, you have more to offer in the job market. You might get a raise or a better job with a higher salary. See what's available.

Does your employer allow for flex time or telecommuting from home? Even if it's only one day a week, you'll save commuting time, transportation costs, and possibly even on child care. If flex time is a new idea at your place of employment, prepare a solid case before you ask. Delineate exactly which tasks you can do from home. What would you need, if anything, in the way of equipment? And if it works out, check with your tax advisor to see whether a portion of your rent or mortgage is now a deduction. You have an official home office!

WHEN SAVING ISN'T PRUDENT

My mother spouted old sayings and proverbs every few minutes. She was the human version of Old Faithful when it came to sharing these little jewels. As a teenager, she drove me crazy. Who could have imagined that one day I would see the wisdom in these words and share them with my readers? One of her favorites was "penny wise, pound foolish." This is a great time to look at a few examples of cost-cutting measures that can create long-term deficits upon close inspection. We all do it. We're sure we have a deal and are so enamored of our good luck that we fail to run the numbers and see the real value of our purchase. Let's vow to be wiser consumers and more astute shoppers.

Bulk perishable items. Remember that bag of bananas I couldn't finish from Costco? That's the perfect food example for penny wise, pound foolish. I felt so proud the first time I bought them—all I considered was the money I was saving. But when they began to rot, I felt foolish.

(I gave them to a friend who is a chef, and she made banana bread for her clients that week.) Always ask yourself if you are really saving with the purchase you are contemplating. Will you be able to use it all before it spoils? Can you store it once you get home?

Gym membership. Let's say it's January and you are hell-bent on getting in shape and losing weight. You join a gym because of the fantastic special they are having. What you haven't considered is how much you hate going to a gym or how many times you have tried this route. Heaven forbid you charge this membership on a credit card. Unless you pay off the balance at month's end, that membership is getting more expensive by the minute! As suggested, take the amount you can afford and purchase some equipment you will enjoy using, such as a bike or great walking shoes.

Airfares. When you spot a deal, ask yourself what the real value of the item is for you and your family. Suppose you are flying home for the holidays and get what appears to be a great airfare. The problem is that you will be traveling twelve extra hours with multiple stops and lots of time in various airports. You'll run the risk of lost luggage. You'll have to entertain and feed the kids. You'll be so exhausted when you arrive, you'll probably miss a day of family activities by staying in bed or you'll come down with the flu thanks to all your fellow travelers. Did you really save in the long run?

Annual physician and dentist visits. Yesterday you might have spent $100 at the dentist getting a check up and a good cleaning. Today your delay may result in thousands of dollars for a root canal and a crown. Likewise, see your doctor once a year for a check-up. And do you have symptoms right now that you have been ignoring? Listen to your body's built-in early warning system. It could save your life.

Your diet. Nutrition isn't the number-one place on your budget to go rock bottom. We've all been outside the home when suddenly hunger pangs hit. It isn't time for a meal but we need *something*. If your habitual choice is to dash into a 7-Eleven, Dunkin Donuts, or Baskin-Robbins for a high-calorie, high-fat snack, try this instead. Travel with a small bag of mixed nuts or a piece of fresh fruit. (Snacks, by the way, can be a good purchase at one of those member-only stores such as Costco. You can stock up and save time, money, and gas.) Invest some of what you save in other areas into your food choices.

A PENNY SAVED IS A PENNY EARNED

If you embrace just two or three cost-cutting tips, you'll be amazed at the amount of money you can save. Don't be surprised if these tips seep into your consciousness and inspire you in ways you can't imagine now. You may find yourself automatically calculating the amount of money you can save wherever you go. ("Let's see. I'd like to see that new movie on Saturday but a matinee is much less expensive than an evening show. Let's eat after the movie!") This kind of mental gymnastics will replace the knee-jerk "How can I comfort myself?" impulse behind most emotion-based spending.

Pretty soon you'll be excited to watch your growing savings account or expanding investment portfolio. These tips are meant not to turn you into a Puritan but to help you find fun in new experiences.

WEEK TWO

Harness Your Marketability

This week, you can

- Examine your skills for ways to make and save extra money
- Consider whether you have a service to offer the community

I READ ABOUT ACTRESS AND ENTREPRE-neur Angela Logan at CNN.com. This is one of those "if she can do it, so can you" adventures. Angela is an actress who, like most in the profession, has had to supplement her income with many side jobs. She is also a mother of three, and keeping a roof over her family is imperative. Earlier this year, she fell behind on her mortgage payments through no fault of her own and was in danger of losing her home to foreclosure. After a credit counseling session, she decided to make apple cakes to sell to raise the amount she needed.

When she put the word out to family, friends, and church members, everyone responded. Soon those in the community heard about this plucky mom and her extraordinary willingness to do whatever she needed to keep her home. The chef at the local Hilton offered its professional ovens so she could accelerate production. Internet retailer Bake Me A Wish! is preparing to mass-produce Angela's Mortgage Apple Cakes and share the proceeds. The company says it already has hundreds of orders for the Mortgage Apple Cake and is developing a line of cakes with Angela.

FINDING A MONEY-MAKING OPPORTUNITY

This week, we get creative and look for hidden opportunities to make more money in your life. There is no telling where thinking outside the box about your talents may lead. The key is to suspend judgment. I'm sure Angela had a million reasons why her Mortgage Apple Cake idea wouldn't work. But she gave it a try and look what happened! Courage, determination, and talent are attractive to other liked-minded individuals. Who knows? Maybe I'll be reading about you on CNN!

Have your financial notebook handy so you can make notes. See which of these ideas appeal to you, but be sure and have a family meeting before you implement any of them.

Teach others a skill. Do you play the piano, for example? With art and music programs being downsized at many schools, you may be able to introduce a love of music to children in your neighborhood. Are you particularly adept at a sport? Are there academic subjects you could tutor? Do you speak a second language? Students and travelers are always eager to practice conversational phrases with a native speaker. Examine your skill sets and see what you have to offer.

Make a trade. If you need to contract services or help with some projects around your home, consider whether you know someone in your circle who could assist you. Perhaps you could barter your service for someone else's.

Take out your financial notebook and on a blank sheet draw two lines down the page, creating three columns. In the first column, list the things you need accomplished. Next to each task, in the second column put the name of a family member or friend who is skilled in this area. And in the third column, write a skill you can offer as payment.

I can hear some of you saying you don't have any skills to offer. Everyone has something! Could you offer several weekends of babysitting? Are you a good cook? Are you a whiz in the garden? You might be surprised how many talents you have that others would appreciate.

Sell a product you love. Would it be possible to have home parties and sell the products you enjoy to others? When I first moved to Los Angeles from New York, Tupperware parties were all the rage. Lately I've been invited to cooking parties, sexy lingerie parties, and skin care parties. If you like this idea, begin your quest with a product line you know and love. You'll be a much more effective salesperson if you're coming from the heart rather than a desperate need for extra cash.

You might have to go outside your home to host these parties. But you store the product and do your paperwork in your home, so be sure you have space for these activities. You'll need an organized file system (to keep track of clients and invoices) and a neat office or work space (so you can think clearly and perform your duties in a professional manner). Storage can be in the form of inexpensive bookcases from a store such as Ikea or utilitarian shelving units at a home store such as Costco or Home Depot. These choices are all well under $100 (and can be used later for household items, books, CDs, and DVDs if you decide not to continue with your business). Also consider climate control. No one will buy your products if they are damaged by excess heat or cold!

Mary Kay (www.marykay.com) and Amway (www.amway.com) are among many popular home-based businesses. Both companies are well-established, multilevel marketing organizations. Caveat emptor: These are businesses and, like any business, you have to make an investment in time, money, and sweat. Operations such as these can't be done on a whim. Be serious before you start. Also, people who get involved in multilevel marketing often begin by marketing to friends and family and fellow employees. Be careful that you aren't too aggressive, lest you start losing friends and irritating family.

Take care of children. Does your neighborhood have young working parents who would gladly pay you to watch their children after school for a few hours until they get home? Before you baby-sit at home, however, check with your insurance broker to be sure you're covered in the event of any accidents.

Become a petsitter. Many people are gone for hours each day, and their pets need bathroom breaks. Would you enjoy being a dog walker? You might want to learn doggie first aid and take a class in dog etiquette first. Make friends with the folks at the local pet store or groomer. Check your local newspaper for ads, the Chamber of Commerce for your area, and sources such as Craigslist and the *Penny-Saver*. See what the competition is doing in your area. With any luck, you won't have any!

Shop, shop, shop. If you have a car or live in a city with a great transportation system, you might be able to start an errand-running business. Not having to shop for groceries, pick up the dry cleaning, or go to the post office would save a busy executive or working mom a lot of time.

Several companies have sites on the Internet recruiting mystery shoppers. You are paid to shop at stores and record your experience. If you like being at the mall anyway, this may just be your ticket. Here are two sites to get you started: http://www.mysteryshoppersamerica.com and http://www.secretshopper.com.

Does your area have a market research firm? They frequently have on-site events. For example, you might be asked to test drive a vehicle or give your opinion about consumer products at a panel discussion. This isn't steady work, but you might get lucky and score a few hundred dollars a year. Check out "Market Research" at your favorite Internet search engine or your local yellow pages to find firms near you. Tell them you want to register for their panels.

PUTTING YOUR MONEYMAKING PLAN IN PLACE

Every year millions of well-intentioned people make New Year's resolutions. Statistically, few turn their resolutions into accomplishments. Ever wonder why? Are these folks lazy? No! They have simply taken on too many resolutions at once or haven't moved from the dream to the fulfillment phase. Be sure that in your quest to earn more money, you don't fall into these traps.

If you're launching a business, you won't be able to do all the following steps in one day, one week, or even one month. And you certainly don't want to cut corners during the preparation to launch. You have some homework to do now. Schedule the steps on your calendar. Give your ideas direction and focus.

Step One: Make a List

Take out your financial notebook and list all the moneymaking ideas that appeal to you. Add additional ideas that come to you during the week. Put numbers next to your entries to indicate which idea is the most interesting and work your way down to the idea that interests you the least.

Step Two: Turn Your List into Steps

Make a list of the steps you have to take to make your number-one interest a reality. Let's say the Mary Kay idea captures your imagination, and you can use your spare bedroom to store products. Time to start researching—the Internet is a great place to start. At a search engine such as www. google.com or www.bing.com, type the words "Mary Kay" and a world of information will come up. Do this for all the ideas that interest you.

In the case of Mary Kay, their official Web site tells you what you need to get started and how the company can support your new business. In other cases, you might discover that you have to take some classes and get certified to move forward. The questions then become, "Can I afford the class and do I have the time to fit school and homework into my schedule?" Be careful not to overwhelm yourself with too many new endeavors at once.

Step Three: Research Business-Related Issues

Next you'll want to know a bit about creating a business plan, billing, and keeping records. Call your local Small Business Administration or check them out online

at www.sba.com and see whether they have any classes coming up. These classes are usually free. As a bonus, on some days you'll find retired executives ready to give you advice on business plans and the like. These execs are part of SCORE (Service Corps of Retired Execs) and generously donate their time. You couldn't find better mentors.

Check with your income tax preparer or other financial consultant to see how an increase in income will affect your tax situation. Speaking of taxes, you'll need a business license and, if you're working from home, be sure and check your local zoning ordinances. SBA can help you with all these details.

You'll want to look professional, and a few business cards will do the trick. You can order them online (along with matching stationery if you want) from sites such as www.iprint.com or www.vistaprint.com. You can also go to your local big-box supply store such as Office Depot. Check out your computer as well. PCs and the Mac come with templates for documents you can print. You'll certainly need invoices so you can get paid!

Step Four: Market Your Business

If you're going to have a business, you need customers. How will you market your products or services? When people approach me about becoming a professional organizer, I suggest that they work with friends and family members for a nominal fee. This will give them experience, a client list, and maybe a few testimonials they can use on their Web site.

On the Internet, you'll have a host of free or low cost ways to promote yourself, starting with a Web site. I have used www.wonderwebusa.com for many years for my Web site. You can also check out www.networksolutions.com. If you aren't comfortable with the idea of promoting yourself on the Internet, you can start with ads in the local *PennySaver* or post flyers around your neighborhood. You can tailor your business to your PR campaign. A dog walker, for example, can use flyers and the local groomer and vet's office to great advantage; someone who wants to sell a product or a personal service would need to reach a wider audience. Online, the world of Craigslist, Facebook, Twitter, and blogging await you.

DREAMING REALLY CAN MAKE IT SO!

Never underestimate the power of the simplest idea to mushroom beyond your wildest expectations. Martha Stewart built an empire from a small catering company. Amos became famous for the cookies he started baking in his home. Angela Logan's Mortgage Apple Cakes may help her join this elite group. You may not become a mogul, but you might just earn a few extra dollars doing what you love.

WEEK THREE

Working with Your Budget

This week, you can

- Avoid common mistakes when creating a budget
- Cut expenses large and small

Unless you find that tracking your formal budget gives you unbridled joy, you might want to set a reasonable amount of time for working with the budget you began to set up in February. Perhaps for six months to a year, you'll want to work with the budget on a daily basis. During this time, you will not only track your expenses carefully but also edge toward your goals, whatever they may be, such as reducing debt, increasing savings, and boosting charitable giving. This week, I help you to fine-tune and make maximum use of the budget you began to create several weeks ago.

AVOIDING BUDGETING MISTAKES

Following are the five biggest mistakes that people make when budgeting. Please re-view these to make sure you don't fall into the following traps:

1. Forgetting to add expenses from previous months. If you pay the bill for your local newspaper subscription once a year, for example, and you paid it several months ago, it is easy to forget to include that expense. Such annual bills need to be divided by twelve and allocated to each month's budget.

2. Setting goals that are too hard to reach. If you are deeply in debt and still outspending your income, don't think you're going to suddenly build a college fund! Rome wasn't built in a day. And the funds to pay for all that Roman construction weren't raised in a day, either.

3. Not having agreements with your significant other. A budget won't work unless all parties involved are fully on board. There would be no point in try-

ing to reduce the monthly utility bill, for example, unless everyone is willing to turn off the lights before they leave the house.

4. Not looking at both sides of the equation. Some budgeters focus obsessively on reducing expenses. Others seek to boost income. Just as the best weight-loss plans involve both getting more exercise and consuming fewer calories, the most successful budgets address both income and expenses.

5. Having only half a plan. Don't simply say that you're going to reduce your transportation expenses. As you draw up your budget goals, include plans to reduce mileage by combining trips to the supermarket and the bank, by carpooling, by asking the boss about telecommuting one day a week, and so on.

CUTTING EXPENSES IN TWO WAYS

When it comes to addressing budgetary problems, two schools of thought exist. One (which I'll call the latte school) tells you to cut down on daily discretionary expenses that are slowly nibbling you into debt: the morning coffee, the French cheeses, the half-eaten muffin on the run. The other (which I'll call the mortgage school) tells you to look at nondiscretionary big items: the mortgage, insurance, cable, and phone bills. Where should you look for ways to save in your budget? We say you should look at both.

Leah Ingram agrees. "My husband and I, once we created a budget and worked on it, were able to save $2,000 a year. It came from both the little daily expenses and the larger, regular expenses." Examples of the Ingram's savings:

Gave up HBO and part of the premium cable package (saved $240/year)

Asked their daughters to give up one of their online gaming subscriptions (saved $80/year)

Gave up the second phone line in their house and now use a cell phone instead (saved $756/year)

Husband stopped eating with his staff in the corporate dining room and now packs his lunch (saved $936/year)

So successful was freelance writer Ingram at budgeting that she turned her newfound frugality into a paying second career with a popular blog called Suddenly Frugal (www.suddenlyfrugal.com), where she shares her budgeting triumphs. The blog has since helped Ingram land a book deal and has created other income opportunities, including a lucrative media tour with Wal-Mart. You may not turn your budget experience into a moneymaking adventure, but you will surely have more control over your finances because of it. Your budget is the foundation of your financial life. Without it you might be robbing Peter—say your 401(k)—to pay Paul—perhaps that four-star vacation you just put on a credit card.

WEEK FOUR

Banking Made Brighter

This week, you can

- Learn how to find the right bank to suit your financial needs
- Get tips on smart banking
- Decide whether a CD, money-market, or savings account is for you
- Understand the protection offered by the FDIC

IN THE 1946 CLASSIC *It's a Wonderful Life,* George Bailey (played by James Stewart) is a small-town banker with a big heart. Today, you have many options for your banking services. You can go to a bank in your own town, hoping to find a George Bailey, or you can use an out-of-town bank, perhaps a conglomerate. You can also choose an Internet bank for some of your banking needs, such as checking, savings, and CDs. And many large "financial supermarkets," such as Fidelity and Charles Schwab, also offer traditional banking services. And let's not forget ye olde credit union. Where does a savvy consumer turn? We're going to sort through the maze of choices this week.

FINDING THE RIGHT BANK

In the next few months we discuss your long-term investments, most of which should not be kept in a savings bank. Savings banks are not for storing your nest egg, if you hope to see that nest egg grow. Investment growth requires stocks and bonds. Savings and checking accounts, and even certificates of deposit, have modest historical track records of performance. You'll be lucky—very lucky—to earn enough in any of these accounts to break even with inflation. Nonetheless, you will need a checking account, and perhaps other banking services, such as an occasional money order or a small loan, so you will need a bank.

Here are some pointers on finding a good one:

Yield (interest rate) is important. Look to see what kind of interest is being paid for checking and savings accounts. Beware of come-on offers, however. Some banks run specials that last for only a few weeks or months. Is it worth the hassle of opening an account if you're only going to move your money next month? (Sometimes, if the offer is good enough, it may be worth the hassle!)

Look beyond interest rates and check the fees. Getting the best yield on your checking or savings account and paying the least amount of interest on your loans are important. But banks rack up considerable money charging various and sometimes frustratingly annoying fees. One bank I did business with once tried to charge me $10 for mailing in a deposit without an "official" deposit form. I refused to pay it! Some banks charge considerably more than others for overdraft protection.

Know the minimums. Some banks charge you a monthly fee if your balance falls beyond a certain point or if the average monthly balance falls below a certain point. Inquire.

What services does the bank offer? Most banks today have Web sites that allow you to pay all your bills online, move money between accounts, and much more. Some Web sites are more user-friendly than others. Play around with a bank's Web site if you plan to use it down the road.

How convenient is the branch office? If you prefer doing your banking in person, how far is the closest branch from your home or office? How many tellers are there, and what is the average wait? Are the tellers friendly and knowledgeable? How good do you feel in the waiting area?

How many ATMs does the bank have and how conveniently located are they? What does the bank charge for ATM usage? (This is a biggie!) Make sure to inquire as to the ATM fees for both the bank's own ATMs *and* the ATMs of other banks.

If you are thinking about a loan, either a personal loan, business loan, or mortgage, how good are the bank's rates compared to other alternatives?

Comparison shop by looking at ads in your local newspaper, and go to several online resources, such as Bankrate.com and Moneyaisle.com, to see what competitors are offering.

Does the bank have "relationship pricing"? In other words, will you get better deals on loans and such if you and your spouse and kids all have accounts at the same bank?

How does the bank treat seniors? If you're over fifty, know that many banks offer special deals, often accounts that pay slightly higher interest or eliminate certain fees. Does yours?

Look for George Bailey. Developing a personal relationship with a local bank may pay off if you ever need a loan or a mortgage. Having a personal relationship can also speed up everyday transactions.

CREDIT UNIONS VERSUS SAVINGS BANKS

Credit unions are cooperative banks, owned by members (customers). Banks are run for profit by investors. Credit unions are typically selective in who they allow in the door. You might have to be a member of a union or an employee of a certain company. Some credit unions may be open only to people who live in a certain neighborhood or belong to a certain church. Credit unions can, and often do, offer all the same services as savings banks. And, yes, they are insured by the government, much like traditional banks. You can often find better deals—for both depositors and borrowers—at credit unions. And the service can be chummier than a typical bank. If you have access to a credit union, it is worth serious consideration. I bank at a credit union based in Los Angeles. Like Russell and his bank in Pennsylvania, all the tellers at my local branch know me on sight and never ask for identification.

Where Russell banks in his small town in Pennsylvania, the tellers never ask to see his personal identification for any transaction; they all know him—and his children—by face, if not by name.

Does the bank offer free cookies? Okay, this is not a major consideration for most people, but Russell's kids, when dragged along for the ride to the bank, do appreciate the chocolate chip ones!

After you read through the preceding, take out your financial notebook and make some notes. Do you feel that your current bank meets all your financial needs? This week, you may want to do a little investigating to see whether you can get a better deal or find a bank that is closer, has more branches, or has staff who make you feel welcome. Do business with a bank that makes you feel like you're in a valued partnership.

BANKING SMART

Once you have chosen your ideal financial institution, you can watch your funds grow in several more ways.

Have your paycheck deposited directly into your account rather than having to make the deposit in person (where you might be tempted to ask for cash back).

Pay yourself first. Arrange for 10 percent of your paycheck to be automatically transferred into a savings account. Chances are, what you don't see, you won't spend. Sock away 10 percent off the top, and your savings will quickly increase.

Getting a tax refund this year? Have it sent directly to your bank account. Simply give the IRS your routing information.

Are you a freelancer? Some clients may find it easier to transfer money directly to your bank than to send you a check. Ask.

Chances are you'll get your payments faster and collect more interest as the payment sits in your account.

DECIDING WHERE TO STASH YOUR CASH

As this book was going to press, interest rates in America were just about the lowest they've ever been. That's good news for borrowers (with thirty-year mortgages running slightly higher than 5 percent) but bad news for savers, especially conservative savers who like to sink their money into savings accounts, CDs (Certificates of Deposit), and such. According to Bankrate.com, the average rate paid on savings accounts nationwide in August 2009 was 1.2 percent. The average rate on a one-year CD was 1.79 percent. Most money-market accounts, where you can store your money at a brokerage firm, are paying less than 1 percent. Don't spend it all in one place!

It pays to shop around for a high interest rate. At any point in time, you might get a better deal on a savings account than a money-market account, or vice versa.

Money-Market Accounts

Keep in mind that money-market accounts, although they rarely lose money, are not as safe as savings accounts or CDs, which are generally Federally insured through the Federal Deposit Insurance Corporation (FDIC). On the other hand, if you are in a high tax bracket, a tax-free money-market account can save you money in April. All the interest on savings accounts and CDs is fully taxable.

Two excellent online sources for comparing rates on savings accounts, checking accounts, and CDs are www.Bankrate.com and www.Moneyaisle.com. Online banks www.HSBCDirect.com, www.INGdirect.com, and www.Emigrantdirect.com often offer top rates.

For top money-market rates, it's hard to beat Vanguard (www.Vanguard.com), which, because of its low costs, often trumps the money-market rates offered by other financial supermarkets and mutual fund companies.

Be aware of any money-market funds that offer what look like exceptionally high rates and feature words such as *Plus* or *High Yield* in the name. Although money-market accounts infrequently "break the buck" (fall to less than one dollar a share, the price you pay to buy in), some do lose money. The Schwab YieldPlus Investor Fund (ticker SWYPX) and Schwab Yield-Plus Select (SWYSX) lost about 20 percent of their value in 2007 and 2008, shocking and angering many investors and resulting in numerous ongoing lawsuits.

Exchange-Traded Funds

Another option for your cash might be certain exchange-traded funds (ETFs), which are similar to most money-market funds except the principal can fluctuate a little. ETFs can be bought and sold at any brokerage house or financial supermarket, such as Fidelity, Charles Schwab, or T. Rowe Price. You pay a small commission (usually around $10) to buy and sell, so ETFs are not good options for very small balances. If you have a few thousand to squirrel away, however, and you plan to let it sit for a while, you should check the rates. Good ETF options for your cash include the iShares Short Treasury Bond fund (ticker symbol SHV), the iShares 1-3 Year Treasury fund (SHY), and the WisdomTree U.S. Current Income Fund (USY). Just like money-market funds, these are uninsured and can lose money, although such a loss of principal is very unlikely given the conservative nature of the underlying investments.

Higher-Yield Securities

The best way to make money on your money, however, is to stash as little in cash as necessary. Most financial experts recommend that you should keep three to six months of your money as cash. Russell and I agree. If you have a major purchase on the horizon, you may want to temporarily build up your cash reserves for that.

It's not a bad idea, especially if your job isn't secure, to keep another three to six months of your money in "near-cash," that is, a short-term, high-quality bond fund that pays slightly more than a money-market or savings account. One good option is the Vanguard Short-Term Tax-Exempt Bond Fund (ticker VWSTX). The rest of your funds should be invested in higher-yielding securities, such as stocks and longer-term bonds, which you can read all about in the next two months.

UNDERSTANDING FDIC INSURANCE

The Federal Deposit Insurance Corporation (FDIC), created after the terrible run on banks in the Great Depression of the 1930s, insures the money you have in an FDIC-insured savings account or certificate of deposit. For many years, up to $100,000 was covered. But given the recent turmoil in the financial industry, Uncle Sam wanted to assure us that our savings were safe, so the government created a new guarantee limit of $250,000 per depositor, per account. That limit will stay in effect through December 31, 2013. Do you still need to worry about the financial strength of your bank, even with FDIC insurance? Your money, in the event of a bank folding, could be tied up for some time, so yes, you should still be concerned. Bankrate.com uses a four-star rating system to give you an idea of the financial strength of a particular bank.

AS APRIL DRAWS TO A CLOSE

This month you have had a lot of work to do regarding your finances. By month's end, however, we bet you'll feel more empowered in terms of your own situation. You're cutting some corners and are probably on the road to making extra money. You know how to save and where to stash it. The goal is to make your money work for you, rather than letting a lack of it rule your life. Next month, we take a long hard look at credit cards. For most people, this is the drain that needs a plug.

APRIL SUMMARY

WEEK ONE

Discover tips that save money, time, and personal energy—and tips that don't.

WEEK TWO

Uncover hidden opportunities to make more money.

WEEK THREE

Create a budget you can live with.

WEEK FOUR

Find the best bank for your financial needs and the best places for your money.

5. MAY

Borrow Smart

Remember that not getting what you want is
sometimes a wonderful stroke of luck!

—THE DALAI LAMA

IT HAPPENS TO ALL OF US. LIFE IS GO-
ing along smoothly and suddenly that
unexpected item comes along we literally
can't live without. It could be a medical
test or procedure. Perhaps the car dies, the
roof leaks, or the dog is hit by a car. Whatever it is, we need cash.

Sometimes, however, we confuse true
needs with emotional ones. We have become a credit dependent society. We whip
out our cards with great abandon. Not that
long ago folks were taking equity out of
their homes to get access to cash for luxury items. What are the consequences of a
credit-financed life?

Many economists argue that the world's
economic turmoil of late is testimony to
the peril of overborrowing. As you'll recall, the recession that started in late 2008
began with financial institutions' over-
indulgence in debt. This crisis is a reminder that we all need to look at our

personal balance sheets to make certain
that debt doesn't eat us alive.

And looking at your balance sheet with
an eye toward debt is exactly what's on the
agenda this month. We'll start by trimming
your use of credit cards—the most expensive kind of debt (unless you frequent a
loan shark)—and move from there to look
at the broader picture of any other debt
you may be carrying, such as a mortgage.

HABIT OF THE MONTH: SAVE YOUR POCKET CHANGE

There's an old saying: "pennies make dollars." This month, see how much money
you can manifest by saving the change
from your pockets and wallets each
evening. Get a piggy bank or use the container of your choice. Try to engage the entire family in this habit. At the end of the

month, add the total. Now multiply that by twelve. At the end of a year, how much do you project you will have? Set a goal for yourself. Is there something you'd like to save for as a year-end treat? Don't be surprised if you decide to save this money.

TOOL OF THE MONTH:
THE DREAM BOARD

The Dream Board isn't for everyone, but it is especially beneficial if you are not a visual person. The idea is to get some poster board and a glue stick at your local office supply or craft store. Next, tear out photos from magazines that represent things you would do or would have when debt has been eliminated from your life and your cash flow has been strongly positive for months. The images will be personal. During the year, look at your Dream Board as a compass: It will help when doubt or fear threatens to knock you off course. Go ahead, dream a little. It's good for the soul.

WEEK ONE

Lower Your Cost of Credit

This week, you can

- Understand what a FICO score is and why it's important
- Correct errors in your credit report
- Learn how to boost your score for cheaper financing

WE ARE DEFINED BY MANY NUMBERS. There's the powerful Social Security number that can give thieves access to your identity. Are you a member of a union? Do you have a bank account? Do you have investment accounts? All these entities have assigned you a number. I know adults who can tell you their SAT scores even though the test was taken decades ago. But of all the numbers that identify you, your FICO score needs to be near the top of your list.

Your FICO score (developed by the Fair Isaac Corporation) is a snapshot of your credit history and a measure of your creditworthiness, at least in the eyes of most lending institutions. In lieu of telling a mortgage bank, car dealer, or furniture salesperson what a reliable person you are, potential creditors simply check your FICO. In other words, how trustworthy have you shown yourself with money up to now? Do you pay your bills on time or are you riddled with late fees? Have you ever defaulted on a loan? How much money do you owe? Did you forget to return some library books? (Library fines that are turned over for collection can lower your score by as much as 100 points!) In this day of instant communication, when you default in one area, all the other aspects of your financial life know about it. And down goes your FICO score.

FICO scores are important because those with the best scores get the best deals, by far, on the credit market. I'd rather you don't borrow at all (aside from carrying a mortgage), but if you must, at least borrow cheaply. Having a sterling FICO store and comparison shopping for credit are key.

CHECKING YOUR CREDIT SCORE

Three credit bureaus—TransUnion, Experian, and Equifax—collect data on you. (Contact information for each appears in the "Resources" section, page 251.) Each bureau arrives at a score based on different criteria. Every year you are entitled to one free report from each of the bureaus; to see your report, log on to www.annualcredit report.com. I spread my requests out so that I can check my credit health throughout the year.

The report (a snapshot of your bill-paying dependability) is free. However, if you want to learn your score, you have to pay the entity a nominal fee. It's worth it.

Many lenders will use only one of these credit bureaus; others will contact all three and take the middle score. Just to complicate matters, Equifax is the only credit bureau that provides you with your actual FICO score. At TransUnion and Experian, the score you purchase is similar to the FICO but based on slightly different criteria. If you want to see your score based on all three reports, go to www.my-fico.com.

HANDLING CREDIT REPORT ERRORS

Once you have your credit report, check it for errors. Be sure all the accounts listed are ones that you opened and maintain. This report is one of the tools you can use to monitor for identity fraud. Do you see any errors? If so, do the following:

- Immediately draft a letter to the credit bureau stating what you believe to be the error.
- Explain why you feel this is a mistake, and attach copies of any material that verifies your story.
- Include a copy of your credit report with the item in question either circled in red or highlighted.
- Request an immediate change in the status of your credit report.
- Send your letter via certified mail with a return receipt request.

The investigation usually takes thirty to ninety business days to be resolved.

You will also want to draft a letter to the creditor who is supplying what you consider to be incorrect information. Your letter to them can be brief. By enclosing copies of the material you are sending to the credit bureau, you are documenting your case. Request that the provider copy you on all correspondence to the credit bureau. Be sure and certify this letter as well. Keep copies of all correspondence in the "Pending" folder you made when you created your new file system. Remember to check your "Pending" file once a week to be sure nothing important falls between the cracks. If you want to save these reports, you have two choices. If everything is in order, you won't need a hard copy. Create a file on your computer that says Credit Reports. I would keep it in the Financial section of your files. Every year let the new report from each agency replace the old one. If you want to keep hard copies instead, shred the old report.

INTERPRETING YOUR SCORE

FICO scores range from 300 to 850. The higher the number, the better. Most people will find themselves in the 600s and 700s. (The average score in the United States is 723.) Anything over 700 makes you a prime borrower, likely to get the best deals in town on any loan. A score below 600, and you'll likely need to pay top dollar to compensate lenders for the risk they will see themselves taking by lending you their money.

BOOSTING YOUR SCORE

If a new car or a home is in your financial sights, you want to have the best FICO possible. It's worth it to dedicate some time and energy to boosting the numbers. It could save you thousands down the line, especially if you are contemplating taking on a new mortgage or home equity line of credit. You can increase your FICO score in four ways, as follows:

1. The number-one way to boost your score is to pay your bills on time. This is why one of the first items we addressed in this book was bill paying. You must have a system. If you aren't generating enough money to stay current, return to April for long- and short-term ideas to help you generate additional funds. If you are unable to make ends meet, don't hesitate to contact your creditors to see what special arrangements they can make for you. You may not be able to

avoid a ding on your credit score, but at least you won't completely obliterate your credit history.

2. If you are new to credit or perhaps recovering from a bankruptcy, foreclosure, or lien, build your good credit slowly. Don't go out and open multiple accounts in a short period of time. This may have an adverse affect on your score. Always take time to demonstrate how responsible you are. Remember too that your *debt ratios*—the amount of debt you carry as a percentage of your total income and as a percentage of your total credit availability—are key factors in determining your FICO. You don't want to max out your credit cards! Nor do you want to have too many.

3. Remember to consider all your credit cards, including department store cards. If you have some that have been inactive, don't close them all at once as a way to raise your FICO. You might just lower it. (Yes, this is tricky business!) Why? You will have potentially adversely affected your debt ratio by lowering your overall credit availability, thus raising the ratio of the amount of debt you carry to that availability limit. By the way, have you noted that department store credit cards usually come with exorbitant interest rates? You'll fare better if you use a Visa, MasterCard, Discover, or American Express card. Of course, if you intend to pay your department store purchase in full when you receive the bill, by all means use the store's card, especially if the store offers a discount or special service

(such as free shipping) on purchases made with the card.

4. Don't continuously open low-interest-rate accounts in an effort to keep your debt "in motion." Paying off your balance is the goal. If you already have a fist full of cards, you are in trouble. You don't need any additional fuel on the credit fire. As you pay off your cards (start with the highest interest-bearing cards rather than the highest amount), literally cut up those cards. You don't want a zero balance to tempt you to get back on the treadmill of debt. On the other hand, if you have only one or two credit cards and feel that opening a third to secure a few months of interest-free or low-interest payments would help reduce your overall debt, take advantage. Remember that over time, with regular payments and a reduced balance, your FICO will climb.

Never pay a fee to a debt consolidation company to raise your score. They can't do it! Only sound fiscal practices on your part can affect your score.

TAKING A BREAK

Take some time this week to find out your current FICO score and consider ways to improve the number. Don't forget to check your report for any errors. And remember that the easiest ways to establish good credit are to consistently pay your bills on time and keep your balances under control. Next week, you'll continue your credit investigation.

WEEK TWO

Curb Credit Card Spending

This week, you can

- Confront your total credit card debt
- Better understand how credit card purchases get out of hand

THERE IS PROBABLY NO GREATER waste of money than maxed-out credit cards, especially those with a high interest rate. If you pay only the minimum, it will be years before the card returns to a zero balance. When you factor in the interest, the price of every purchase will be much higher than the original sales slip indicated. And don't forget that this interest isn't like that accrued on your mortgage: You can't deduct it. It's just eating away at your financial security.

How much will it be eating away? Glad you asked! Suppose you have a balance of $1,000 on your credit card, and you are paying an annual interest rate of 18 percent. You pay the minimum amount each month, $24.85. It will take you 114 months (9.5 years) to pay down that debt. In the end, you will have paid the credit card company $932.32 in interest. Many Americans do just that. What a waste!

No, I didn't do that calculation in my head. I went to the credit card calculator on Bankrate.com, and so can you, at http://www.bankrate.com/calculators/managing-debt/minimum-payment-calculator.aspx. Plug in your credit card balance, the minimum payment, and the percent you're being charged, and you'll instantly see why paying off credit card debt sooner rather than later is a wise move.

Just think—instead of making those monthly payments, you could be building your savings and your investment portfolio. Suppose you didn't have that $1,000 debt, and instead invested that same $24.85 every month into a diversified portfolio earning you 8 percent on an annual basis. After 114 months, instead of being $932.32 in the hole, you'd have a portfolio worth $4,275.83!

Let's devote this week to getting a handle on your credit card debt. It's worth it.

This is a good time to stop unwanted solicitations from credit card companies. Go to www.optoutprescreen.com.

DETERMINING YOUR TOTAL CREDIT CARD DEBT

Grab your statements from the last few months. By the way, aren't you glad that you set up a working file system? There was a time you might not have been able to put your hands on these papers. Now it's a snap. I hope you're beginning to see the value of the work you've accomplished to date. Budgets, file systems, and bill paying aren't exciting tasks, but they make the work required for the remainder of the year that much easier.

If you didn't add your total credit card debt when you worked on your budget, be sure you do so now. Very often when you're in credit trouble, the only number you see is the minimum amount due. The total may shock you, but it's the reality. Paying only the minimum required each month will keep you tied to your debt for years to come, as we saw in the preceding example. Bankrate.com has a nifty calculator that enables you to see exactly how long it will take you to pay off your credit card debt if you pay the minimum each month. When you pick yourself up off the floor, you'll be ready to continue reading the material for this week!

DISCOVERING THE REASONS FOR CREDIT CARD DEBT

High balances generally accumulate for one of three major reasons: unconscious spending, illness, and what I call magic money. In this section, we look at all three reasons in turn.

Unconscious Spending

The most common way that credit card debt grows is through unconscious spending. You see something you want and the idea of checking your budget goes right out the window. You feel empty inside and the void gets temporarily filled with this purchase. Here's my advice. Leave the credit cards at home if you know you have little or no self-control. When you see something you want, go home and think about it. How important is it to your health and safety? Will it improve your life? Is it a status purchase? Are you trying to impress your friends? Take out your financial notebook and make a list of the pros and cons of this purchase.

Then, before you make a final decision, give yourself a cooling-off period of at least a day or two. Make a wise decision based on the financial reality of your situation. You can do it.

Getting financially sober is a choice. If you feel that overspending is a serious personal issue for you, consider attending a few Debtors Anonymous meetings, which are part of a twelve-step program. You can find a meeting by consulting your local phone book or the Yellow Pages online (www.yellowpages.com).

Illness

Another major source of credit card debt is medical expenses. If it's an urgent medical matter for you or a loved one, these charges are more than understandable. Try and negotiate the fee before the charge is made. I realize that this isn't always possible in an emergency. Let's say you are overwhelmed with debt from a hospital stay. You have insurance but the portion that isn't covered is astronomical. Don't hesitate to call the business office at the hospital and ask to have the total amount due lowered. Then ask for a payment plan that suits your budget. We tend to think of hospitals as places we visit to get well, but the hospital is in fact a business. And like all businesses, it is in quest of a profit.

Never hesitate to negotiate. And don't accept no for an answer the first time you call. If the finance office can't help you, consider going to the top of the corporate food chain. Find out where the decision-making buck stops. If this kind of phone call isn't your forte because you feel shame or embarrassment or you run from confrontation, find a trusted, polite colleague, friend, or family member who can negotiate on your behalf. We're going to talk about medical advocates later in this book (October, week one).

In addition to asking friends and family for help, you can find a professional advocate to speak on your behalf. They not only interface with medical personnel, they can negotiate with insurance companies and business offices. You will find them at most large metropolitan hospitals. If your local hospital doesn't have any on staff, ask to speak to a social worker. They aren't likely to negotiate for you but they often can direct you. Don't ruin your financial life because you are too proud to ask for help. Trust me: You won't be the first person who needed help. Nor will you be the last.

Let me share a personal experience I had negotiating a reduced payment. When I had cancer surgery more than seven years ago, I had no medical insurance. I was so busy dealing with the emotional upheaval of a cancer diagnosis and the need to negotiate the basic expenses that I forgot about the pathology report. When it arrived, I nearly fell over. I had assumed it would be a few hundred dollars. The report was ten pages long and cost roughly $1,000 a page!

When I called the lab, they weren't happy to receive my request. They wondered why I hadn't called before the report was made. I explained that I had no clue how expensive these reports were and that I had assumed I could handle it. The gentleman I dealt with wasn't very kind to me. He treated me as if I were trying to pull a fast one. However, I didn't have a spare $10,000 under my mattress, so I had to swallow my pride and soldier on. The financial office eventually reduced the fee and gave me a low monthly payment plan. Three years later, I received a call from a rep at that office. I had never missed a payment, so they were forgiving the rest of the debt! Speak up for yourself.

Magic Money

Finally, the least likely but occasional candidate for out-of-control debt is paying bills by credit card. Automatic bill payments through credit card are a good idea in theory: It can be wonderful if, say, your car payment is automatically charged on the same day every month. You don't want to be late with such an important bill. And it's great if this is a credit card with perks. Charging the expenses you have to pay anyway could help you rack up the frequent flyer miles, maybe enough miles for a long flight by the end of the year. The problem arises when you cannot afford (or don't remember) to pay the credit card amount charged each month. Credit cards can often feel like magic money. If you're building your debt with bill payments, however, you're not only asking for trouble, you're tacking on interest. Your car just got a lot more expensive. See whether you can avoid charging your bills to credit cards. Maybe you need to get a less expensive car as a way to lower your payments.

If you do use credit cards, always shop for the best deals and pay off the balances as soon as possible. If you find you must carry a balance, remember that you are never wed to one credit card. If you find a lower interest rate elsewhere, you can always shift your balance on one or more cards to the cheaper card. Check to see if the offer includes a fee to transfer a balance. You might want to shop around for one that waives that transfer fee or find a lower fee.

Before switching companies, however, call your existing credit card companies and ask them to lower the interest rate or reduce the yearly membership fee, if there is one. If you have a good payment history, you can usually make a request every six months. Try making your call midweek rather than on weekends because you are more likely to encounter a more experienced crew member.

Some people ask whether they should be paying down credit if it means they can't save for retirement. A diversified portfolio in your retirement account might be expected to grow at a rate of perhaps 8 percent a year. Chances are that you'll be "making" much more than that by paying off your credit cards first.

WEEK THREE

Reduce and Rejoice

This week, you can

- Think of additional ways to reduce debt
- Make a debt-reduction plan

LET'S SAY YOU WERE UNAWARE OF THE importance of your FICO score. And let's assume that the amount of credit card debt you were carrying each month was a surprise when you totaled it. You understand you need a plan of attack so you can eliminate the debt and start building for your future. Don't fret over the score or the debt total. Instead, make a plan and stick to it.

BRAINSTORMING TO REDUCE DEBT

Sisyphus rolled one rock up the same hill for eternity. He expended a lot of effort but made no progress. Needless debt and high interest rates are your rock. You can't make any real progress until they are eliminated.

We looked at ways to reduce your expenses in week one. Those methods will essentially reduce your credit card debt if you put the savings toward paying off your balance. In this section, we look at further ways to reduce debt:

You can get a second job or work overtime at the one you have.

Give yourself a weekly allowance and practice "tough love." When the money is gone, it's gone until next week. (Practice this approach with your children's allowance too.) Carry cash rather than using plastic or checks. And carry large bills: You're more likely to spend one dollar bills than break a twenty.

Use a home equity loan, perhaps, to pay off high-interest-rate credit cards. Home equity loans will cost much less than credit card debt and the payments are usually tax deductible. The one catch with a home equity loan is that you use your home as collateral. Make sure you have the means to pay off the loan.

Cut up all but one of those cards so the problem doesn't recur.

Are you self-employed? Ask your tax advisor if you might scale back on your quarterly tax payments, and use the saved funds to pay off your credit card debt. (Even if you have to pay a penalty, it might be less than the interest on the cards.)

If you don't itemize your deductions on your tax return, check out the possibility of reducing your tax bill by doing so. Use some of the cash you save to reduce those pesky credit card balances.

RUNNING THE NUMBERS

It's time for you to run the numbers, look at your situation, and draw up a battle plan for reducing debt. Determine how much debt you can pay down in the next month, two months, and six months. Remember that whatever steps you take, the plan has to be realistic. It can't just look good on paper. Too much austerity with money is the equivalent of a Spartan diet. You simply aren't going to stick to it. And of course it could cause a relapse of spending when you stop midstream. Binging isn't solely about ice cream and cake.

WEEK FOUR

Protect Your Identity

This week, you can

- Take some steps to protect yourself from identity theft
- Take steps if you are a victim of identify theft

I ONCE HAD MY CREDIT CARD NUMBER taken and used without my permission. I'll never forget the discovery: Someone had charged more than $300 in costume jewelry from a TV shopping network. The purchase was made here in California. The product was sent to a man in Florida. When the credit card company rep asked me if I was sure this wasn't my purchase, I said: "I don't buy jewelry from home shopping networks for starters. And I would never send jewelry to a man!" It took six months but the purchase was reversed and all interest was credited back as well. Most banks will handle such matters more quickly.

Credit card fraud such as I experienced is but one type of identify theft. Others involve government benefits, electronic bank transfers, bank account debits, check cashing, and Internet purchases. All told, the Federal Trade Commission logged more than seven million identity theft complaints from 1997 to 2009, and the number is growing each year. Victims have seen money disappear from their accounts, their credit destroyed, and their primary assets confiscated.

PROTECTING YOURSELF AGAINST FRAUD

Protect yourself from identify theft starting today. The credit bureaus offer credit-monitoring services for a hefty price, but these are often unnecessary. In this section I give you tips for doing it yourself.

Set up an online account with your credit card company and check your credit card statement and balance each week. It takes about two minutes. If someone uses your card without permission, you will find out sooner than month's end when the statement arrives.

Shred credit card offers you receive in the mail, investment reports from your broker, and bank statements after you've reconciled your balance. See March, week one, for tax papers that can be shredded. Shredding paper can be fun! Make it a habit.

Don't carry your Social Security card in your wallet. If it's stolen, ID thieves have a piece of gold. Don't send your Social Security number through e-mail to anyone. If the request is legitimate, call the person and provide it directly.

If a known vendor such as your phone company or a credit card account wants to use your Social Security number as a form of security ID, politely refuse and ask what else you can offer.

Keep your blank checks and all financial paperwork in a safe place at home. If you don't have a literal safe, keep them under lock and key in a file cabinet. Store here as well all the credit cards and debit cards you aren't carrying.

If you invest in a home safe, try and build it into a wall or the floor or make it so heavy a thief would need more than a dolly to carry it out!

Watch out for several computer-related issues. Beware of phishing, which is an e-mail or a pop-up that looks legitimate but isn't. The e-mail or pop-up asks you to click a link and then provide personal information. Forward phishing e-mails to spam@uce.gov. Use antivirus and antispyware software, as well as a firewall, and update frequently. Be careful about downloading attachments from sources unknown—or known!

TAKING ACTION IF THE UNTHINKABLE HAPPENS

If you believe you have been a victim of identity theft, call the toll-free fraud number at any one of the three major reporting agencies (Experian, Equifax, or Trans Union) to place an alert on your credit report, your name, and your Social Security number. The agency you contact will alert the other two. With an alert in place, you are entitled to a free report from each of the agencies. This will help you determine the extent of the fraud. The numbers are

Equifax: www.equifax.com or call 1-877-576-5734

Experian: www.experian.com/fraud or call 1-888-397-3742

Transunion: www.transunion.com or call 1-800-680-7289

After you have made your report, call the lenders in question to close the accounts and file a report with the local police. If you know where the fraud took place, call police in that area as well. Unless a huge sum of money was involved, local police departments may not do very much. However, the report you make may help them in their overall efforts to curb identity theft. You should also contact the Federal Trade Commission at ftc.gov/idtheft.

Keep papers related to this operation in your "Pending" file. (You don't have to print copies of all your letters. Have a file on your computer for them.) If the print-outs multiply and threaten to take up the entire folder, make one called "Identity Theft" and place it behind your "Pending" folder. When the matter is resolved, you might want to keep a permanent record of the resolution with your archived files for a year or so, just to make certain that the matter is fully resolved, before shredding the papers.

Be sure to keep a list of your credit card numbers along with their emergency toll-free numbers. My clients always ask me how they should file this information. I tell them to use a code only they will remember. (You don't want a thief going through your file cabinet thanking you for the file called "Passwords" or "Credit Card Accounts.") One of my clients files this information under "Feng Shui." If you have a safe, that's the ideal spot.

CLEARING THE DEBT DECK

Entire books have been written about identity theft, credit card debt, and FICO scores. The material offered this month has been a primer, but getting a start is pivotal to your financial success. Paying off debt is not an easy or a quick process, but it affords you an opportunity to build for a secure future. Instead of sending your money to credit cards, your liquid assets can now be directed into savings and investing. If you run the numbers and remain stumped as to how you will ever pay off your debt, consider ways to increase your income or cut costs. April and May work hand in hand.

MAY SUMMARY

WEEK ONE

Understand your FICO score and how to raise it.

WEEK TWO

Discover ways to lower your credit card balances.

WEEK THREE

Find more ways to reduce credit card debt.

WEEK FOUR

Avoid becoming a victim of identity theft.

6. JUNE

Build a Nest Egg

Goodness is the only investment that never fails.

—HENRY DAVID THOREAU

So you've been busy cutting expenses and saving money for several months. This is the work of youth and middle age, isn't it? There comes a time, however, when you may want to take it easy, and quit your day job or work part-time. The only way to make that happen is to do just that: Make it happen. And that's what this month and the next are all about: learning how to accumulate enough so that, one beautiful day, you can call yourself retired.

The focus this month is on achieving financial independence—getting to the point where, if you want, you can get by on the cash flow from your investments and no longer have to punch the clock every morning. We want balance, however, so that you're not so burned out and exhausted that when you get to that blessed point you no longer have the ability to enjoy it. Or worse, you won't get there but your money will and others will get to en-

joy the fruits of your labors. Make liberal use of the tool of the month. After all, friendship is the glue that holds you together, especially on days when the markets are down.

HABIT OF THE MONTH: READ ABOUT INVESTING

Before you become an expert investor, you need to learn about diversification, the trade-off between risk and return, the tax ramifications of investing in stocks and bonds, and the best use of retirement plans. With a topic this broad, why not dedicate just ten minutes a day to reading about it? As you peel back the layers, you will find yourself becoming more and more confident.

Caution: Much of the investment literature available to the public may not be impartial. Many financial magazines, for example, are supported more by their advertisers (such as mutual fund and annuity companies) than by their subscriptions. Keep in mind, too, that some television shows, in an effort to boost ratings, are often prone to crass sensationalism. "NOW IS THE PERFECT TIME TO INVEST IN THESE 10 STOCKS!" "SELL NOW!" "10 BEST FUNDS FOR THE NEW YEAR—DON'T GET CAUGHT OUT IN THE COLD!" Investing is not an action sport. Building wealth is a slow and reasoned process, with lots of academic research behind it. We suggest that you start your reading by picking up a few books by John Bogle (a fabulous investing primer is Bogle's *The Little Book of Common Sense Investing,* Wiley 2007) or any of the other investment books listed in Resources at the end of this book.

TOOL OF THE MONTH: FRIENDSHIP

Think of four ways you can relax, spend little or no money, and enjoy the company of others. What pops into my mind are watching a big weekend sports game at home with a buddy; meeting your best friend at a coffee shop after work and getting caught up in person rather than through IM or Facebook; visiting a local museum with your partner one afternoon; or spending some volunteer time at a place such as a homeless shelter or retirement home. We live in a world of instant communication. And yet the very instruments of communication that help us stay in touch keep us physically isolated. Reach out and literally touch someone at least one weekend this month.

WEEK ONE

Establish a Retirement Plan

This week, you can

- Learn the basics of saving for retirement
- Know your contribution limits

WHEN YOU'RE IN YOUR EARLY TWEN-ties, building a nest egg is as much of a priority as, say, learning Turkish. It's only when we see the value of compound interest that we start to appreciate the value of saving money early in life. Do you want, for example, to have a cool $1 million in the bank by the time you're sixty-five? If you don't start investing until age fifty, assuming an 8 percent rate of return, you have to sock away $2,889.85 each *month* to reach your goal in fifteen years. However, if you began saving at the age of ten, you would need to save only $84.10 each month to be a millionaire by age sixty-five. Pretty huge difference! Start saving for retirement as early as you can. If you don't have a retirement account, open one this month.

Maybe retirement feels so far off that it doesn't seem worth worrying about yet. But one day you will be in those shoes. All you really need to do is remember one powerful four-letter word: save. It's the golden key.

BUILDING A PORTFOLIO: THE BASICS

To build a bountiful retirement portfolio requires several steps:

1. Save, save, save, on a regular basis. A retirement portfolio doesn't spring up out of nowhere. You must feed it.
2. Invest your money wisely. That means diversification; don't place all your eggs in one basket, lest your life savings wind up scrambled.
3. Take maximum advantage of retirement plans such as 401(k)s and IRAs.

How much your nest egg will grow depends not only on the amount of money you save and which investments you choose, but also on which containers you put those investments into. You can choose from three styles of container:

- Plain retirement plans, such as the company 401(k), the IRA, or for the self-employed, the SEP-IRA. These are all tax-deferred vehicles; you pay taxes on the monies invested but generally only after you retire.
- The Roth-IRA and the Roth 401(k) plan. These are tax free, as long as you play by certain rules. These rules can be extremely complicated (discuss them with your accountant), but typically they involve leaving your money untouched until at least age $59^1/_2$. Anything you invest into these two vehicles can double, triple, or even quadruple, and you'll never have to pay the IRS a dime.
- Brokerage or savings bank account. Except for certain select investments, such as municipal bonds (munis), all earnings on your holdings are taxable.

401(k) and IRA

Although many tax-advantaged retirement accounts are available, the most common are the 401(k) and the IRA. Both have a traditional and a Roth variety. The 401(k) is an employer-sponsored plan whereby you put away part of your salary; your employer may or may not match all or part of what you invest. In a traditional 401(k) plan, the money you save is tax-deferred until you take it out. In a Roth 401(k), the money is tax free upon withdrawal, but

you won't get any tax deduction the year you put the money into the plan. Either way, you generally need to wait until you're $59^1/_2$ to withdraw, or you'll be subject to a 10 percent penalty.

The IRA, which stands for Individual Retirement Account, works much the same as a 401(k), but no employer is involved. You open the IRA on your own. You can contribute up to $5,500 a year or $6,500 if you're over fifty, although these figures will likely go higher in years to come. The money that goes into an IRA must be earned income, money you make from working. You can't put in gift money, for example. And the IRA and the 401(k) are not mutually exclusive. You can have both.

Consequences of Different Plans

How much does it matter which container you choose? Lots. Suppose you're an average middle-class person paying the government (Federal and state) 30 percent of what you make. Next, suppose that you have $30,000 you've already paid taxes on and are ready to stash it away for the long haul. You find an investment, say a high-grade corporate bond fund, that is yielding 5 percent, and you lock your $30,000 away for fifteen years. Now, if that investment is held in your regular brokerage account which requires that you pay taxes on the interest each year, at the end of fifteen years you'd have a pot worth $50,260. Not too shabby. But if you hold that same $30,000 bond fund in your Roth-IRA—which isn't taxed each year nor when ultimately tapped—after fifteen years you'd have $62,368, which is an extra $12,108.

In general, 401(k) plans come with certain expenses and a limit as to what kinds of investments you can choose. For that reason, if you leave a place of employment, and rolling over your company's 401(k) plan to an IRA becomes an option, it is often best to grab that option. Roll, baby, roll! It's easy to do, and any brokerage house (such as Fidelity, Vanguard, or Charles Schwab) can help you do it.

UNDERSTANDING RETIREMENT ACCOUNT LIMITS

Unfortunately, the amount of money you can put into retirement accounts is still limited, although the law has allowed the sum to grow over the past several years. For example, in the most commonly used retirement accounts, the IRA and the Roth-IRA, the maximum contribution amount for 2009 is about $5,500 for those under fifty and $6,500 for those over fifty. (The final amount is based on inflation, and at the time of this writing the IRS hadn't announced the official number.) Other retirement plans, such as the 401(k), have higher limits, but there is always a cap. (Again, you need to talk to your accountant; the formulas can get complicated.)

Prioritize Investment Accounts

So given those limitations, which investments should get utmost priority and go first into your retirement accounts and which are best left out? Follow these primary principles.

You do not want any investment that generates regular taxable income you want in your retirement account or any investment that throws off little or no taxable income. Thus, tax-free municipal bonds, which typically generate no taxable income, definitely do not belong in your IRA. Neither do tax-advantaged vehicles such as tax-managed mutual funds or variable annuities sold by insurance companies. (If an annuity salesman suggests you use your IRA to fund a variable annuity, run!)

In general, fixed-income investments, such as CDs or bonds (other than municipal bonds), benefit more by being housed in your retirement account than do stocks or stock mutual funds. Recall our example of $30,000 at 5 percent for fifteen years. Bonds and CDs benefit so greatly because their earnings generally come entirely from interest, and interest is taxed at your ordinary income tax rate. On the other hand, the return from stocks, whether from dividends or long-term capital gains, is usually taxed at a lower rate.

Keep your emergency funds out of your IRA. Any money you think you may need to withdraw in a hurry should be kept out of retirement accounts. Withdrawing money from a retirement account can often be tricky, possibly involving stiff penalties if you are not yet $59^{1}/_{2}$ and often triggering taxation. You don't want to have to worry about such things when you need money pronto.

You need to keep other considerations in mind when deciding where to house your investments, especially the more exotic varieties of investment. *Real estate investment trusts* (REITS), for example, are best kept in a retirement account, because the dividends they generate, unlike most other stock dividends, are usually taxed as ordinary income. On the other hand, mutual funds, especially index funds that are made up principally of foreign stocks, are perhaps best kept in your taxable account. That's because the U.S. government reimburses you for any taxes your fund paid out to foreign governments, but only if you have that fund in a taxable account.

Retirement Account versus Taxable Account

Before you decide where to put your investments, refer to these guidelines:

Generally best kept in a retirement account
Corporate bonds
Zero-coupon bonds
High-yield junk bonds
Inflation-indexed Treasury bonds
Stocks you plan to trade often
Real-estate investment trusts
Mutual funds with high turnover
    rates

Generally best kept in a taxable account
Cash reserve for emergencies
Municipal bonds
Tax-free annuities
Tax-managed mutual funds
Index or exchange-traded funds
Individual stocks you plan to keep
    for many years
Foreign stock funds

Talk things over with your spouse or partner, tax advisor, financial planner, or whoever is on your team. Is it time to expand, contract, or rearrange the way your funds are allocated? Even if you have taken advantage of everything mentioned here, keep this in mind: Tax laws change all the time, so you should review your portfolio every year or two to make sure you have your assets in the right "containers."

But I am an artist!

When I work with new clients, some try to wiggle out of the need to be organized by assuring me that artistic types simply can't be organized. They have no idea that I used to be an actress or that I write books. I assure them that being organized creates a firm foundation from which their artistic temperament can take flight. An organized environment is your launching pad, not your jail.

I can imagine that some of you may balk at this month's material. Perhaps you work in the arts and have no intention of retiring. This is frequently the case with actors, writers, musicians, and painters. If you relate to this, remember that building a retirement nest egg will afford you the luxury of working for as long as you want. You don't want to be, as a friend of mine once put it, an "old artist" who has to work until they drop because it never occurred to them to save. And in the event of an emergency, you will be covered.

WEEK TWO

Calculate How Much You Need to Save

This week, you can

- Decide how much you should be saving to satisfy your long-term goals
- Develop a reasonable expectation for a return on your investments

HOW MUCH DO YOU NEED TO BE SAVing for retirement? As we saw in the example at the start of this month, that question largely depends on how old you are and, of course, how much you already have stashed away. Most experts say that a good place to start, for most adults, is at least 15 percent of your income. I know. Keep breathing. But the fact is, if you want to maintain your lifestyle after retirement, Social Security probably can't be your sole support.

You should plan on living on roughly 75 percent of your pretax salary. Your savings and investments, unless you are lucky enough to have a fixed pension, will be the key ingredients in the equation. Depending on your age and how much you already have saved and invested, that 15 percent might adjust up or down. Stuart Ritter, CFP with T. Rowe Price, provides

the following example. You can adjust the figures to reflect your income.

If you are earning $100,000 a year, you need about $75,000 a year to keep the same lifestyle. Typically, here's where that money may come from:

- $50,000 from investments
- $20,000 from Social Security (you can go to www.ssa.gov to get an estimate of what your Social Security payments will be when you retire)
- $5,000 from other sources (part-time work or pension)

Mr. Ritter continues: "Our guide is you can withdraw 4 percent of your assets from your investments the first year, and increase by 3 percent for inflation each year. So in the example, if you need to pull $50,000 from savings the first year of retirement, you will need to start with a port-folio of $1.25 million."

What if you anticipate needing more or less? In general, says Ritter, provided you retire at roughly the normal retirement age, which is mid-sixties, you should have twelve-and-a-half times your salary saved and invested well to maintain your life-style. To run the numbers for your situa-tion, use the online retirement income calculator at www.troweprice.com/ric.

One of the keys to Mr. Ritter's analysis is the "4 percent" that you can withdraw from your investments each year. This percentage is based on many studies that have done something called Monte Carlo analysis to help determine a sustainable rate of withdrawal from an average portfo-lio. In short, if you have had a reasonably well diversified portfolio of stocks and bonds (I discuss this more next week), most thirty-year periods (a reasonable re-tirement period) throughout history would have seen your portfolio produce enough return so that a 4 percent initial withdrawal, with yearly adjustments for inflation, would have seen the portfolio last the three decades.

Put another way, a well-diversified port-folio, over the long run, should produce at least the 7 or 8 percent return necessary to cover the 4 percent withdrawal plus the 3 percent or so that inflation can be ex-pected to eat into the portfolio.

Based on this research, here is the sim-plest formula I can give you for how much money you'll need to call yourself finan-cially independent.

X = Amount of money you'll need to live on each year
(include money to pay taxes) – income from other sources
(Social Security, pension, and so on)

X ÷ 4 percent

Voila! That's what you'll need to get by for thirty years or so.

Here's an example. Richard and Vicky estimate they will need $75,000 a year, which means a pretax income of around $100,000. Social Security will provide them with $30,000 a year, and Vicky's pension from work will provide another $10,000 a year. They will therefore need $60,000 a year from their portfolio. Be-cause $60,000 is 4 percent of $1.5 million, Richard and Vicky will need a nest egg of $1.5 million to call themselves financially independent.

WEEK THREE

Assess How Much Risk You Can Afford

This week, you can

- Learn to create a portfolio that will serve your needs
- Understand how to diversify your portfolio to balance risk

THE KEY TO BUILDING A PORTFOLIO starts with some introspection. You need to have a long-term plan. In other words: Why are you investing (in a broad sense that may include anything from greater freedom to leaving money for charity) and what are you investing for (in terms of material wants, such as a cottage by the sea)? You'll want to save an appropriate amount and select diversified investments that together provide an appropriate level of risk and potential return. Having solid goals and objectives makes saving money and determining an appropriate level of risk easier.

Let's get specific. Are you saving for a new car? What about a (new) home? Is a child's education your responsibility? What items are on your list? Open to a fresh page in your financial notebook and draw a line down the center of the page.

Identify items as short-term or long-term goals. For example, if your current vehicle is falling apart, a new car is a short-term goal. If your only child was born last month, his college tuition heads the long-term list.

Eventually you'll need to build a nest egg to carry you through retirement. How do your future needs match the amount you're currently saving? Perhaps the most important question of all—but one that can be answered only by first tackling the others—is to know your time horizon. In other words, when might you first need to withdraw from your savings and how much would you need at that point? For most people, the biggest expenditure by far is getting through retirement years. The need for cash today, tomorrow, or twenty years from now is what should determine the investments you plug into a portfolio.

UNDERSTANDING RISK RATIO

All investments qualify as either *equity* (stocks and, to a lesser extent, real estate) or *fixed income,* which represents money you've loaned in return for interest (bonds, CDs, and money-market funds). Historically, stocks have provided much greater returns than fixed-income investments but have also been considerably more volatile. A well-diversified portfolio includes a mix of both stocks and bonds. Investment professionals say that these two kinds of investments have *limited correlation,* which means that stocks and bonds tend to not rise and fall together. In a year when your stocks are shooting high, your bonds may lag. The next year, stocks may fall, but bonds may rise. Having both stocks and bonds in a portfolio usually helps to smooth out your returns.

Stocks represent ownership in companies. Bonds are essentially IOUs issued by companies or governments. Both stocks and bonds can be purchased individually or grouped in investments called *mutual funds* or *exchange-traded funds* (ETFs). For most people, funds are often better than individual purchases because funds offer diversification, and diversification means greater safety. The best funds are *index funds,* which represent lots and lots of stocks and bonds and charge lower *expense ratios* (the ongoing fees you pay to the mutual-fund company) than so-called *actively managed funds,* which attempt to beat the market but, as research clearly shows, rarely do. (Any of the authors men-

tioned in the Appendix explain index investing in depth.)

What is the best ratio of stocks to bonds to cash? You don't want too much in stock because your portfolio may be too volatile. You don't want too much in bonds and cash because, over time, they tend to return much less than stocks.

Your *time horizon*—the time you have before you need money from your portfolio—becomes an essential factor in determining the optimal mix of investments. Generally, you want to keep in cash or fixed-income investments (bonds and cash) any money that you might need to tap within the next four to five years. Money that won't be needed for five or more years, such as money for retirement, you may want primarily in stocks. Typical thirty-year-olds who are saving for retirement, for example, might want to allocate 70 to 80 percent of their portfolio to stocks, depending on how much risk they can take. Typical fifty-year-olds might want to allocate closer to 55 to 65 percent to stocks, because they may be less able to

> This is a good time to check your risk tolerance. September and October are historically the most volatile months for the stock market, so June is a good time to ask yourself if you can handle the heat. Perhaps it's time to scale down stocks and stock funds and beef up on more conservative bonds.

weather a 50 percent drop in the market, like the one we saw in 2008–2009.

Money needed within the next four to five years should be invested so there is minimal risk to the principal. Beyond four to five years, taking the added risk of the stock market is usually a fair trade-off for the expected greater return. But people have different risk preferences. You need to ask yourself how much you're willing to see your portfolio drop in any one- or two-year period.

You may have heard simple formulas, such as "Take your age, subtract that number from 100, and that's how much you should have in stocks." The problem with such simple formulas is that they lump together all people of the same age. A forty-year-old with a solid job, a healthy nest egg, no debt, and family members who could bail him or her out in a cash crunch can afford to take more risk in the market than another forty-year-old with little in savings, no solid job, and a limited support system.

As a very rough guidepost, I recommend that most people start crafting their portfolios from a position of 60 percent stock and 40 percent bonds and cash (a *60/40 portfolio*). That mix, studies show, is where you are going to get good growth without undue risk. If you feel you need less growth and less volatility (if, for example, you are nearing retirement age and already have a nice nest egg), you might think more along the lines of a 50/50 portfolio or a 40/60 portfolio. If you are looking for real growth and can stand

substantial volatility (as would be rational if you are under forty and plan to be working for at least another decade or two), you might think along the lines of a 70/30 portfolio, 70 percent stock and 30 percent less-volatile bonds and cash.

Many brokerage houses and mutual-fund companies offer "target retirement date" or "lifecycle" funds that get more conservative as you get older, but these are not for everyone. These companies use very simple formulas that assume that all people of the same age should have the same risk. That is not the case. And as we've seen recently when the stock markets collapsed, some of these funds are much more aggressive than others. There is no industry standard.

DIVERSIFYING

How do you know how to diversify your portfolio and minimize risk? Let's examine the common denominators. Just as stocks and bonds tend to have limited correlation, different kinds of stocks and different kinds of bonds similarly have limited correlation. Diversification is important for all your investments, but it is especially important on the stock side of the portfolio, where risks are largest. Savvy investors who have built up sizeable portfolios typically will make sure to have domestic and international stocks, stocks in large companies and small companies, and value stocks and growth stocks. The savviest investors will do all this with index funds, which are low-cost funds that track large segments of the market and don't attempt to cherry-pick individual stocks or bonds.

Growth stocks are usually defined as shares in fast-growing companies in—you guessed it—fast-growing industries. *Value stocks* are typically shares in more sedate industries, but the price of the stocks may be depressed (because many investors are out there chasing the growth stocks). Despite what you may think, value stocks tend to do better over time. Different asset classes perform differently under various market conditions. That's the very heart of diversification.

After you have all the broad asset classes covered, you might consider branching out into narrower (but not too narrow) kinds of investments. Possibilities would include high-yield bonds, small international company stocks, commodities, and certain industry sectors of the economy, especially those that tend historically to have limited correlation to the market at large, such as real estate and energy.

It is hard to achieve the kind of solid diversification described by investing in individual stocks or bonds. Unless you have a ton of money, it is virtually impossible to own a sufficient number of stocks so as to be diversified across the board: domestic and international, companies of different sizes, and different industries. Owning index mutual funds or exchange-traded

funds makes achieving good diversification much easier.

Exchange-traded funds (ETFs) are akin to index mutual funds, but they trade like stocks. Generally, you pay a commission to buy an ETF, so mutual funds generally will make more sense if you are contributing regular, small amounts to your account.

One caveat: Pay little attention to which asset class happens to have performed especially well in recent months. The vast majority of investors make the mistake of pouring money into hot sectors and then selling when those sectors cool. They are continually buying high and selling low. That is exactly the opposite of what you should do.

Based on how much risk you can handle, and how much return you need, choose an allocation and stick with it, unless your situation warrants change. Don't forget your goals. Don't panic and sell when the market drops. Lots of people sit on the sidelines, keeping their money in cash, waiting for the right moment to buy. That's a mistake. You stand to lose more than you stand to gain. And don't watch the market every day as a guide to your ability to be happy. My mother and I had to tiptoe around my dad when the stock market was down. When it rose, my dad was the happiest guy in Brooklyn. In the end, this kind of behavior is an addiction. Just say no!

WEEK FOUR

Max Out Where It Pays

This week, you can

- Start a matching 401(k) at work, if possible
- Know the difference between 401(k) plans

I HAD DEAR FRIENDS WHO SKILLFULLY planned for the financial aspects of their retirement. They sold their big house and got a much smaller one in the country. It took about a year to get the new home up to their standards. The last year in their old home was filled with downsizing activities. One day the work was finished. The new house was perfect. The old one had been sold and all possessions that didn't make the move had new owners. And then a funny thing happened: boredom set in. My friends never gave a thought to what their retirement years would be filled with! They couldn't really volunteer because they had moved into the woods, so to speak, and only he drove. Nor had they considered the weather. When the snow, ice, and freezing cold arrived, they realized why people usually retire to warmer climates. While running the numbers for the financial aspect of your retirement is key to

your survival, don't forget to run the emotional numbers! What are you going to be filling your days with? Is the weather something you will enjoy or will it isolate you? How close are family members? Do you have existing friends in the new community? Cover all of your bases. A dream board might be just the ticket (see May's "Tool of the Month").

THE GOLDEN MATCHING 401(K)

Perhaps the very best retirement deal you'll ever find is your 401(k) plan at work, if your employer offers a match. About one-third of all U. S. employees have such plans, and where the employer offers a match, it is typically to the tune of 50 percent of whatever you invest, to a maximum of 6 percent of your salary. Do whatever you can to make that 6 percent contribution.

According to numerous studies, most employees don't do this—or even come close to maxing out. One study, by Hewitt Associates, found that 39 percent of employees at large companies don't participate in their 401(k) plans at all, and of those who do, 40 percent fail to max out their contributions to take full advantage of the employer match. What a shame. No other investment guarantees you an instant 50 percent return.

The return is so good on a 401(k) plan with employer match that this is the one retirement plan that makes sense funding even if you are paying off credit card debt. (Otherwise, you're almost always better off paying the credit card debt first, before funding your retirement accounts.) Beyond maxing out to meet your employer's match, you can contribute up to $16,500 to your 401(k) if you are under fifty, and $22,000 if you are over fifty. Do it, do it, do it, if such savings are possible after paying all the bills.

A White House initiative announced in September 2009 began automatically enrolling employees in their employer-sponsored 401(k) plans for the first time. It remains to be seen how this will affect overall participation rates. Employees still have the option of asking not to participate. But you, of course, would not even think of opting out!

Part of the same initiative now makes it easier for you to contribute overtime pay and money for unused vacation time to your 401(k). Talk to the 401(k)-point-person in Human Resources for the details.

TRADITIONAL 401(K) VERSUS ROTH 401(K)

Some employers, perhaps yours, have recently started to provide the option of contributing to a Roth 401(k) plan in lieu of, or in addition to, a traditional 401(k) plan. These Roth options work in the same way as Roth and traditional IRAs. With the traditional version of either retirement plan, you get a tax deduction today for every dollar you contribute to the plan, and you pay income tax when you take the money out (after age 591/2). With the Roth versions, you get no deduction today, but you pay no income tax when you take the money out.

Which is better? It depends.

If you think you will be in a lower tax bracket when you plan to withdraw the money, take the deduction today, and pay the taxes later. If you think you may be in a higher tax bracket in years to come, you're better off, generally speaking, with the Roth 401(k) plan.

Of course, your future tax bracket is unknowable. You can't be sure how much money you'll be making in the future, nor can you be sure what Uncle Sam or your state government will require in taxes years down the road. That's why many financial experts recommend tax diversification. Try to squirrel away some money in traditional savings accounts and some money in Roth varieties.

MAKE YOUR MONEY
WORK FOR YOU

This month's information may be something you act on immediately. Or you might be the kind of person who needs to do a lot of research before you engage a broker or financial planner. There is no one way to approach this material. There is no right way to take action. There is, however, the need to ultimately do something so that you feel you are truly directing your own life rather than simply reacting to outside forces. You want your money to work for you as a force for good in your life and in the world. Investments are your ticket.

JUNE SUMMARY

WEEK ONE

Learn to build for a secure retirement.

WEEK TWO

Find out how much you need to save for the future.

WEEK THREE

Assess how much risk to take and reduce risk through diversification.

WEEK FOUR

See how maxing out the humble 401(k) may provide a secure financial future.

7. JULY

Make Long-Range Financial Plans

I'd like to live as a poor man with lots of money.

—PABLO PICASSO

BUILDING A SOLID FINANCIAL CORE for yourself and those you love takes time. This month we turn our attention to asset management over the long-term. How do you find a financial planner? Do you in fact need one? After that we move on to the world of portfolio maintenance. A *buy and hold* portfolio, such as the one we set up last month, is the best kind of portfolio; but *buy and hold* does not mean *ignore.* A portfolio needs wise monitoring and care.

We close the month with a discussion of transferring your wealth and making sure that the assets you have accumulated during your life are passed along in accordance with your wishes. Grab a cool drink and your financial notebook and let's begin.

HABIT OF THE MONTH: GO GREEN

The summertime is a perfect time to go lightly on the earth and save money at the same time by visiting the Worldwatch Institute Web site at worldwatch.org/resources/go_green_save_green. This month, choose four tips on the list and try working them into your daily lifestyle. Perhaps start with washing your clothes in cold water and air-drying them. Or try making your own household cleaners from inexpensive items such as vinegar and baking soda; they work just as well as the commercial brands and will save you a bundle. And if you're feeling especially green this month, go to the Environmental Protection Agency's Energystar.gov, click the "Federal Tax Credits" icon, and find out what energy-saving upgrades to your home might earn you a refund at tax time.

TOOL OF THE MONTH: REWARDS

This month, reward yourself for the progress you've made so far. The big argument I hear from clients and students against rewards is that they don't deserve them. "Why should I get a reward for something I *should* have been doing?" To this I say, "Poppycock!" If you work hard, you deserve a reward. And remember a great reward doesn't have to cost a dime.

Most cities have beautiful parks, some are huge with walking paths and others are like tiny jewels waiting to be discovered. You can sit in a library for hours and transport yourself around the globe with books. How long has it been since you have flown a kite? Visit a public tennis court, pool, or track. You can even go to a high-end mall and just window shop. Magic is all around you. What's in your area?

WEEK ONE

Decide Whether You Need a Financial Advisor

This week, you can

- Evaluate financial or investment advisors
- Know the questions to ask about investments
- Remember ten important tips for investing

IF YOU'RE LIKE MY FRIEND RUFUS, you may have shied away from working with a financial professional. Rufus is a charter member of the "I can do it myself" club. (My mother was on the board, so I know this mentality.) This type of person usually has trouble asking for help or delegating tasks at work or at home. Here's the issue: No matter how brilliant, capable, or trustworthy you are, no one can learn everything about every subject. (Even the president has dozens of advisors!)

HIRING A FINANCIAL ADVISOR

If your financial life reaches a certain level of complexity, someone with more expertise might be able to help make your assets grow, your debt shrink, and outline a strategic plan for your money. Why not consider working with a professional who has made a serious study of such matters? Although not everyone requires a financial planner, many people could undoubtedly use some help, at least from time to time. Here are a few tips for finding someone who may be able to help you succeed financially.

Ask yourself what you need. Financial planners (whose business cards may also say financial advisor, financial consultant, or wealth manager) vary widely in their practices and expertise. Most, if not all, planners manage or provide guidance on investments. Others may offer counsel on everything from how to balance a checkbook and reduce debt to how to lower taxes or set up an estate plan. Some will work with you for a day to help you get your fiscal affairs in order. Others prefer longer-term arrangements. Take a good look at your own strengths and weaknesses about money, and ask yourself where you most need a helping hand.

Gather names and brochures. Start by drafting a list of potential planners. Begin close to home. Ask family, friends, and business colleagues for referrals. You can also contact the National Association of Personal Financial Advisors (847-483-5413) or the Financial Planning Association (800-647-6340) and ask for a referral. Some people are okay working with a planner from afar, perhaps even in another state, but others want to work with someone close by.

Look for experience and credentials. Unlike, say, someone calling himself a physician or a dentist, just about anyone can call himself a *financial planner*. And just about anyone does. That's why other more standard credentials are important. A business degree, such as an MBA, is a good thing. Some CPAs and attorneys specialize in financial planning. In addition, over the past several years, the designation CFP (certified financial planner) has become widely recognized as a mark of competency. To attain the CFP, a planner must meet certain educational requirements, pass a fairly tough exam, and then have a requisite amount of practical experience. A CFA (chartered financial analyst) is somewhat similar to a CFP.

Check their registration. An investment advisor (or his employer) should be registered with the Securities and Exchange Commission or home state securities commission (which go by different names in different states). Larger firms must register with the SEC; smaller firms are typically registered by the state. Find out a firm's registration status—if the firm isn't registered, run!—by asking to see a candidate's *ADV* (advisor) *form*. Anyone who gives investment advice professionally is required to provide such a form. It will give you lots of interesting information about the planner and his practice, such as how long he's been in business, how many clients he has, and how much money he manages. (Note: Some investment advisors do much of their business on an hourly basis, so you may see only a small amount of money under direct management. It doesn't mean that the advisor lacks experience or clients.) It will also tell you about any disciplinary history for unethical conduct.

Check, too, with the local Better Business Bureau and the Certified Financial Planner Board of Standards (303-830-7500) to make sure the planner isn't prone to lapses of good judgment.

Stroll into the office. After you've gathered a list of planners who look clean on paper, it's time to chat. Even if you're no expert in the field, you can still get a good sense as to whether a planner knows his stuff. Ask what sets him apart from other planners. Ask for his philosophy on money and whether he has a clearly defined strategy for financial success. As for investing, ask how he does it, and whether his choices in investments are based on hunches or on research. If a planner can't answer these questions quickly and confidently, think twice about hiring him.

Check out the bill. Be clear about how, and how much, a planner will charge you.

Financial planners charge by the hour, by a percentage of your assets under management, or by commissions from the products they sell you. I feel that many fee-only planners—planners who do not sell products or take commissions—can be more objective in their advice and investment suggestions.

Make sure you will get along. Financial planning can get personal. A competent planner working on your long-term financial goals should be asking you questions about your retirement dreams, your health, and perhaps even the quality of your marriage and your relationship with your children and grandchildren. ("Do you want them in your will or not?") If you're going to be working with a planner for a long time, the two of you should click. You should feel comfortable together.

EVALUATING POTENTIAL INVESTMENTS

Understand what you're investing in! Sounds self-evident, doesn't it? Don't just give your money to a financial entity with a great name or a list of impressive investors. Bill Gates once tried to get Warren Buffett to invest in Internet stocks and Buffett refused. He preferred traditional businesses such as insurance or restaurants. Do you understand the business you're being asked to invest in? Until you do, take a pass. Get more information. Don't ever worry about hurting your advisor's feelings. After all, look what great friends Warren and Bill have become.

Ask questions, and expect direct answers. It's your money and your advisor works for you, so ask for all the clarification you need.

Unsure what questions to ask your advisor about your investments? Here are some things you should know—and your advisor should certainly know!—about any investments that you are considering:

- What is the total cost of this investment in management fees?
- What is the historical return of this security?
- How risky is this investment? (How much did it lose, for example, in the recession of 2008 and 2009?)
- How well does this investment mix and match with my other investments? Will it tend to go up when my other investments go up and down when my other investments go down (not good)? Or is it uncorrelated to my other investments (good)?
- How lightly or heavily will I be taxed on any profits made from this investment?
- How often do I need to look at this investment or adjust my total mix of investments?

TOP TEN TIPS FOR INVESTING ON YOUR OWN

Want to be your own investment manager? Here's how to make the most of your efforts and avoid the most common pitfalls:

1. Realize the trade-off between risk and return: Anything that gains 50 percent in a year can lose 50 percent (or more) in a year. Take only as much risk as you can handle.

2. Invest in stocks only for the long run (at least five years).

3. The most successful portfolios are those with the lowest costs, typically those made up mostly of index funds.

4. Make efforts to minimize taxation.

5. Keep your portfolio in proper balance. (For example, if you set out to have a portfolio that is 50 percent stock, and the market has soared so that your portfolio is now 70 percent stock, your portfolio is out of balance.)

6. Most investors are overconfident, and you probably are, too. Realize that you aren't smarter than every other investor out there.

7. Don't listen to the talking heads on television every night that chatter about the markets' every twist and turn. Listen to soothing music instead or watch a good police drama.

8. Pass on the "How to Get Rich Quick" stories, and read something more realistic, like a science fiction novel!

9. Don't assume that what happened in the markets yesterday will happen tomorrow. Financial markets are unpredictable.

10. You've heard this one before, but if something is too good to be true, it really is too good to be true.

GETTING INVOLVED

Remember that you don't have to work with the first financial planner you meet. Nor do you have to stick with him or her if you feel the relationship isn't working out. It's like dating: A good relationship is worth everything when you find it.

If you are ready to invest, you want to take your time, do your research, and make wise decisions. The research you do today can affect your financial well-being for years to come. Do a few minutes of financial reading every day this month. Whether you wind up managing your own money or hiring an advisor, your reading will make you an informed partner in the investing process rather than a passive bystander. Bernie Madoff's former clients wish they had followed this advice.

WEEK TWO

Maintain Your Portfolio

This week, you can

- Discover what organizing and finance have in common
- Keep your portfolio in balance
- Learn the do's and don'ts for portfolio maintenance

L ET'S SAY YOU SET ASIDE AN AFTER-noon to pick up around your house. You might wash all the dishes in the sink, toss out old magazines and newspapers from the family room, and do a load of laundry. But if your only goal is to "get rid of this mess," I'm going to make a bet. The mess will soon be back. Why? Because tidying up and getting organized are not the same. The former is temporary and the latter is about putting systems in place. Systems also need to be able to grow and evolve over time. You change and so should the way your life is organized. And what is the glue that holds those systems in place? Maintenance.

It's no different when it comes to personal finance. You might set aside a Saturday and tend to some aspects of your financial life, while other parts get put on your mental to-do list, and you assure yourself that you'll come back to them

eventually. When? "Oh, one day when I have the money," you tell yourself. It's as if that day will arrive without any real planning on your part. This is called magical thinking, and we do it all the time. But just as you need to schedule time each year to handle routine chores such as cleaning the gutters and washing the windows, so do you need to make time regularly to maintain your finances.

Let's say that today you work on reducing your debt and securing an emergency fund. Maybe you have to wait six months or a year before you start investing in saving for college. Very few people can do everything that is suggested in this book all at once. What's important is that you make a plan to guide you from financial step to financial step so that no aspect falls through the cracks. And part of this plan that moves you forward must be steps to check on the progress you have made. Notice your credit card rates. Be sure you have the best rates on your insurance policies. Research new investment opportunities from time to time. Money is energy and you don't want it to stagnate!

REBALANCING YOUR PORTFOLIO

After you have created your portfolio, it will need your attention from time to time. A buy-and-hold portfolio, which I strongly advocate, is not synonymous with a portfolio you ignore. It can't just sit there forever and maintain itself, for the primary reason that portfolios get out of whack. Suppose you have one that is a reasonable mix (for you) of 50 percent stocks and 50 percent bonds. That portfolio may evolve, through no fault of your own, into one that is, say, 70 percent stock and 30 percent bonds, which is way too risky for you.

When the asset allocation in your portfolio becomes uneven, you'll need to rebalance it and get back to your original allocation. If your stock allocation has risen beyond its original set point, rebalancing means selling stocks and buying bonds. Or you could perhaps avoid selling your stock holdings by directing new purchases into bonds.

Many financial experts recommend that you look over your portfolio every year or two. I think eighteen months is fine for most people. (Mark the date in your calendar or planner.) If the urge strikes you to shuffle things around more often than that, resist. Buy-and-hold investors (but not ignore-your-portfolio-entirely investors!) tend to be the most successful investors over the long run.

The main reason to rebalance your portfolio is to mitigate risk. For instance, it may become seriously overweight in stocks as a result of a gangbuster year in stocks. If the following year is a gangbuster as well, what was once a nice mix of stocks and bonds may find itself with the lion's share in stocks. So what? Well, more stocks mean that your portfolio has become more aggressive. And as you grow older, it should probably be adjusted to become more conservative, not more aggressive. Otherwise, if you are just about to retire, and suddenly the stock market falls 57 percent, as it recently did, you can say good-bye to your long-awaited retirement.

Proper rebalancing requires more than reallocating your stocks and bonds. It means putting all your investments back in place. Again, you can do this by either selling your winners and adding money to investments that have sagged in the past months (easier said than done) or directing new savings into your "down" investments. Let's take a look at a sample portfolio, and how it might be rebalanced.

Suppose in March 2010 you set up the following simple portfolio, after a careful analysis that it is the right one for you:

American large-stock index fund:
  15 percent
American small-stock index fund:
  10 percent
Foreign stock index fund, developed
  nations: 15 percent

Foreign stock index fund, emerging-
market nations: 10 percent
Government bond index fund:
30 percent
Corporate bond index fund: 20 percent

Let's assume that the next eighteen
months are gangbuster months for stocks,
especially foreign stocks, and especially
stocks of emerging-market nations
("emerging-market nations" is a euphe-
mism for poor countries that we hope are
emerging). At the end of eighteen months,
your portfolio looks like this:

American large-stock index fund:
17 percent (2 percentage points
over target)
American small-stock index fund:
13 percent (3 percentage points
over target)
Foreign stock index fund, developed
nations: 21 percent (7 percentage
points over target)
Foreign stock index fund, emerging-
market nations: 16 percent
(6 percentage points over target)
Government bond index fund:
20 percent (10 percentage points
under target)
Corporate bond index fund: 13 percent
(7 percentage points under target)

What should you do now that you find
yourself with a portfolio that was 50 percent stock and is now 67 percent stock?
You'll need to sell off some stock, especially the foreign funds, and buy bonds.
It's the only way to keep your portfolio on
an even keel. In the example, you'll want to
compare the numbers in each of the two
lists, and sell and purchase accordingly.

Buying and selling may involve transaction
costs, and sometimes selling means having
to pay capital gains tax. You'll need to
compare these expenses with fine-turning
your portfolio too much. In general, I
wouldn't worry much about rebalancing
until any one part is more than 5 percent
out of whack in either direction.

SUMMARIZING THE POINTS OF PORTFOLIO MAINTENANCE

The last section described rebalancing
your portfolio. But maintaining your portfolio in proper working order requires
other tasks, which are listed in the following table.

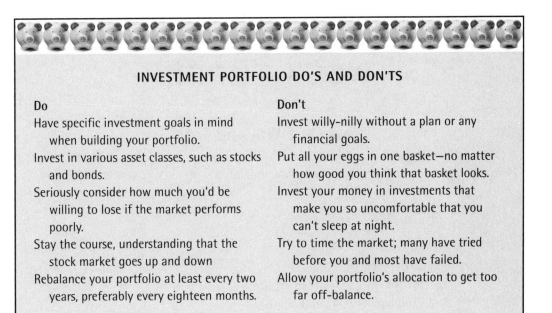

INVESTMENT PORTFOLIO DO'S AND DON'TS

Do

Have specific investment goals in mind when building your portfolio.

Invest in various asset classes, such as stocks and bonds.

Seriously consider how much you'd be willing to lose if the market performs poorly.

Stay the course, understanding that the stock market goes up and down

Rebalance your portfolio at least every two years, preferably every eighteen months.

Don't

Invest willy-nilly without a plan or any financial goals.

Put all your eggs in one basket—no matter how good you think that basket looks.

Invest your money in investments that make you so uncomfortable that you can't sleep at night.

Try to time the market; many have tried before you and most have failed.

Allow your portfolio's allocation to get too far off-balance.

WEEK THREE

Draw Up a Will and Trust

This week, you can

- Make a will
- Create a trust
- Provide for the care of your children
- Make your funeral arrangements

IF YOU FOLLOW THE GUIDELINES IN this book and do the dedicated work involved, you will be able to achieve a level of financial security. You will acquire things you care about and enjoy. Don't you want to know that they will be handed down to the people *you* designate? Nothing is sadder than watching family members squabble over who gets what personal treasure from a dearly departed member of the tribe. Has this happened to you or someone you know? Let's examine some ways you can avoid this scenario.

WRITING A WILL

Drawing up a will isn't the most exciting task, and it may be tempting to skip it or put it off this week. But make the time to visit your attorney's office. You're going to feel responsible and secure when you have this important paperwork taken care of.

A will is an important legal document that is best drafted by an estate attorney. You don't want your estate to fall victim to a legal loophole. If your estate is complex, vast, or varied, you really have no choice. There may be people you want to include and those you want to exclude. My favorite provision is one I've seen in the wills of the rich and famous: "If you contest this will, you forfeit all claims to anything in it." It certainly gives you the last word. Don't forget to review your will every few years.

On the other hand, if you have few assets, you can go to www.lawdepot.com, www.legalzoom.com, or a similar site that provides forms to do your own will. If you are a member of a union, have you checked your benefits package? Often inexpensive legal counsel is included. You might pay a nominal fee and have an attorney read the document you created. You know what they say: Better safe than sorry. You won't be around for the sorry part, but your heirs will. And you want them to sing your praises!

Finally, if there is a law school near you, often new graduates will do work pro bono or for a modest fee. They want to practice and build a client base. Call the registrar at the school and see whether someone can assist you. This option makes sense only if you have few assets.

A will isn't the only paperwork you want to prepare to help determine what happens to your belongings should you die or become incompetent.

A *durable power of attorney* is a simple document that provides someone with the legal right to act on your behalf should you become incapacitated and no longer able to handle your affairs.

A *medical power of attorney* (sometimes called a *healthcare power of attorney*, a *living will*, or an *advance directive for health care*) gives someone else the right to make medical decisions on your behalf if you are not capable of doing so. A lawyer can prepare this form for you, but it is straightforward. The form is available through your state government; to find it, search online or contact your state representative. If you feel you don't fully understand the possible repercussions of this document, discuss it with your doctor.

Pages 136–137 show Pennsylvania's standard advance directive for health care. (Most state forms will look similar.)

SETTING UP A TRUST

If you have substantial assets (such as a home or a portfolio) and you want to minimize the taxes owed by your estate or your heirs upon your death, you might want to consult an estate attorney about setting up one or several trusts. Trusts can be complicated, but in essence they provide perfect legal loopholes that allow the avoidance of estate or inheritance taxes at the Federal level, the state level, or both. (Congress is debating the future of the estate tax, so anything is possible by the time you're reading this chapter.)

The most common kind of trust is known as a *bypass trust,* sometimes referred to as a *credit shelter* or *type B* trust. The way it typically works is that a married man or woman leaves his or her money (half the marital estate) to the kids, but allows the spouse to use that pot of money to withdraw living expenses. Simply by having this document in place, your heirs can often be spared a bundle in taxes. Trusts, unlike, say, living wills, are not do-it-yourself documents. If you have substantial assets and you care what happens to those assets when you die, hire a competent estate attorney familiar with your state laws to set up a trust for you.

The following is the Advance Directive for Health Care statutory form:

DECLARATION

I, _____, being of sound mind, willfully and voluntarily make this declaration to be followed if I become incompetent. This declaration reflects my firm and settled commitment to refuse life-sustaining treatment under the circumstances indicated below.

I direct my attending physician to withhold or withdraw life-sustaining treatment that serves only to prolong the process of my dying, if I should be in a terminal condition or in a state of permanent unconsciousness.

I direct that treatment be limited to measures to keep me comfortable to relieve pain, including any pain that might occur by withholding or withdrawing life-sustaining treatment.

In addition, if I am in the condition described above, I feel especially strong about the following forms of treatment:

I do_____ do not_____ want cardiac resuscitation

I do_____ do not_____ want mechanical respiration

I do_____ do not_____ want tube feeding or any other artificial or invasive form of _____nutrition (food) or _____ hydration (water)

I do_____ do not_____ want blood or blood products

I do_____ do not_____ want any form of surgery or invasive diagnostic tests

I do_____ do not_____ want kidney dialysis

I do_____ do not_____ want antibiotics

I realize that if I do not specifically indicate my preference regarding any of the forms of treatment listed above, I may receive that form of treatment.

OTHER INSTRUCTIONS:

I do_____ do not_____ want to designate another person as my surrogate to make medical treatment decisions for me if I should be incompetent and in a terminal condition or in a state of permanent unconsciousness.

Name and address of surrogate (if applicable):

_____

_____

_____

Name and address of substitute surrogate (if surrogate designated above is unable to serve):

_____

_____

_____

I do_____ do not_____ want to make an anatomical gift of all or part of my body, subject to the following limitations, if any:

_____

_____

_____

I made this declaration on the _____ day of _____(month, year)

Declarant: _____

Signature: _____

Address: _____

The declarant, or the person on behalf of and at the direction of the declarant, knowingly and voluntarily signed this writing by signature or mark in my presence.

Witness: _____

Signature: _____

Address: _____

Witness: _____

Signature: _____

Address: _____

PROVIDING FOR THE CARE OF YOUR CHILDREN

If you have minor children, remember to name the adult you want to function as their guardian in the event of your death. The majority of Russell's clients find that when considering their own deaths, the issue of childcare is their most agonizing decision. For example, perhaps you don't want your sister, who is your closest blood relative, caring for your children. You want your best friend Amanda to care for them instead. Don't forget to check with Amanda before you sign the document. You might even give your sister the heads up.

I am an animal advocate so I have to remind you to include your pets in your will. You don't have to earmark millions for their care like Leona Helmsley, but you do want to designate their new owner. I do a lot of volunteer work with animal rescue organizations and can tell you that one of the main reasons pets are abandoned is a death in the family. Be sure everyone in your care is provided for in your will.

MAKING FUNERAL ARRANGEMENTS

My dear friend John passed away a few years ago. Cancer took him long before those of us who loved him were ready to bid him farewell. He knew he had a terminal illness and worked with the funeral home to plan every detail of his service. He made a video telling the story of his life through pictures and then he delivered a personal farewell to us. I think we all felt embraced by John as we sat in the chapel that day.

This week, you might give some thought to your funeral arrangements. Do you want a formal burial or does cremation better suit you? What about donating your body to medical science? It's a bit creepy, I know, but making arrangements for burial plots and caskets before they are needed can save your heirs a bundle. If a funeral home or large cemetery is near you, make a visit or give a call. They have planning kits to help you.

You can leave detailed instructions for your wake. Do you want flowers or donations to a favorite charity? Will there be one night of viewing your remains, a week, or perhaps no public viewing? Will the casket be open or closed? I could go on but you get the idea. You don't have to write it all down if you find this too disturbing. You can tell your wishes to your spouse and children or a few good friends.

THE FINAL FAREWELL

I was blessed to have parents who not only made final arrangements part of their financial plan but also who openly discussed things such as death. It certainly takes the onus off the topic. It also takes the guesswork out of the funeral arrangement if you are the only survivor in charge.

Remember: If you don't make these plans, someone else will! It's the final celebration of your life. Don't you want to be in charge?

WEEK FOUR

Review Your Beneficiary Forms

This week, you can

- Determine your beneficiaries and change them if needed

Remember when you opened that IRA account in 1991? Or when you bought that life insurance policy in 1987? You were asked to fill out a beneficiary form for each. Whose name appears on those forms? Quick!

CHANGING BENEFICIARIES

Did you know that your listed beneficiary has a legal right to your assets when you die—even if your will stipulates that you want your money to go elsewhere? *That's right—your beneficiary forms take legal precedence over your will.* For example, let's say you wrote the name of your sister, Agnes, the one who never remembers your birthday, doesn't even know your kids' names, and still hasn't returned your copy of *Catch-22*. When you go to that great reading room in the sky, unless you affix your spouse's name or those of your kids to the policy, Agnes still gets the loot. Beneficiary forms, unlike wills, are easy to do. Most banks and brokerage houses require a simple letter of instruction.

Take the time this week to locate and review your beneficiary forms and make changes, if necessary. Remember to review the forms once every several years—put the reminder on your calendar right now. Also, if you move your money from one bank to another or sometimes even open a new account at the same bank or brokerage house, you'll need to redo your forms.

One final word on beneficiary forms: If you have an employer-sponsored retirement plan, such as a 401(k) plan, and you are married, your employer will likely designate your spouse as the beneficiary automatically. If you want to make someone else the beneficiary, your husband or wife will need to consent in writing.

TAKING CHARGE OF
YOUR ESTATE

It's natural for most of us to react negatively when the subject of wills and beneficiary forms is brought up. In some Asian cultures it was once considered bad luck to draw up these documents because it meant you were going to need them sooner rather than later. Acknowledge those fears when they come up—and then let them go and do what is required. It takes time, effort, skill, and dedication to build an estate. You have been in charge of the building process; now it's time to direct its disbursement.

Don't forget to indicate whether you want your assets left to your heirs *per capita* or *per stirpes*. Suppose you have two heirs, Homer and Marge. Homer has two children and Marge has three. What would happen to your assets if you left them *per capita* versus *per stirpes*?

Per capita: The money is split equally among all descendants.

Per stirpes: Homer and Marge split the money equally. If Homer dies before you do, Marge gets half and Homer's two kids split the other half.

CHANGING OUR FOCUS

This has been a cerebral month, with lots of research and reading. Next month you'll be up on your feet tearing through the house decluttering. And with any luck, you'll make money in the process.

JULY SUMMARY

WEEK ONE

Decide if you need a financial planner.

WEEK TWO

Learn the ins and outs of savvy portfolio maintenance.

WEEK THREE

Decide who will inherit, starting with creating a will.

WEEK FOUR

Understand how beneficiary forms work and review yours periodically.

8. AUGUST

Refinance and Downsize Options

Nothing is as it appears.

−BUDDHA

AUGUST MARKS A TURNING POINT IN the year. The lazy days of summer are upon us but the busy fall season looms on the horizon. We're about to shift from rest to ramp up. This month we clear the house of unnecessary items. Whether they get tossed, shredded, or donated will be the result of decisions you'll make as we go through the month. You can receive a tax deduction for donations and make a little extra cash with a yard sale or cyber sale.

This elimination process can have a broader application. You can take steps to do away with some huge financial drains from your life. Is your house too big for your current needs? Do you need that fancy car or the second car that is rarely driven? Eliminating on this level is called downsizing. Although it may sound as if I'm asking you to live a diminished life, downsizing is actually an invitation to embrace a bigger life. My vision for you is a life with more funds, less obligations, and a lot more freedom.

HABIT OF THE MONTH: WRITE IT DOWN

This month, write in your financial journal each day. The optimum time is just before you retire in the evening. It will take only a minute. I want you to record one thing you did that day toward achieving your financial goals. Perhaps you reached out to an old colleague who has connections in a field you'd like to explore? Maybe you finally posted an ad on Craigslist for that dresser you've wanted to sell? This habit will instantly build your self-esteem.

TOOL OF THE MONTH: FANTASY STOCK PICKS

Last month you read about financial matters, including investing in the stock market, and maybe you were thinking, as most beginning investors do, that choosing winning stocks is easy. Before you actually dive in, why not spend one month (at least) making fantasy stock picks and tracking the progress of the stocks you feel are winners. I think you'll find that choosing stocks, just like timing the market (jumping in just as you think the market is going to soar), isn't easy. In fact, most professionals who try fail. That's why smart investors invest most of their money in low-cost index funds that mirror the performance of entire markets, such as the entire U.S. stock market, the European stock market, or corporate bonds. Almost any investment book will further explain *index investing*, which is the way you should do investing in the real world. "Fantasy" stock picking, however, using fantasy dollars, can be fun.

WEEK ONE

Look for Downsizing Opportunities

This week, you can

- Rethink downsizing
- Determine if a smaller home makes sense
- Assess the emotional and economic value of big-ticket items in your life
- Think about simpler, more cost effective, transportation

DOWNSIZING CAN BE A PRETTY SCARY word. The knee-jerk reaction is to feel that downsizing of any sort represents a failure. How? Some people think that having fewer things means you are letting the world know you can't afford the "big life" you have experienced to date. Or maybe to you downsizing means leaving the big house where you raised your family. If you aren't sure about your next phase of life, scaling back can cause emotional upheaval.

DEFINING DOWNSIZING POSITIVELY

The demon with downsizing is an erroneous perception of what it means. Let's create a definition that is in keeping with the financially responsible lifestyle you're trying to create: *Downsizing* is letting go of items that are draining you financially, emotionally, or physically. These items can be as big as a car or as small as a ring. They can have intrinsic value or be frivolous. What all these items have in common is that they drain rather than enhance or serve your life.

Instead of failure, let's use another f-word to describe the aftermath of a substantial downsize: freedom. The American dream has long been to amass material status, but if material things become a burden, it might be time to "86" them. Your home might contain lots of items that you have outgrown; these items are waiting to be recognized. I have had clients who couldn't drive their car into the garage because it was filled with old toys. They kept the stash to be prepared should family and friends drop by with children. The reality, however, was that they had an emotional grip on a time in life that had passed. What does your garage look like? Can guests use your spare bedroom? Is your finished basement a place where the kids can hang out or is it a dumping ground?

Downsizing can lead to making more money (renting out the garage or guest room); saving money (riding a bike instead of driving a fancy car); enjoying more freedom (home or condo ownership versus renting); or simply having more space. In the end, though, downsizing is about freedom.

In your financial notebook, make a list of the top five big-ticket financial drains or space-taking items in your life. Here are a few common ones: multiple big-screen TVs and computers (these two take up space and use electricity), a second or third car, motorcycles, boats, and excess clothing, jewelry, or art objects. Draw a line down the center of a page and work out the pros and cons of ownership. Very often seeing this information in black and white can wake us up to new possibilities. In the end that's the essence of downsizing: embracing new possibilities.

Be creative as you make this inventory. One word of caution: Don't make immediate plans to sell or donate an item without consulting your family, especially the person most involved in the original purchase. We're trying to save money, not start a family feud!

DOWNSIZING YOUR HOME

Dallas is one of my favorite cities. One year a client drove me around one of the newer exclusive areas that has mansion after mansion. I asked what the average person in the neighborhood did for a living. Diana told me that most were midlevel execs in the oil industry. Much to my surprise, she also told me that most of these homes were not furnished. The owners would have a bed, a table, and chairs. When I asked why, Diana told me that these homes were purchased to impress others. The money down, the taxes, and the mortgage were barely affordable, so the owners couldn't do any entertaining. This is an extreme example of well-meaning folks who need to downsize. (And, yes, these purchases were made before the economic crisis that began in 2008.)

Home ownership is special. We are emotionally connected to our home, which means making a change requires more than considering the tax breaks. One's home, however, comes with huge responsibilities. You have a yearly tax assessment. If you carry a mortgage, in most states you must have a homeowner's insurance policy. You have to heat the home in winter and cool it in summer. Homes have yards, and even the smallest home needs tending whether you garden yourself or hire one. If you have a pool, you have a pool service bill to pay. Have you ever heard of a home that didn't need repairs? Pipes burst. Paint peels. And tree roots uproot your foundation. As Roseanne

Roseannadanna from *Saturday Night Live* used to say, "It's always something!"

Is it time to downsize your home? This is a big, long-term decision, so make it after a careful assessment. Here are some questions to consider:

Do you have more space than you need? Are the kids off to college, or grown and out of the house? If the answers are yes, what keeps you in your home?

Are you living in a home that you have difficulty affording? Many Americans purchased their home during a better economic climate and now the monthly payments are more than they can handle. If this has happened to you, pinpoint the problem. Did you have an adjustable-rate mortgage and the rate has increased? Have taxes in your area gone up? Did you lose your job? Be specific. Now that you have a budget, can you make up the monthly deficit without selling?

Remember too that although our focus is on the family home, you may need to consider a move if you rent. I live in a rent-controlled area in Los Angeles. I know when and by how much my rent will rise each year. If you're in an unprotected area and without a lease, your ability to afford your apartment may be in question. Do the same kind of calculation I'm suggesting for homeowners to see whether a move might be beneficial. And consider a rent-controlled area or ask for a long-term lease to lock in your payments. In the current economic climate, renting can be a more economical decision than home ownership.

If your property taxes just went up, could you have your home reappraised? Perhaps the tax is based on a value that no longer reflects today's market.

Does it make sense to refinance your mortgage, meaning to swap your old mortgage for a new one with a lower interest rate? Call your bank and see what they can do for you.

If you own your home, might you consider renting it and moving to a condo or smaller home in another part of town, the state, or elsewhere in the country? Do you have unfulfilled dreams that could make this move a pleasure? For example, have you always wanted to live abroad? I live not too far from Mexico, where an increasing number of Americans are finding the home of their dreams for a fraction of the price they would have paid north of the border. Large ex-pat communities have sprung up also in Costa Rica, where Americans find their dollars stretch far. If this choice feels right to you, you can always rent your home for a year or two as a test. If you love your new community and don't miss your old home, make the change permanent. If it doesn't feel right, you can have the satisfaction of knowing you gave your dream a shot. (A word of caution: Being a long-distance landlord is not without risk; you can lessen that risk if you have a trusted relative or friend who can keep on eye on your property.)

If you are planning to sell your home, consult with your tax preparer, tax advisor, or tax attorney to find out the ramifications of a sale. In addition, consider working with a rental agency or real estate agent rather than handling the transaction yourself. People frequently want to save the agency fee or the real estate agent commission, but they are forfeiting the expertise. Realize that commissions, especially in a down market, are often negotiable.

If you are moving to a smaller space, it's always best to sell what you can't take with you rather than rent storage space. I have clients who are still paying for multiple storage units that they haven't been inside for years. Don't waste money. Make some decisions.

If you are ready to downsize but overwhelmed by the prospect of going through all of your stuff, it can save money in the long run to hire a professional organizer who specializes in downsizing. Ask family and friends for a direct referral, call your local Chamber of Commerce, or contact the National Association of Professional Organizers (856-380-6828 or NAPO@napo.net or www.NAPO.net). You can also contact The Zen Organizer herself at www.reginaleeds.com.

LETTING GO OF STATUS ITEMS

Let's say you decided that camping would be a bonding experience for the entire family. Before you thought about it (or held a family meeting to see if everyone was on board), you went out and purchased first-class camping equipment.

I could retire if I had a dollar for every time I've seen these items languishing in a garage. I would bet that a family of diehard campers would relish these items. Simply post a classified ad. After you make the sale, you'll have gained cash and space, and someone else will be using the equipment. "But Regina, what if in years to come my family decides to camp?" I can hear you now. Then it will be your turn to check ads on Craigslist and rescue a family who got involved with their hearts, not their heads. Cross that bridge if and when you get there.

Is a big-ticket white elephant living in your home? Significant purchases can derail your budget for months or years. Beyond the initial price, there's often the interest accrued if you paid by credit card. If you paid cash, did you borrow from your emergency fund to do so? What about the cost to maintain the item? When you add all the factors, these big-ticket items are more expensive than the sticker price.

When the economy was booming did you indulge in something for the family that you could live without? Try giving it up now.

Did you purchase a piece of artwork you didn't love but thought it would make a good investment? Consider selling it at an auction. Does the camper in your driveway get used every weekend or has it become a monument? Do you have a boat docked in the local marina? Saving the insurance, dock rental, and maintenance

SELLING THAT PRICEY CAR

Did you purchase or lease a vehicle for emotional reasons and now find that your payments are stretching you too thin? Here are some of the basics for selling your car:

Before doing anything else, take the car to the car wash. Wash the outside and vacuum the inside thoroughly.

If you are selling a vehicle you own, consult www.Edmunds.com for the most reliable pricing guide.

If you have had the vehicle for a while, put your repair bills in a file folder for presentation to the new owner. It's proof that you have maintained the vehicle. If you use a dealership rather than a private mechanic, all maintenance records will be on file on the dealer's computers.

If you have a leased car, try to find someone who is willing to take over your payments. The preferred source is your place of business, house of worship, or a club. Why? You will have to take your perspective buyer for a spin in your vehicle, and it's best to be in a car with someone you know rather than a perfect stranger. If you come up dry, you can advertise on eBay (fee-based), Craigslist (free), or your local paper, or you can drive around with a sign in your vehicle.

If you have a leased car and someone wants to take over the lease, you need proof that he qualifies. His bank or credit union must supply you with a document that verifies that this person can afford the payments. Note that lease agreements can be tricky to transfer. They vary in complexity, so read yours carefully before you begin this process. You must contact the financial institution that currently owns the vehicle you are leasing, and they will handle the transfer.

If this is a car you own and someone wants to buy it, ask for a cashier's check. Do not take personal checks or money orders.

You must take the person to your local DMV or Auto Club to be sure that you transfer all necessary documents to that person. Otherwise you are legally liable should the buyer have an accident.

Some dealerships will take your vehicle on consignment and try to sell it for you. You pay a fee up front or after the sale.

You can of course return your vehicle to the dealership and buy your way out of your agreement. But if you have the cash on hand to do this, I doubt that making your payments is much of a struggle. The bottom line once again is to get into a vehicle you can afford. My Saturn isn't as sexy as the Mercedes I used to own, but it's beautiful and reliable and the payments don't keep me up at night. I think that's pretty sexy!

alone could put a tidy sum back into your budget. Did you indulge yourself with a new car when a used car in great condition would have been wiser?

Have you long dreamed of mastering an instrument or a sport? Did you rent a Steinway piano or purchase expensive golf clubs, but then realize you weren't interested in making the effort to achieve your dream? Cancel the lease or sell the items.

If you have a large family and a garage, you probably have a second freezer. This is a great way to store specials at the supermarket. But if the kids are gone and it's just the two of you, how practical is that freezer? It gobbles up electricity as well as space. Perhaps one of your kids wants it? Or maybe a local school, shelter, food pantry, or day care center would appreciate a donation?

NEGOTIATING

You can't put off a new roof when you need one, but in today's marketplace, don't assume that the price of anything is fixed. An attorney once gave me advice that I now live by: Everything is negotiable. Although not every request may be granted, you won't know until you ask. (Just remember that the vendor, consultant, or expert with whom you're negotiating has his or her own bills to pay.) Remember: Nothing ventured, nothing gained. Here are some techniques to help remove any stigma you may feel about the need to ask for a deal:

- If you are dealing with a new vendor, ask whether there is a range on the published fee schedule. For example, if someone wants to work with me, I charge by the hour, not the job. If they can't afford my hourly fee, I suggest they purchase a consultation. This choice gives them ninety min-

utes with me. I look at a project and take you step-by-step through the process. If you follow my instructions, you are your own Zen Organizer. Ask your vendor for all price options available.

- You might barter for the full amount of the service you are seeking or at least a portion of the fee. This works if you have a legitimate service that the other vendor might need. Please check with your tax advisor regarding the tax implications of bartering. Uncle Sam wants to hear from you!

- Be prepared to walk away from your negotiation. I once asked a medical specialist what the cash discount was for her services. She reacted as if had just insulted her. I continued my quest and found an expert who offered me the option of seeing her outside the hospital at a satellite office, reducing the fee by half. When she found out I was a cancer survivor, she not only reduced the fee again but waited a year before she sent me a bill. Continue your quest until you find the right person for you. It isn't one size fits all for vendors, from doctors to shoemakers. Negotiate.

- You have a right to negotiate any item. Don't feel embarrassed or guilty (as many Americans do). Negotiation is an everyday part of life in most of the world. Remain friendly. State your objection to the price offered. Allow the other side to make the first counteroffer. And be prepared to walk away.

DOWNSIZING YOUR TRANSPORTATION

I had a client who drove the hottest BMW sports car you can imagine. It was a thing of beauty. But none of her coworkers knew that she lived in a shoebox-sized apartment because most of her paycheck went toward paying off the car as well as paying for gas and insurance.

Does a sizeable chunk of your income go into maintaining status? I'm not suggesting you buy the oldest, most beat-up jalopy on the car lot, but consider choosing a different vehicle so that you can live better or invest more. Often, a less expensive car not only means lower monthly car payments but also lower auto insurance, especially so if you are paying for collision insurance (covering damage to your own vehicle).

The cost of gas is a major factor in how much you spend on transportation, so it pays to choose a high-mileage vehicle.

Lease

Usually, buying a car costs less than leasing one, so have a conversation with your tax preparer before you make the decision to lease a vehicle.

Most people choose leasing because they want a new car for their image. In some cases this is legitimate. Leasing is great, for example, if you are on the road for business and can deduct the lease payment on your tax return. It works well also for people who use their car to transport clients. If you're in a status-conscious profession, you may want a new vehicle every two to three years, and leasing could be your best bet.

When your lease is up, it's typically best to return the car rather than buy it, unless you can negotiate a particularly good deal. You want to factor in how much of a down payment you made and the current Blue Book value of the vehicle. Check Edmunds.com and kbb.com for auto values. Also go to www.swapalease.com to investigate how much you can get to turn your lease over to someone else. The same Web site might be used to shop for leases, if you are determined to go that way.

Buy

Buying a good used car, rather than a new one, is almost always the best option for private transportation. The cost of buying, when you think about it, should be less than leasing. After all, the middleman collects a check from you every month. If you must have a high-end car such as a Lexus or a Mercedes, buy a three-year-old one and save $10,000 or more.

And don't forget to factor in the price of fuel—not at today's price, but over the entire time you plan to drive the car. The price of gas will likely rise again. Consider a hybrid, for both economy and ecology. When choosing a used car, check *Consumer Reports* to find out the most reliable models. You can subscribe to *Consumer Reports* or pick up the magazine and special auto guides at your local public library. In addition, before you buy any used car, be sure to have the vehicle fully inspected by a trusted (and independent) mechanic. An inspection should cost around $100. And it can save you a small fortune in return.

I purchased a high-profile car when I moved to Los Angeles. My Mercedes was six years old when I brought it home and in mint condition. I used to say I paid more for gas than I did for repairs. But as the car aged, the situation changed dramatically. I was hooked emotionally, so I neglected to see how absurdly expensive the repairs were becoming. Let me give you an example. Every other year the state of California requires a smog certificate to show that your car is not polluting the air. One year my old Mercedes failed. It needed a new transmission, and the law stated that it had to be an original transmission. It took six months of searching the country before my mechanic found a usable transmission from another 1973 Mercedes. Only a fool would sign up for this drama. And I was a fool.

In the final years of my time with that old Mercedes, travel was a crapshoot. Whether the car was going to start or stall at a light was always in question. Eighteen years after I purchased the car, I finally donated it to a charity when my mechanic refused to work on it again. Even a mechanic thought the car was dead! My attachment was absurd.

Today, I drive a Saturn. It doesn't command an immediate second look like a Mercedes, but it also never, ever fails me. My insurance payments are affordable and regular maintenance is inexpensive. And I've learned to not let my car become an extension of my ego.

Public Transportation

As I travel the U.S. organizing clients, I am shocked to see rush-hour gridlock on the highways in just about every major city. In some locations in the United States (and many more abroad), public transportation makes travel a breeze. If you live in an area blessed with good public transportation, this may be the best option for commuting to work. Consider how much you spend on gas and tolls in a given week. Contrast that to the cost of public transportation. How great will your savings be over the course of the next year if you leave your car in the garage? If you are driving less, let your insurance carrier know because it may reduce your insurance premium.

When comparing the cost of public transportation versus driving a car, make sure you factor in all the costs of your automobile, including its purchase price, financing, fuel, maintenance, insurance, parking, tolls, and cleaning and waxing. To get a rough idea how much it costs to own and operate a car, consider that the IRS's business mileage deduction rate is 55 cents a mile.

Also, if you could do some of your work during a morning train commute, add that as a plus for public transportation, too. Aside from the money you will save, you will also be gaining time. Of course you can always use that time to study the landscape and rest your mind. If this makes you more productive at work, it's priceless.

You may decide you don't need a car after all. You can always rent one for special weekend or vacation trips.

THE ROAD TO FREEDOM

Your road to freedom is paved with good decisions about downsizing! The most important takeaway message from this week is the willingness to eliminate some items from your life. If the items are no longer needed or used or are costing you a fortune in maintenance, you are better off without them. By getting beyond your emotional attachment and paying attention to what the item is really costing, you can make an empowered decision. However, don't eliminate a lot of items in a short time span. Offloading any major purchase is an important decision that should be made with care. After this week, you have the tools.

WEEK TWO

Clear the Clutter, Room by Room

This week, you can

- Find temporary storage for items to sell or donate
- Clear the clutter from your home with an eye toward making money and gaining space

WE'RE GOING TO MAKE USE OF TWO powerful tools in the Zen Organizing arsenal this week. First we're going to use the "fresh eyes" technique to look at the major rooms in your home and see them as a stranger might. We tend to look past our own clutter. It's simply part of the landscape. But a stranger entering the room for the first time sees everything. He sees the stacks of unread magazines and the clothing tossed on the chair. He sees the empty jewel cases in the family room languishing in search of the music or movie they are meant to house. He sees the cracked dishes and the chipped tea cups. He wonders why this home has so much stuff! After this week, there will be nothing for our imaginary stranger to do but marvel at the serenity of the environment.

The other tool is the powerful speed elimination. This is a time of action. It's not the moment to savor memories or weep over what might have been. There's no time for recriminations about how this stuff got like this. Nor is it the week to chastise family members for not doing their part. We're moving. We're on a mission. The literal clock is ticking.

August is the perfect month for this kind of work. When you feel you need a break, you can go outside with a tall glass of cold lemonade or a cup of iced tea. August provides us with the ability to escape our work environment. But before we get going, we need to do a little planning, so grab your financial notebook.

UNEARTHING A HIDDEN STASH OF CASH

Would you be excited if I told you that right now you have money hidden in your home? Whether it's enough money to pay

> This is a good time to take a stand against clutter-to-come. Opt out of catalogues so you won't be overwhelmed when it comes time to shop for the holidays. Go to www.cataloguechoice.org and select your favorites (and save some trees). In fact, you might find that your favorite catalogues are available as online editions and you can eliminate the printed version altogether.

the mortgage this month, some spare cash for a long weekend by a lake, or a few bucks for your 401(k), you'd be thrilled. Who wouldn't? Well, that's exactly what I am telling you. You're sitting on a sweet stash of cash.

This week we're going to find it. It's hiding in plain sight. It's all those possessions you no longer need or want. It's the items you have outgrown or purchased in error. Some of them will bring you cash. Some will make your heart happy as you see others make use of them in a way you long abandoned. All will leave you with space.

FINDING TEMPORARY STORAGE

Before you jump up and start work, however, I have a crucial question to ask. Where are you going to store all the discards? Next week we're going to look into how we turn the objects into cash. We'll plan for a yard sale, contact charities, and consider eBay and Craigslist. But in the meantime, we need a temporary place for all these items.

A project like this engenders a lot of excitement. People are ready to toss out and clean out with great abandon. After a few hours, the typical scenario sees the rest of the family return home. The house looks like a war zone. The air is fast escaping the Zen Organizing balloon. Even Fido looks annoyed with you. The danger here is that we can start feeling depressed and overwhelmed, and all the items will stay in the middle of the floor for months. We can't have that happen, can we?

If you live in a large house, you can make use of a space in the garage or perhaps a spare room. If you don't have one central room to use, designate an area in every room for what you intend to sell or donate. I've made a list of the major rooms in the average home. You can tweak my instructions to suit your particular situation. You can also use the basic guidelines for a room I haven't covered.

CLEANING THE CLUTTER

As you move through your home or apartment, carry your financial notebook with you and list any big-ticket items you'd like to sell. Do you have the original purchase receipt? Do you know how much the item currently sells for? (More about that next week.) Keeping track of the sellable contents of each room will also save time later.

If you feel that you have nothing to sell or donate, remember that you probably do have items to toss or recycle. You may even find items that should have been returned to friends or family months ago. Use this week to create space in your home. When my clients do this work, they tell me it's easier to think clearly or breathe more deeply. Some even lose weight. What have you got to lose? And what will you gain?

In each room of your home, place the following items:

- Heavy-duty garbage bags for trash
- Heavy-duty garbage bags or a box for recycling
- A box for items to donate
- A box for items to sell

Have a single box on hand to transport items to other parts of your home. You can empty this box as you complete your work in each room and then use it for the next room.

Set your stopwatch, alarm clock, or cell phone for fifteen minutes. You may need more time, but for now let's keep the intervals short. Shut out all distractions and focus on the room before you. If your phone rings, let the call go to voicemail. If you would like music, crank it. This is a treasure hunt! For the next fifteen minutes, I want you to move as quickly as you can.

The work you're doing now is the first step of the Magic Formula. When you have lightened the load in a room, follow the other two steps in the Magic Formula: Keep related items in categories and then organize the categories for easy retrieval. (An entire chapter in the first book in this series, *One Year to an Organized Life,* is dedicated to completely organizing each room in the home.)

The Kitchen

This is one of the most important rooms in the home. Traditionally everyone gathered here for fellowship. You know the old joke: No matter how big the home, everyone is in the kitchen. In today's world we have upped the ante because the kitchen is now also a makeshift office. Let's get this room in shape so we can make easy use of its original purpose: to prepare nutritious food for the family.

I'd suggest you work in this order:

1. Counters
2. Upper cabinets
3. Lower cupboards
4. Kitchen table
5. Pantry (if separate)

I bet you'll find the following:

- Old newspapers and magazines
- Invitations for events that have passed
- Flyers for sales that have passed or that don't interest you
- Mystery tools that you picked up at a cooking or Tupperware party decades ago
- Food that has expired

- If children are in the home, you'll no doubt find schoolbooks, homework, and school flyers

What else did you unearth? While you're working, if you come across items that belong in other parts of the home, toss them in your transfer box and deliver them to their proper place at the end of your last speed elimination. (Depending on the size of your kitchen, you might do this several times.)

When deciding whether to toss or donate something, remember that charities such as Goodwill can fix broken items and then sell them in their stores.

The Dining Room

The dining room is often used as an adjunct office, so you may find yourself dealing with lots of papers, magazines, catalogues, flyers, and mail. Recycle or trash as appropriate. Box up important papers that you need to keep for transport to your real home office or work area later.

What else are you likely to find?

- Worn, faded, and threadbare table linens are best thrown away or torn up as dust rags.
- Extra dish sets, serving pieces, and decorative items might best be sold or given to other family members. How will you know you have too many? Look around. Does it look like a family dining room or a cluttered shop? You have your answer.
- Children's toys should be corralled and taken to your children's bedrooms or the family room. Designate an area for play so that your entire home doesn't turn into a toy shop or, worse, a place where you can't invite people over. While you are gathering the toys for transport out of this room, pull out those that can be donated or sold. If you have family and friends who need toys and children's clothing, by all means take care of them first.

The Bedroom

For our purposes, we're going to put every possible bedroom (master, guest, and children) under one umbrella. Here are the most common items you will find in search of a route to a new home:

- Clothing that is frayed, ripped, torn, or worn should be tossed. This includes hanging items as well as garments in your overstuffed drawers.
- Clothing that is no longer worn, whether because it is out of fashion or the wrong size, should be tossed into the sale box. This includes shoes.
- Check all accessories, including belts, jewelry, scarves, hats, and gloves. You either wear it or you don't. Your stopwatch is ticking, remember? How much can you clear out in fifteen minutes?
- Threadbare linens can be donated to your local animal shelter, vet, or animal hospital. Be sure you have a usable set before you strip the bed and cart the sheets off.

- If you have sheet sets or towels that are in great condition but are no longer in use, consider them for the sale or donation box.
- Is there too much furniture in the room? What about lamps, rugs, and decorative items? These are great for yard sales or donation. Clean out the drawers for any items of furniture you want to sell or donate but don't cart it down until the day of the yard sale. If you know you want to donate, be sure you have a charity that will make a house call.
- Do you have extraneous items in your closets? If you aren't using those fans and free weights, consider selling or donating them. Items like memorabilia boxes and photos should be whittled down and stored elsewhere. For today, move them if you can. Schedule the whittling for a day when you have extra time.

The Family Room

The family room often becomes a dumping ground because so many people use it. The key is to assign chores and ask each person to clean up their own debris when they are ready to leave the room. It doesn't take more than about two minutes to return music or movies to their jewel case or binder and fold the afghan. Children can put their toys away. If they are too young to do it on their own, let them help you. On your way out, return to the kitchen the dishes and glass you used for a snack. Magazines and newspapers should have homes so they don't spill all over the room.

What are you looking for in this room?

- Old magazines and newspapers that can be recycled (donate magazines to a retirement community).
- Books, CDs, and DVDs can be sold or donated. (If the music is on your iPod, for example, you don't need the CD. And if you have seen the movie or read the book, are you likely to view or read it again?
- Toys that have been outgrown are great candidates for donating or selling.
- Items related to hobbies that are no longer being pursued can be sold or donated.
- Are you displaying too many decorative items? Can you part with any of them? Store them if not.
- What about photos? Are your children toddlers in these photos but raising families in real life? Time to downsize or at the very least swap out the old photos for some current ones.
- Are the afghans in this room in need of being replaced? Donate them with the towels and sheet sets to the local vet.

The Storage Areas: Garage, Basement, and Attic

The garage, basement, and attic are usually full of a great mixture of trash and treasures. Why? Because these areas hold items that we couldn't make a decision about. It's a new time in your life. Decisions keep the environment clear. Decisions are the engine behind all your organizing efforts. If you avoided decisions in the past, now you embrace them.

You might find the following items in these areas:

- Sports and gym-related items no longer in use. These are great for garage sales and donation.
- Furniture and decorative items we no longer use but have felt guilty giving away or getting rid of. Now is the time.
- Memorabilia from when your children were young. It's wonderful to save some items, but if you have gone overboard, why not photograph the items and then let them go? You can make a digital scrapbook and send it to your kids. They will appreciate that more than the actual items.
- If you find enough holiday ornaments to decorate the White House, sift through, pare down, and donate or sell the rest.

Bathrooms

Check the bathrooms for old towels to donate to the animal shelter, vet, or animal hospital. They will also be appreciated. The only other items you're likely to find are those you feel guilty for having purchased in the first place: the amazing skin cream that did nothing; the expensive shampoo that left your hair lifeless; the deodorant that didn't work; the makeup that looked freaky when you got it home; the hair gel that left your hair frozen in place. We all make mistakes. You don't have to live with them forever. Toss them now and have the space for the items you enjoy.

The Living Room or Great Room

In the living room or great room, you may find items of value that are best sold on eBay or at auction. If you have quality furniture and accessories, you certainly don't want to sell them at a garage sale. If the value is great, try an auction house like Christies or call a broker.

REWARDING YOURSELF

After a day or two of speed eliminating, you are ready for a reward. I hope you'll do something that takes you out into nature. Summer is waning and soon you won't be able to take a stroll in the park, walk through the zoo, or sit by the water and watch the boats go by. You've worked hard this week. Let nature restore you.

WEEK THREE

Hold a Yard Sale

This week, you can

- Learn the secrets of hosting a successful yard sale
- Consider other options to create space in your home

IN THE LAST TWO WEEKS, YOU LOOKED through your possessions to see whether there were any items you no longer needed, wanted, or found useful. Did you find any that you might sell? A good old-fashioned yard sale can help some of our possessions find wonderful new homes. Are you entertaining the thought but feel lost? This week has lots of ideas to help you get started. Your yard sale requires planning and some elbow grease to be successful, but it will also be fun and lucrative. To get started, I'll break the process down into steps.

STEP ONE:
DECIDING WHAT TO SELL

When the going gets tough, you'll want to have that trip, investment cash, or boost to your IRA in mind to help motivate you. A few years ago, my friends Herb and Laurie were about to move and planned a big yard sale with the hope of downsizing their possessions. They made well over $800 in one morning. And the more they sold, the less there was for them to haul to their new location. It was win/win for everyone.

When it comes to the specific items to be sold, you want variety and quality to lure in the best customers. However, don't decide for other members of the family which of their items are no longer needed. The exception is very young children. Be sure they aren't present or you will be dealing with unhappy toddlers when your customers want your attention.

Invite friends, family, and neighbors to participate. The more the merrier and the greater the selection. You'll also have more companionship on the big day and help setting up and tearing down your sales tables and clothing racks. And of course a big neighborhood yard sale means more customers. Have a firm date when you call or e-mail so that you don't waste time negotiating the date for the sale. If someone isn't available that day, ask them if they can deliver their goods the night before so you can sell their items for them. (Do this only if you are both comfortable with this arrangement.) Establish a rain date as well. (When choosing your dates, be sure to check the extended weather forecast.)

Go to a few local sales before you start your advertising campaign. Ask them what they know at the end of the day that they wished they had known from the start. Learn from their mistakes.

STEP TWO: CREATING CATEGORIES

Categories immediately put you in charge. Yard sales require a tremendous expenditure of time and energy. You're going to want to make as much money as you can to justify the amount of time and energy you are pouring into this endeavor. To help things run smoothly from "sort to sale," we're going to create categories.

If you have large items to sell, they can stay where they are for now, but be sure you have lined up the muscle to move them on the big day. Can you persuade your family and friends to help?

Some of your shoppers will be browsers but others will be on the hunt for specific items. Make their quest an easy one. The best-case scenario is for you to store items in your garage or backyard. If you are an apartment or condo dweller, try and keep the items organized in a specific location. Don't scatter them all over your home. You'll start to resent the sale before it happens. This way too it will be easier to transport previously sorted items to the street the day of the sale.

Mend, wash, iron, or repair items so you can get the most money for your possessions. Think of the discord at the average sale rack or sale table. It's hard to see what's available. Set up your sale so that it feels like a high-end store rather than a junk shop.

Encourage your children to participate by allowing them to keep the money they earn. Depending on their age, there should be two caveats: You need to approve what items they want to offload and how they plan to spend their loot. If you have enterprising children, encourage them to set up a lemonade stand.

STEP THREE: CONSIDERING YOUR LOCATION

As your real estate agent might say: location, location, location!

If you live on a lovely cul-de-sac, how will people find you? Put up signs with arrows the day of the sale. Or consider having your sale at the home of a friend who lives on a busy street. High-volume foot and auto traffic can be a huge help. If you take this route, remember you'll need muscle to transport your items and you'll want to post flyers and the like in your friend's neighborhood rather than yours. This can't be a last-minute decision.

When you have set your location, remember to warn your neighbors. You don't want an angry neighbor crashing your sale and scaring off potential buyers.

STEP FOUR: ESTABLISHING A MARKETING PLAN

You want to attract as many buyers as possible. How will you reach them? Plan to advertise.

Establish a specific start and end time for the sale. You don't want strangers ringing your bell at 7 a.m. if the sale doesn't start until 9!

Create flyers and post them around the neighborhood. Start two weeks before the big day to build momentum. Choose specific locations rather than use the shotgun approach. Check your locations periodically to be sure the flyers are still there.

E-mail friends and ask them to spread the word. Is there a (real or cyber) bulletin board at work? What about at your house of worship? You might consider placing an inexpensive ad for your sale in a local newspaper. Alternatively, if you're in a city, put an ad on Craigslist for free. Post photos of some of the best items to lure folks.

STEP FIVE: SETTING PRICES

You'll want to tag your items for the sale. This will enable others to help you. It will also let visitors know whether or not they can afford the item. But how will you know what the price is? Keep the basics in this section in mind.

People are looking for a bargain, so be realistic. You aren't going to get top dollar for your items. By the way, don't be surprised if most of your customers during the first hour are dealers and professional online sellers. Yard sales are one of the top ways they get their merchandise. These pros are counting on you to undervalue the good items.

Go to as many yard sales as you can. Get an idea of the price range in your neighborhood. Everyone is selling pretty much the same type of items.

Research the price of your most valuable items at online sale sites such as eBay and Craigslist. You might even print the information and put it in a binder. When people start to bargain with you, you can mention (or show them) the online price of the item. You can more easily command your price (or close to it) if you can assure your customer that your price is a deal. Know how low you are willing to go before you look into the eyes of a bargain hunter.

Remember that part and parcel of life at a yard sale is the art of haggling. If you know you want $.50 for a particular item, tag it for $1.00 or $2.00. You'll get the price you want and your customer will have fun negotiating down. But if you price a $.50 item with a $10.00 tag, you will have to deal with your treasures at the end of the day because they won't have found new homes.

STEP SIX: PLANNING YOUR PHYSICAL SETUP

The last part of planning your yard sale is to think of the physical setup. This involves asking yourself the following questions.

Do you have folding tables? What about chairs? Do you have portable clothing racks? Are there enough hangers in your home?

Did you purchase tags so that every item has a clear price marked?

Who will help you at the sale? You don't want to do this alone. Someone has to be watching the merchandise while you are negotiating a sale. Have snacks and water for your crew.

Do not allow any strangers into your home for any reason. Keep the doors locked. This is a great time to have your dog on duty. If someone needs a phone for an emergency, offer to make the call on your cell phone. If they need a bathroom, know the nearest gas station. You're in business today. You aren't trying to find new friends.

Secure a portable cash box with fifty or a hundred dollars in small bills and some coins so you can make change. Your money should be under lock and key. Never stash the box under a table or leave it on your chair. It must be with someone at all times.

Don't forget to have a collection of bags, boxes, and newspaper so that your purchases can leave for their new homes in style.

STEP SEVEN: CLEANING UP

What will you do with the "remains of the day"? Here are some ideas.

Many people have a charity stop by at an appointed time to pick up whatever didn't sell. You'll have a possible tax deduction, and that free space you were hoping for will materialize. If no charity will make a pick up, do you or a friend have a truck so you can load and deliver the items yourself?

Who is helping you return chairs and tables to your home? Who is going to load the truck or (Heaven forbid) return items to the house? Is anyone on garbage detail? You'll have empty water bottles, trash from customers, and food wrappers or paper plates depending on what and how you fed your volunteers. You're all going to be exhausted. Be sure everyone has an end-of-the-day assignment when the day starts.

USING CRAIGSLIST AND EBAY

Selling individual items on Craigslist— www.craigslist.org, a free classified ad site—may take a bit longer than selling them at a yard sale, but you'll have an easier time in terms of preparation. You can post an ad for any item, from furniture to old sports equipment. The trick is that you'll need to advertise for your local area because the key to success is easy pick up. Upload a photograph with a thorough description and the right price and you're in business. That said, be careful when it comes to letting strangers into your space. If you live alone, before prospective buyers stop by, ask a friend to join you—you know, that nice burly six-foot five-inch friend with the fuzzy pit bull.

If you're not already familiar with eBay—www.ebay.com—there can be a learning curve when it comes to using it, so you have to ask yourself if you are interested enough in selling your items on eBay to invest the time. However, with eBay you can reach prospective buyers all over the world. Many people sell on eBay full time and make money selling an astonishing array of items. If you're a novice, small items will be easier to send. Just be sure the buyer picks up the shipping tab for larger items. If you don't make that clear, you will get stung and your profit margin will tumble.

In addition, local storefront businesses and private entities can handle your eBay sale for you for a commission. For the storefront closest to you, check out your Yellow Pages or go to www.yellowpages.com. The caveat is that these folks take a hefty portion of the sale. Be sure it's worth your while; very often a solid tax deduction will be just as rewarding for you.

THE BOTTOM LINE

You have options when it comes to finding new homes for items you have outgrown emotionally or physically. These options all come with a certain amount of hard work, so choose the one that best fits your needs. I have friends who live for yard sales and others who love selling online. My choice is to donate the item to the right charity. Shelters for battered women, for example, need clothing and furniture in all of our large cities. I've had clients give me valuable items and, with their permission, I have sold them on eBay and then donated the funds to my favorite charity, The Search & Rescue Dog Foundation in Ojai, California. I had a client with a practically new Mac laptop she decided she didn't want. We donated it to a school that had just had their students' new laptops stolen. Donating can be a creative as well as a rewarding endeavor.

WEEK FOUR

Determine If You Should Refinance

This week, you can

- Understand the basics of refinancing
- Learn about second mortgages, home equity lines of credit, and reverse mortgages
- Find out whether you should refinance your mortgage

INTEREST RATES GO UP. INTEREST rates go down. The mortgage payments you make every month probably account for a major block of your budget, and as interest rates go up and down, so too does the cost of your mortgage if you have an *adjustable-rate mortgage,* or *ARM.* Most people have a *conventional mortgage,* with a fixed interest rate (say 6 or 7 percent) for a fixed period of time (most often thirty years). If you have a conventional mortgage and interest rates go up, you are sitting pretty paying yesterday's rates. If interest rates go down, you will find yourself paying more, sometimes substantially more, on your mortgage payments than if you were to take out a mortgage today. Solution? You can refinance.

LEARNING REFINANCING BASICS

A *refinance,* sometimes called a *refi,* is essentially swapping a higher-interest rate mortgage for a lower one. A difference of only 1 point in your mortgage—let's say from 7 percent to 6 percent—can make a difference of nearly 10 percent in your monthly payments. (The monthly tab of a thirty-year 7 percent $150,000 mortgage is $997.95. The monthly cost of a thirty-year 6 percent $150,000 mortgage is $899.33.) So why doesn't everyone refinance whenever interest rates drop? Well, more people should, but there are costs to consider.

This week we help you to weigh those costs against potential savings. By the way, most people who refinance do so to save on their monthly payments. But even if you don't need the extra money, you can refinance and reduce the life of your loan. Using the preceding example, if you have a thirty-year, 7 percent, $150,000 mortgage, you are paying $997 a month. If you were to refinance to a 6 percent mortgage and continue paying $997 a month, you could pay off the mortgage in twenty-four years, not thirty. Still, there are those costs to consider.

RESEARCHING REFINANCING COSTS

Start your research into the refinance process by going to www.bankrate.com. It's a great resource for many financial questions. Information on this Web site, along with perhaps the bank advertisements in your local newspaper and a chat with one or two mortgage brokers in your area, will give you the lowdown on today's mortgage rates. Conventional wisdom suggests that it is time to refinance when your mortgage rate is a full percentage point or more above current mortgage rates. That conventional wisdom is based on the costs of refinancing, which eat up any gains made when you save, say, one-quarter of a percentage point. Jeffrey Bogue, CFP and principal of Bogue Asset Management, suggests that the "one-percent point consideration" is not a bad guideline, but it is only the beginning. Here are four factors Bogue says you also need to take into consideration:

- The details of your current mortgage, including interest rate and time until the debt is paid off. (Eighteen months or less until your mortgage is over? It's very unlikely that it will pay to refinance.)
- All closing costs—inspections, deed search, courier costs, and such—involved with the refinancing. It doesn't make sense to pay $3,000 in closing costs to save a few dollars a month.
- The full terms of the proposed mortgage, including interest rate and maturity date. Beware! Many people pay close attention to the interest rate and the monthly payments, but how long will you be making those payments?
- How long you expect to live in the current house. If you think your boss may ask you to take a job halfway across the country next month, refinancing may be a costly mistake.

What to do once you've taken a bite and digested these four factors? Find yourself an online mortgage calculator, which will do something that your $2.99 calculator can't do: It will help you to compare the *net present value* (the value in today's dollars) of all the remaining payments of your current mortgage (both principal and interest) with the net present value of payments (principal and interest) of your proposed mortgage. Then it will compare the two, and make a suggestion.

In general, you'll usually find that it will be worthwhile to refinance if you are saving at least 1 percentage point and are going to be staying in your home for at the very least two years. This is only a rough rule because closing costs—as well as all other terms of a mortgage—can vary substantially. Remember too that closing costs and the interest rate on the mortgage itself are often negotiable. In fact, everything in the world of real estate is negotiable—especially these days.

Compare the figures for the old mortgage and the new mortgage (or have the calculator do it for you). Make sure you get an accurate picture of all the costs involved with the refinance. Voila! The lower cost is the option that you should choose. Many online mortgage and refi calculators are available. Perhaps start with www.bankrate.com, www.moneychimp.com, or www.Mortgage-calc.com. Refinancing has become much easier with the advent of online calculators.

Always keep in mind that although you may intend to stay in your house for the next fifteen or twenty years, you may not. After all, life is unpredictable. When considering refinancing, always figure out how long it is until your break-even point. In other words, how many months' savings do you need to pay yourself back for everything you gave to the bank, the deed company, and the inspector to get your refinance? The online calculators can help here, as well. Or talk to your realtor or financial advisor. If your break-even point isn't for three years, and you think there's a good chance that you might have to move within two years, pass on the refinancing; you could get burned.

As you compare different refinancing options, create a file for saving your worksheets. You can have one in your file cabinet or, if you do your calculations solely online, keep a file on your computer. Call the notes "Refinance." After you have your deal in place, you can shred these notes, but of course save in the "Financial" section of your file cabinet any legal documents generated during the process.

DETERMINING THE X FACTOR

You are expecting a caveat about now, right? Two additional factors may affect a refinancing decision: your age and liquidity. Let's say you can reduce your monthly mortgage payment by refinancing. Sounds great, right? But what if you are sixty-five and currently have a mortgage that will mature in twelve years, and your newly refinanced mortgage would mature in thirty years. Do you want to be paying off a mortgage into your eighties and nineties?

As mentioned, the other consideration is *liquidity*—how much of your cash is tied up in your home? Remember that whenever you take on a mortgage or refinance, that home equity can be useless in times of emergency. Most financial experts recommend that you always have at least three months' living expenses in cash. Keep that in mind before you spend your cash reserves on an attractive refinance. Refinancing may save you money in the long-run but could prove disastrous in the short-run if an emergency occurs.

The more money you can put down, the lower the rate you may be able to secure from the bank. If you can cough up at least 20 percent of the value of the home, you'll get a much better rate because the private mortgage insurance (PMI) disappears.

PREPAYING YOUR MORTGAGE

Whether or not you decide to refinance, you might consider at some point speeding up the repayment of your mortgage by, say, making an extra payment each year. Mortgage companies often encourage this by showing you that with one extra payment a year, you can greatly reduce the amount of time you'll be paying off the mortgage. That's true, but don't be too quick to prepay. Many people do who really shouldn't. Keep the following in mind:

- Your mortgage is probably your cheapest loan, especially because the payments are usually tax-deductible. Pay off your other loans (credit card, auto, and so on) before you pay off the mortgage.
- Make sure you have enough in cash for an emergency. If you need money in a flash, the equity you have in your home isn't going to help much. Real estate is not a liquid investment.
- If you haven't maxed out on your 401(k) at work—taking optimal advantage of any employer match—do that before prepaying your mortgage. You'll be getting a much higher return on your money.

UNDERSTANDING SECOND MORTGAGES AND HELOCS

Second mortgages and home equity lines of credit, or HELOCs, are loan types secured by the equity you have in your home. Caution: That means if you don't pay the home equity line back, the bank may be able to repossess your house. Often, people use a home equity line of credit to upgrade their home or to pay off a considerable high-interest credit card debt.

A home equity loan is often a better way to borrow than using a high-interest credit card. But "all that glitters is not gold." Let's consider some tips that will help you make a wise decision. As we all saw during the recent economic crisis, home values can go down rather than up. If you owe the bank $200,000 for your home, and you can't make the payments, and selling the home would not land you anything close to enough to pay off the loan, you may find yourself in deep trouble. You want to be a prudent real estate owner rather than an emotionally driven one who finds himself in foreclosure.

The *prime interest rate* is the interest rate charged by banks to their most creditworthy customers (usually the most prominent and stable business customers). The rate is almost always the same among the major banks.

How Second Mortgages and HELOCs Work

A *second mortgage* pays a lump sum to the borrower at the beginning of the loan. It has a set and steady interest rate and the borrower usually makes fixed-dollar payments over a period of time, traditionally from ten to thirty years. In contrast, a *home equity line of credit,* or *HELOC,* acts very much like a credit card. You are provided with a credit limit that you can tap for a certain period. The interest rate floats over time and is usually based on the current prime rate of interest plus or minus a certain percentage.

The amount that you can borrow is limited to a certain percentage value of your home less the current balance of the first mortgage. The interest rate charged is a function of current market rates and your creditworthiness. (Did I hear someone say FICO?) Usually a minimum monthly payment is required. The determining factors in how large your payment is are the current balance (if any), the interest rate, and the remaining term of the loan.

The Upside

Second mortgages and HELOCs provide two big advantages over most other kinds of borrowing. The first is that you'll often get a great interest rate. And why not? The bank is securing its loan with your home. The second advantage is that the interest is tax deductible in most cases. Due to the complexity of this potential perk, however, consult with a tax advisor to make sure you are deducting home equity interest correctly. IRS Publication 936 provides details on the limitations involved.

The Downside

The biggest disadvantage to second mortgages and HELOCs is that these types of loans are secured by your home. Most people use home equity to consolidate their higher interest rate debt. Given the difference in interest rates between a typical HELOC and a typical credit card, this can be a great moneysaver. But if you are not living within your means, the consolidation can make things better in the short term and possibly worse in the long-run (because you put your home at risk). You have to be careful because the problem may not be the expensive debt you have but your overall spending habits. There's no point in wiping out debt if you're just clearing the tracks to start over. Weigh all the alternatives and make sure that this is the most efficient course of action. For example, you may find that a disciplined strategy to wipe out current debt within two or three years may be less costly than taking out a home equity loan over ten years. Finally, compare home equity options to other financing options on an after-tax basis. That is, consider the value of the tax deduction you'll get on a HELOC; this deduction will be worth more to you if you are in a higher tax bracket.

The Bottom Line

If you decide to use home equity debt, the best type depends on your needs. If the dollar amount of your need is known and you want certainty on what your monthly payment will be, a second mortgage usually makes more sense. If your needs can vary over time, you are looking for flexibility, and you are willing to accept a varying interest rate, a HELOC is usually more appropriate. HELOCs and second mortgages can be the emergency funds of last resort.

Again, be careful because the debt is secured by your home. Home equity loans are a great tool to use, but keep in mind these loans aren't necessarily the best option.

UNDERSTANDING REVERSE MORTGAGES

A *reverse mortgage* is a loan against the value of your home that you don't have to pay back as long as you live in the house. Sounds like a cool idea, right? Well, not necessarily, according to Jeffrey Bogue. "A reverse mortgage should be a resource of last resort, used for only the basic necessities of life once other planning options are fully exhausted. Reverse mortgages are very costly and inefficient for anything other than making ends meet."

These loans should *not* be used if you

- Plan to sell your home in less than two years, because the savings will likely be less than the expenditure you'll make in the closing
- Want to use the proceeds to buy luxury items, such as a sports car, an exotic vacation, or plastic surgery because, hey, do you really need these things now? Can't they wait until you have some cash in hand?
- Are eligible for public assistance because liquidity received from a reverse mortgage can jeopardize your eligibility for SSI benefits

A reverse mortgage is generally available to anyone sixty-two and older. You don't need a certain level of income to be eligible. You remain the owner of the home, so you have to continue to pay real estate taxes and insurance as well as keep the house in good condition. The balance of the reverse mortgage is due upon the death of the last surviving borrower.

These loans include origination fees, third-party closing costs, and mortgage insurance premiums upfront as well as servicing and mortgage insurance premiums on an ongoing basis. Couple this with a loan that could go up on a continuous basis (if you have a HELOC, the rates are variable) and you see why a reverse mortgage can be an expensive avenue to access cash flow. If you feel that this loan is right for you, however, consider the credit-line reverse mortgage payout option rather than a lump sum or fixed-payment plan.

The credit-line option works like a home equity line of credit, where you tap into the reverse mortgage as needed. If you can be flexible and tap into the reverse mortgage only when needed, the credit-line option will save a lot in interest over time.

Finally, understand the implications of a reverse mortgage for your heirs. The only option available may be for the estate to sell the house. If the home has special meaning for family members and they want to keep it in the family, a reverse mortgage may not be the right avenue for you.

Online calculators at www.Golden Gateway.com and www.AARP.org can reveal the pros and cons of a reverse mortgage. But be sure you speak with your financial advisor before you make your decision. The question of any kind of mortgage should be dealt with in concert with someone who has your long-term financial goals in mind and who understands the intricacies of the tax code.

AUGUST SUMMARY

WEEK ONE

Decide whether it's time to downsize to safeguard your financial present and future.

WEEK TWO

Follow a room-by-room guide to clearing the clutter from your life.

WEEK THREE

Offload your clutter by donating it or selling it at a yard sale or on eBay or Craigslist.

WEEK FOUR

Determine whether you should refinance.

9. SEPTEMBER

Children and Money

You are the bows from which your children
as living arrows are sent forth.
—KAHLIL GIBRAN

MY FATHER WASN'T A GREAT TEACHER when it came to money, in the sense that he wouldn't have been the go-to guy for a prepared lecture series. He was, however, the man who taught by example just how a responsible adult handles the financial aspects of life. After eight months of organizing your finances, I trust that your children have watched the transformations in your life and learned from your example. This month we devote to them: the education they receive with us, as well as the one that happens in the classroom.

HABIT OF THE MONTH: READ ADVERTISEMENTS CAREFULLY

Read advertisements with a discerning eye. As you go through the daily paper this month, or you and your children watch television or pass billboards, choose one advertisement a day to discuss. The local

hospital claims to have "the best surgeons"? Ask you children who is defining "best" and how accurate is the claim. One local supermarket claims "the lowest prices in town"? Ask your kids if that is necessarily true. A daily examination of advertisements for one month can leave your children questioning claims forever.

TOOL OF THE MONTH: A MONEY MANAGEMENT BINDER FOR CHILDREN

One of my clients created a money management binder for her children. I hope you'll find it as creative, inspiring, and instructive as I have. Each child receives an allowance for doing specific chores. After they verify that they have earned their allowance (you'll find detailed information on allowances this month), they collect it and then divide the amount under their mother's watchful eye. Here's how it works.

Place three zippered pouches in the binder. Earmark one for spending money, the second for savings, and the third for charity. The children read about different groups and decide which they would like to help. Their financial education includes sharing what they have. Could you do something like this with your children?

WEEK ONE

Frugality for Parents

This week, you can

- Be conscious of the fiscal example you set for your children
- Examine the relationship between an allowance and chores

I WORK WITH LOTS OF SUCCESSFUL people whose time is managed down to the minute. Sometimes I observe an interesting phenomenon. Their children are gifted with lavish presents. Their birthday parties cost as much as a small wedding. The children go on trips most adults will not experience in a lifetime. I often wonder if this great outpouring of generosity comes from guilt. "I can't spend as much time with you as I'd like, so I'm giving you this (a fabulous gift or an outrageous party) so you will know how much I love you." All parents do this, albeit in less extravagant ways. Perhaps you took your children to an amusement park but spent the day on your Blackberry, dealing with work. You felt guilty so you bought them every stuffed animal they admired or every sugary dessert they pointed to. Perhaps you have to travel and miss a school presentation. At the airport on the way home, you pick up sweatshirts, dolls, and tee

shirts. But is this the precedent you want to set? Just as there *should* be a tie-in between allowances and chores, there should *not* be any connection between guilt and gift giving. This week we're going to sort through these thorny issues. This is also a great week to share key financial lessons with your children.

SPENDING MORE TIME WITH YOUR CHILDREN

The average working parent today spends a scant forty minutes a week playing with his children. (Compare that to the six hours a week parents spend shopping.) What a loss for both parents and kids! Are you looking for satisfying ways to spend more time with the kids? Try making free time literally free-of-charge: an old-fashioned song circle, storytelling, ball games when it's nice outside, and board games on rainy days. At nighttime, try a family outing to stargaze.

Here are some more low-cost or no-cost ideas:

- Work with your child to draw a map of your house, your block, or your neighborhood.
- Plant vegetable or flower seeds and watch them grow. Enjoy the bounty.
- Make puppets out of old socks.
- Fly a kite.
- Peruse your local newspaper for field trips.
- Visit arts and crafts stores such as Michaels for fun projects.
- Get a book on making items you and your child can give as holiday gifts, such as soap or candles.
- Spend an afternoon exploring at your local library.
- Visit your city's botanical gardens, museums or historical sites.

You'll notice that none of these activities cost very much money. What's the price of a ball, some seeds, or a board game? They are paid for in those other currencies: time, energy, and love.

This is an ideal time to begin shopping for holiday flights if you plan to visit your parents or take a vacation this November or December. The earlier you shop, the more you are likely to save. And if you start making your own gifts such as soap and can-

dles now, you'll be all set for a stress-free holiday.

TEACHING CHILDREN ABOUT MONEY

If you have been an over-the-top parent, I suggest you scale back the treats and put the money you save into a fund for retirement or your children's education. We have seen in the economic downturn of 2008 that nothing in life is guaranteed. Many retirement account balances were (at least temporarily) cut in half. People lost their homes. Even the most seemingly secure jobs were eliminated. The bottom line for our purposes is that you give yourself to your children rather than giving to them from your wallet. But let's go deeper with this concept.

Money Management for Children

How can any child learn to appreciate money if everything is handed to him? My best friend's daughter, Molly, frequently gets a strong desire for something pricey. One year she wanted to swim with the dolphins and another year she wanted a top-of-the-line iPod. My friend Susie requires her daughter to earn the money for these purchases. You'd be surprised how often things get forgotten because it's too difficult to raise the money required. It's a powerful lesson because no one gets everything they desire in life. As a result, at age thirteen, Molly has a more realistic grasp of money than some forty-year-olds I know.

I have a client who insists that her children learn how to take care of themselves by the time they reach eighteen. In addition to obvious tasks such as laundry, cleaning, and driving a car, managing money is at the top of her list. She told me a great story about one of her daughters. This young woman loved to go to parties and proms. At the start of her junior year of high school, she was given a clothing allowance. She promptly bought some beautiful party gowns. Lo and behold, the weather turned cold and she didn't have enough money for a new winter coat. When she went to her mother to ask for additional funds, she was told there would be no more money. The amount she had been given was adequate for the year. She had been free to spend it as she wished. Since party dresses had eaten most of her budget, she would just have to wear last year's coat again this year. Lesson learned.

Jobs for Children

Instead of *giving* money to your child, why not guide him in the steps it takes to *earn* it? Help him find an age-appropriate job. My client with the daughter who loved party dresses gave each child (she has seven) a cleaning rag and a spray bottle of water when they were eighteen months old. You'd be surprised what's at eye level that could use a good wipe. Young children can help set the table and remove their own dishes. They can be taught to make their beds, even if that means just smoothing a comforter into place. Military corners are not required! No matter what age-appropriate chore we

A COOL CARD GAME

I'd like to share a story with you about another of my favorite clients. Every year before school starts, Alice's children receive a laminated card. On it are listed their household duties. If they want to receive their allowance, they must check off their duties as they are accomplished. Of course children always want extras. Alice passes out a second laminated card, and this one has bonus tasks the children can perform to earn extra money. Her nine-year-old is quite adept at polishing the family silver!

When her children decide they want to earn extra money to purchase something special, Alice asks them to explain why this item is important. Is it better than what they already have? Is it educational? Is it good value for the money? This sets in motion the process of understanding what a purchase means to you. Too often we shop based on emotional whims. This method instills in children the need to ask: Do I really need this and why?

mention, help your child fulfill his duties in a responsible way just as he will be required to do in his career.

Every year, young men and women head off to college across the country with no clue how to take care of themselves. Laundry and making the bed aren't sexy tasks, but unless they are moving into the dorm with a personal maid, children need

> 🐷 This is a good time to anticipate next summer's fun needs and gardening equipment. Check out the end-of-summer sales with your children. You'll find the best deals right now, by a long shot!

to go to college with these skills under their belts.

A Wealth of Good Examples

Billionaire Warren Buffett once said that two institutions destroyed character: welfare and trust funds. Neither he nor Bill Gates is leaving the bulk of their fortunes to their children. The money will instead go to charitable foundations that will do good for millions around the world. Journalist Anderson Cooper, the son of Gloria Vanderbilt, said during an interview on *Oprah* that when he was growing up, his mother told him and his brother that they had many advantages because of her wealth. (In addition to being an heiress, she headed a design empire.) She would pay for their education and then they would have to get jobs and earn their own money. Cooper's first job was a modeling gig when he was around ten. He said he couldn't wait to earn his own money.

Create Balance

Your example (like Mr. Buffett's "be charitable" or Ms. Vanderbilt's "plan to work for a living like I do") exerts a powerful influence on your children in another way:

How do you take care of yourself? If you spend your nights and weekends at the office, what is the message? "Life is about sacrifice. You work only for others. It's okay to be a workaholic." Show children how work not only brings in money but allows you to fulfill yourself. Teach them the power of money to create balance in life.

For example, when you go on a family holiday or day trip, set your phone to vibrate and answer only emergency calls. Be truly present with your children. Share with them that you are compensated for the work you do outside the home just as they are for their chores. Let them know that your vacation or field trip (or whatever you choose for this teaching moment) has come about as the result of your earning a living. Make the connection. And if you love your profession, be sure and communicate that to your children as well.

Let me share an exchange I had with my own mother, one that unfortunately occurred often. I would suggest that my mother do something for herself. Maybe she needed a new dress for an event she was going to with my father. Or perhaps it was a visit to the doctor or dentist. My mother's response was always the same: "I'm not going to do that. I'm going to save the money so there will be more for you." My mother was a child of the Depression. She was trying to show me how much she loved me. But this behavior only made me feel guilty and depressed. Balance by example is a greater legacy than a fat bank account.

LAYING THE GROUNDWORK

As your children head back to school, they will be geared up for change. This is the perfect time to institute changes in the way you teach them about money: how to earn it, manage it, and give it away. Feel free to tailor the suggestions we've offered to suit your situation. A family meeting is a great way to start. And don't forget to let your children express their opinions. If they are a bit older, be sure you ascertain their current level of financial knowledge. You might just be pleasantly surprised.

WEEK TWO

Educate Your Children about Money

This week, you can

- Increase your child's understanding of money and finance at any age
- Talk openly with your children about your financial situation

YOU BEGAN YOUR FINANCIAL JOURNEY this year by examining your childhood relationship with money. I'm sure you were astonished by how powerful your early experiences were. Let's continue our work this week to be sure your children are on solid footing.

TEACHING CHILDREN AGE-APPROPRIATE MONEY LESSONS

The first principle of organizing is to remember that the whole of anything is overwhelming. You need to break your project down into manageable chunks to achieve success. Fretting over the size of a project will get you nowhere. Incremental moves forward will take you across the finish line.

You don't have to teach your child about money in one day or even over several. You want to demonstrate sane financial practices over a lifetime so your child sees how it all works. Here are a few crucial lessons you can teach your children about money, and an appropriate age to give the lesson.

Under age eleven: Teach patience. If your youngster wants a new bicycle that costs $120, don't simply walk into the store and buy it. Consider giving the child a regular allowance and explaining that by saving $10 a week, he will be able to buy that shiny new bicycle for himself in only twelve weeks.

Introducing your child to money at a young age makes financial matters a natural part of life. Let them surf over to www.centsables.com and meet six super-hero friends named Franklin, Jackson, Grant, Hamilton, Penny, and Suzie B. They live in Centsinnati and can "grow to gargantuan height, run like the wind, and control the elements." And they do it all in the service of giving the target audience (six- to eleven-year-olds) super money-management skills. Youngsters can enjoy the Centsables online in a series of games and comic books. Topics include "How kids earn money" and "Taking stock of the market."

Age eleven–twelve: Explain your values. When your child clamors to have you buy something, use that as an opportunity to speak of your values. Don't simply say "no" or "I can't afford it" or "I don't have the cash right now." Rather, explain why you *really* don't want to make that purchase. Tell your son or daughter that having two pair of jeans is enough, and that rather than purchase a third, you'd rather save that money for their college education or some other long-term goal.

Age twelve–thirteen: Demonstrate charity. Part of a healthy attitude about money is knowing when you have enough and sharing anything above that. You can raise more giving and healthy children by modeling charity. That means not only giving to charities but involving children in the process. Perhaps gather clothes and food to donate to the local shelter, or participate in a family walk or run for a cause you believe in. Volunteer to feed the homeless at a shelter once a month. Whatever you can do as a family serves to teach your children an important and positive lesson.

Age thirteen–fourteen: Show them the future. Compound interest, according to Albert Einstein, is "the most powerful force in the universe." He may have been joking. But then again, perhaps he wasn't.

Consider this: If your thirteen-year-old were to sock away $1,000, invest it at 8 percent (a reasonable return for a good long-term investment), and add $50 every month, by the time she's sixty-five she would have $577,596! Show your youngster how it works with an online calculator such as the one on the Web site www. dinkytown.com; click "Savings Calculator."

Age fourteen–fifteen: Forget about fate. One of the most important things you can teach your children about money (or life, for that matter) is that they have the power to affect their own futures. Sure, luck plays a role in a person's life, but personal action tends to play a bigger role. Teach your children that when it comes to money—making it, spending it, investing it, or giving it away—they have control.

Age fifteen–sixteen: Provide incentive. Reinforce the importance of saving by offering a bonus for doing so. Just as your employer may match any money you put into a 401(k) retirement plan, you might work out a similar arrangement with your youngster. For every dollar he or she agrees to save and invest rather than spend, you agree to add another dollar to the pot.

Age sixteen–seventeen: Demonize bad debt. Americans are drowning in debt, and credit cards are a big part of the problem. Explain to your children—who may soon be off to college, where credit-card companies hunt for kids like big game—that buying with a credit card can cost two or three times more than paying cash. Paying the minimum $24.85 a month on a $1,000 debt at 18 percent interest would cost you a cool $932.32 in interest over 9.5 years.

DESCRIBING THE EFFECTS OF A RECESSION

Teach your children how the world economy touches all our lives. Look at the auto industry: When a large company such as GM goes into bankruptcy, it has a ripple effect: If GM can't pay its bills, neither can its suppliers. If workers are laid off, production goes down and unemployment ranks swell. Perhaps you own a GM car that gets serviced at the local dealership. Where will you go for service if the dealership closes or your car breaks down and parts are difficult to find? Whatever example you choose, whether it's GM or your own company or the donut shop in the downtown area, find ways to make the economy's "cause and effect" immediate for your child. And be sure and explain that recessions are part of the natural business cycle.

Have you lost your job? Do you have enough savings to ride out the storm? Does your child need to sacrifice his allowance? We can all deal with things if we understand what is happening, why it's happening, and how it is being handled. If your child is in school, other families in his circle may have gone through changes. He may be wondering how it will affect his family. The way you handle the crisis will be a pivotal teaching moment for your child.

What if you are going to lose your job but your home is secure because you have socked away a large emergency fund? This is a great way to demonstrate the power of savings to a child. Suppose you aren't sure your job is secure, so you have a family meeting and work as a unit to discuss alternatives. Could you show the importance of communication in a more powerful way? Downsizing from a huge home to an apartment isn't as great a tragedy if your child sees that you are moving as a solid family unit. Remember: "Stuff" is passing, family is forever. There's no better time to demonstrate this reality.

WEEK THREE

Save for College

This week, you can

- Get the scoop on 529 plans
- Set up a 529 plan: a great way to pay for college
- Find out about the American Opportunity Credit and Hope Credit

WITH THE AVERAGE TUITION AT A four-year private college now running about $25,000 a year (about $7,000 a year for a public school), paying for a college education can be overwhelming for most parents. And many parents fret about it for years before college begins. But it isn't just the money aspect. It's the reality of seeing your child leave home and become an adult. You've been working toward this since you brought your kids home from the hospital. But now the rubber of reality hits the emotional road and watching them leave the nest may not be easy. Take this part of the journey one step at a time. And by all means involve your child.

Here's the good news: As much as you want to provide a college education for your child, it isn't appropriate to stash away money for this purpose and ignore your retirement. Your child doesn't have to go to Harvard, Yale, or Princeton. It is his job to get the kind of grades that merit scholarship consideration. It is his responsibility to have part-time work that will enable him to either contribute to his own education or at the very least pay for the basics of off-campus life. Have well-defined expectations and communicate them clearly to your child. What are you willing to pay for? What is his responsibility? Remember that it is possible to attend a two-year college near home, work part-time, and then transfer to a four-year university. Are you starting to breathe more deeply? I thought so.

This week we'll look at one good way to start saving for college early: the 529 plan.

UNDERSTANDING 529 COLLEGE PLANS

A 529 college plan, administered by individual states, is a savings plan that allows you to sock away money and watch it grow, 100 percent sheltered from taxation, provided you use the money to pay for higher education. The different state plans (and some states have more than one plan) differ in terms of overall expenses, investment options, and special tax benefits.

Many states, for example, allow you a deduction from state income tax for any money put into a 529 plan. Some states take it a step further by offering outright grants to residents for opening a plan. Maine, for example, provides $500 to newborns for whom a parent opens a Maine 529. In other states, such as Minnesota and Colorado, similar grants are also available, but only to families with modest incomes. Several hundred colleges

are offering matching grants for parents who put away college savings.

CHOOSING A 529 PLAN

Opening a 529 plan is no more difficult than opening a savings account at a bank. You fill in a form, and you send in your check. The harder part is choosing which 529 plan to go with. The best place for information on 529 plans is on the Web at www.savingforcollege.com. Start with the calculator (click the "Tools & calculators" link) to get an idea of how much you need to be saving, and then proceed to the menu of individual plans.

Start by looking at your own state's plan, but know that you can shop around. In some states, however, a (state) tax deduction is available only if you contribute to your own state plan; in other states, that doesn't matter.

Following are some important considerations in opening a 529 plan.

Will you spend the money? Any money you put into a 529 plan that is spent on higher education will grow tax-free. Any money you don't spend on higher education will be taxed, *and* you will pay a penalty of 10 percent on the earnings. You can, however, transfer most 529 plans from one beneficiary to another. If your son doesn't go to college, you can give the money to your daughter or a nephew, for example, or wait until you have grandchildren. You can transfer to a non-family member, too. (There may be

CONTRIBUTING BEFORE YOU HAVE A CHILD

If you're sure you're going to have children, but the little darlings haven't yet arrived, you can still set up a 529 college plan. You simply list yourself as the beneficiary, and then, when the Big Day comes, change the beneficiary on the account from you to your newborn. It's that easy.

tax ramification if you go outside the family, so check with your tax advisor before you do.)

Know the maximum you can contribute. Amounts contributed to a designated beneficiary's 529 account are treated by the IRS as gifts. According to current tax law, contributions of up to $13,000 a year can be made to a single beneficiary without incurring Federal gift tax. In the case of the 529 plan, you are allowed to contribute a lump sum for five years, for a total of $65,000 ($130,000 for a married couple). If you put that money into your child's 529 plan, the assumption is that you will then make no additional gifts to the child for five years thereafter. Most people, of course, do not have this kind of money sitting around, and instead make regular, smaller contributions to their children's college funds.

Choose a low-cost plan with good investment options. 529 plans come with fees, and those fees come in two basic flavors. The plan itself will charge you money. And the investments within the plan—usually mutual funds—will charge you more money. You need to add the two components to come up with a total charge. In some cases, such as the Utah UESP 529 plan (where Russell put money for his two kids' college educations), the total cost (depending on the exact investment option) can be less than $1/3$ of 1 percent a year. For other plans, such as the Arizona InvestEd plan, the total cost can be well over 2 percent a year. About half of the 529 plans charge more than 1 percent

a year in fees. Don't go there. Stick with those plans whose combined fees are less than 1 percent a year.

Also look for plans, such as Utah's, that offer index funds (usually through Vanguard or TIAA-Cref). Avoid plans (like Arizona's) that charge you a load (sales commission) to buy into individual funds. Other inexpensive options: Louisiana's START plan, the Ohio CollegeAdvantage plan, and the Virginia VEST. Among the most expensive options are Alabama's Higher Education 529, Wyoming's Direct Portfolio College Savings Plan, and Maine's NextGen College Investing Plan.

Choose plans you can directly invest. Some plans are sold through financial advisors and brokers, and others you get directly from the plan itself. Some plans, such as Maine's, come with two versions. The least expensive plans are almost always those you buy directly, leaving out the middleman. Yes, if you go through the middleman you'll get some professional advice on which options in the plan to choose, but do you really need that advice? After all, there aren't usually that many options to choose from, and you can always go with the simple lifecycle option that adjusts accordingly, moving from more aggressive to more conservative as your child grows. You may recall that I argued against lifecycle funds for retirement accounts. That's because you and your neighbor may be on different retirement trajectories. But if your children and your neighbor's children are both headed for college in two years, you are more or less on the same trajectory: You are both going to need cash for tuition in two years. So even though one-size-fits-all isn't a perfect solution for 529 plans, it is the easiest, and it makes more sense here than it does in a retirement account.

Go with an age- and risk-appropriate portfolio. Most 529 plans offer lifecycle funds that start aggressive when your child is young (mostly stocks) and become more conservative (mostly bonds and cash) as the child approaches college age. These funds are often a good option. Other investment options allow for static investing. You can choose, say, all stocks or all bonds. These, too, can be okay, but realize that there is a trade-off between risk and return. If you go with an all-stock portfolio in your 529, you are more than likely to see the greatest amount of growth. But if you are still in that all-stock portfolio just as your child is about to start college and the stock market takes a fall, you'll need to cough up tuition from other sources.

A 529 plan is a great way to save for your child's higher education. But we'd be remiss if the discussion stopped here. Next week there's more information on this important subject. For the moment, decide if the 529 plan is right for you and, if you can, open your account(s). Just remember Russ's initial advice: Don't sacrifice your own retirement. Whether your child becomes an accountant, a surgeon, or a National Park Ranger, he wants to know you

can take care of yourself. He'll also be primed to teach his kids the same lesson. Fiscal responsibility is truly the gift that keeps on giving.

QUALIFYING FOR COLLEGE TUITION TAX BREAKS

As a general rule, higher-education expenses are tax deductible if the courses the student is taking are advancing an existing career. They are not deductible if the courses are developing a new career. However, a special tax break called the American Opportunity Credit, which is available only through the end of 2010, may allow you to take a tax *credit* of up to $2,500. (The tax credit is better than a deduction because it comes off the top of your tax payments.) To qualify, you must have a modified adjusted income (gross income, generally speaking) of less than $90,000 ($180,000 per couple), you must be paying higher-education expenses for a student enrolled in a degree program attending class at least half-time, and the student must be your dependent.

After 2010, tax credits may still be available through something called the Hope Credit, but that is limited to people of more modest means. Whether you do your own taxes or someone does them for you, make sure you apply if you think you qualify for either the American Opportunity Credit (before December 31, 2010) or the Hope Credit (after December 31, 2010).

Note that interest payments on a qualified student loan may also earn you a tax deduction (not a credit). There are thresholds for income here, too. And the amount of interest payments that may be deducted is generally no more than $2,500.

WEEK FOUR

How Your Child Can Contribute

This week, you can

- Help your children find ways to fund their own higher education
- Show your children how to research different colleges
- Check state options

THE COST OF SOME COLLEGES RUNS over $50,000 a year, and the median household income in America (before taxes) runs around $50,000 a year. So to send a child to four years of college, the average American family is going to have to jump some serious hurdles, find an inexpensive college, or carefully navigate the world of financial aid, loans, and scholarships. The earlier you can plan and save for your children's education, the easier it will be.

FUNDING COLLEGE:
THE BASICS

According to the not-for-profit organization College Board, more than $143 billion in student financial aid is available to those willing to do the digging. Part of that money is issued by the government, espe-cially in the form of Pell grants, available to children whose parents earn less than about $50,000 a year. (See www.ed.gov/programs/fpg for more information.) Some of the aid comes from corporations and organizations. Much of it comes from the colleges themselves, which make all sorts of special grants, sometimes for brainy kids, brawny kids, kids in need, kids of certain racial or ethnic backgrounds, or kids of alumni. (See www.collegeboard.com for all sorts of tips on finding scholarships.)

Student Loans
When the cost of the college is still more than savings and scholarships will cover, you may have to turn to loans to fund the remainder. Fortunately, student loans have always come cheap, and that's especially true these days. The least expensive avenue is to go to the government first. The

Stafford Loan program (http://www.staffordloan.com) offers loans of up to $57,500 for an undergrad education at rates as low as 4.5 percent (an interest rate slated to remain in effect through 2011).

Choosing an Affordable College

Of course, key to affording college is choosing the right school, with the right tuition, in the first place. Your child's high-school guidance office can offer direction. Some of the newer software programs available at most high schools provide an amazing analysis of the best schools, using your own criteria regarding price, geography, major, and other factors.

One cost-saving option for higher education that has taken off like a rocket in the recent recession is the use of community colleges. Let's say your child goes to the top-tier school of his dreams. He can still, most likely, take some credits at a local community college during the summer. He'll be eliminating those classes from his required curriculum. But he'll save more than time: He'll save money. Going to community college for the first year or two and then transferring to a better school can be an enormous moneysaver, especially if your child is continuing to live at home.

Finally let's not forget the great universities and colleges to the north in Canada. These institutions tend to cost a fraction of their American counterparts. Here's a Web site to help you do some research and see if this is a viable option for your child: http://www.aucc.ca/_pdf/english/publications/canada_universities_e.pdf.

RESEARCHING COLLEGES

Just as all institutions of higher learning and all financial avenues to pay for an education are different, so too are all students. It's important to toss your child's natural abilities and life goals into the mix. This is by no means a one-size-fits-all proposition. Involve your child—he can learn a lot about research and finance through this process. What does your child want to do with his life? Which school would be the best place to prepare for that profession? Encourage your child to do some online research for each school that interests him. What are the pros and cons of attending that particular school? How much will it cost? Are there scholarships? Is there student housing or would an off-campus apartment be more cost effective? Ask him to request literature from his top choices. Encourage your child to not wed himself to one particular school, especially if that school's tuition is unrealistic. Huge differences exist in tuition, scholarships, and aid at colleges of relatively the same quality. Be a smart education shopper.

At the beginning of this year you learned how to set up a working file system. The college application process is a great time to teach your child this skill. Why not show him your system and offer the supplies you used to create it? Perhaps you can brainstorm the best way to keep these materials. I'd consider using a box-bottom hanging file folder for each college and keep the schools in alphabetical order in a file drawer.

If the materials from all the schools tend

to fall into a pattern, you might create individual folders for each of the schools and keep those in the box-bottom file folder. Now when you need one piece of information from a particular school, you won't have to fumble through everything they provided. (Toss any papers that don't apply to your situation.) In terms of individual folders, you might have "Campus information," "Degree programs," and "Financial aid information." You'll develop your categories as you begin to receive the information from each institution. Help your child see the power of dividing information into categories to make it more easily accessible. He'll become a Zen Organizer.

Getting organized is about more than the right file system or always being tidy and on time. At its heart, the skill of organization helps you plan your life. Long-range goals come true when we make them happen. Wishing doesn't make it so but getting organized can.

A wealth of information, including scholarship tips, is available at www.collegeboard.com. If your child is interested in service before school, he or she should check out www.americore.com and www.peacecorps.com. Another great online source for scholarship assistance is www.studentaid.ed.gov. The Web sites of many individual colleges also offer a wealth of information on available scholarships.

INVESTIGATING STATE AID

Most states offer some kind of assistance to residents. For example, I'm a graduate of Hunter College in Manhattan, which is part of City University of New York. Residents of the five boroughs (Brooklyn, Queens, Manhattan, the Bronx, and Staten Island) can get a first-class subsidized education at any one of the colleges making up City University. Ask the guidance counselor at your child's school about resident programs provided for colleges located in your home state. A higher education may cost a lot these days, but if you think outside the box, you will no doubt encounter aid you didn't realize existed. What's at stake is your child's future, so it's more than worth the effort.

COMMUNICATING YOUR CHILD'S RESPONSIBILITIES

Your child's biggest responsibility is to have good grades. These open the door to scholarships and student loans. I have a young friend who wants to be a drummer. His parents helped him research the schools that would offer training for a career as a professional musician. After pouring over literature from the Berkeley School of Music in Boston and Julliard in New York, their son wisely opted to test drive the schools by attending summer sessions. He'll increase his drumming expertise, experience life in new cities, and have an opportunity to live away from home.

Along with grades, your child's extracurricular activities carry weight. Is he an active member of an organization such as the Boy Scouts? Does he do volunteer work at homeless shelters or retirement homes in your community? Experiences like these will not only make him more valuable to college recruiters but also enhance his self-esteem.

A part-time job during the summer can teach your child the value of money quickly. Sometimes a part-time job in the field he hopes to enter is available. Think creatively. My friend the drummer was part of a band that played at social functions. They received experience and made some money doing what they love. What creative options are available in your area?

MANY ROADS LEAD TO ROME

Again, there is no one answer when it comes to the question of paying for higher education. The information this month is meant to spark communication in your home and foster the quest for creative solutions.

SEPTEMBER SUMMARY

WEEK ONE

Set a financial example for your children, and have them earn money.

WEEK TWO

Teach your children how to manage money.

WEEK THREE

Embrace the simplicity and power of the 529 college savings plan.

WEEK FOUR

Identify additional ways to help your child pay for his education.

10. OCTOBER

Protect Your Assets

He who knows that all things are his mind,

That all with which he meets are friendly,

Is ever joyful.

—HUNDRED THOUSAND SONGS OF MILAREPA

WHEN I WAS IN GRAMMAR SCHOOL, there was an accident in our Brooklyn neighborhood. People from two city blocks were evacuated from their homes. When the accident happened, my dad was home alone, I was in school, and my mother was shopping downtown. It was hours before we were reunited as a family. (This was before the age of cell phones.)

While others struggled with what to grab when they were given minutes to exit their homes, my dad was as cool as a cucumber. He took two things. Over the years, I've asked people if they can guess what items he felt were important. What did he take? He grabbed all the insurance policies because he said with them he could replace what he owned. And he took our collie, Queenie, because life, he said, was precious and irreplaceable. I have to note that dad was organized, and he knew exactly where all his insurance policies were. My father taught me volumes about the value of "stuff" and life that day.

This month it's time to make sure you have adequate insurance. You are working hard to build a solid financial base for your life. You don't want some unforeseen event such as an illness, theft, a travel emergency, fire, flood, or an automobile accident to derail your best efforts. Be aware, however, that you don't need some forms of insurance and others you might need only for a time. Insurance isn't a one-size-fits-all proposition. You need to ask your insurance broker or agent savvy questions, and you need to know how to make wise decisions. And that's what we investigate this month.

HABIT OF THE MONTH: PROTECT YOUR HEALTH

By now you have discovered that some of the suggested habits were easy to acquire, some you avoided, and others went by the wayside after a month. Don't fret: It's the rare individual who acquires all twelve habits and uses every tool. This month we discuss several types of insurance, and insurance is important, especially health insurance. But good health is arguably the most important thing in our lives. Without good health, we are paupers indeed. And with good health, we can rise up and meet all the challenges life has in store for us.

In your financial notebook, note nightly what you did that day to safeguard your health. Your insurance premium is only one part of the equation. Was it a walk in the park or a yoga class? Did you forego a cheeseburger for lunch in favor of grilled salmon? Nothing is too small to note.

Keep your list in one section of your notebook so later you can see at a glance all the positive steps you took this month.

TOOL OF THE MONTH: A DIGITAL INVENTORY

Everyone has a few expensive items they would be loathe to see damaged, lost, or stolen. If disaster strikes, you don't want to be caught short. This month use a camera to create a digital record of the contents of your home. And now that your file system is set up, you no doubt have receipts for those big-ticket items in one area. Scan them into your computer and keep a copy safe with your video. If you ever need to make an insurance claim, you'll have a clear record of the items and in no time you'll be well on your way to recovery. For more on home inventories, see week two.

WEEK ONE

Medical Insurance

This week, you can

- Know the difference between a PPO and an HMO
- Gain insight into securing the care you need if you can't find insurance
- Learn about the importance of a medical advocate

MEDICAL INSURANCE IS ESSENTIAL, it can be outrageously expensive, and unless you have access to a group policy (typically through your work) you might have to deal with preexisting condition clauses that greatly reduce the value of the insurance. You want to shop around, but you also want to be sure you are with a respected, recognized company (such as Blue Cross and Blue Shield) or private hospital (such as Kaiser). Ignore the cheaply photocopied advertisements for "affordable health insurance" that you see. You want to deal with a large, established company with proven resources to honor your claims. If you decide on a smaller company, check them out first to be sure they are legitimate. Make sure what you're buying is *real* medical insurance and not a discount card disguised to look like insurance. Contact the Better

Business Bureau. Call your doctors and the local hospital to see if their billing office has a relationship with this firm.

Unlike many developed countries, the United States does not have national or universal health care. A sudden medical emergency can wipe out your savings and bring you to bankruptcy court. In fact, this is the most common reason for that drastic legal resource. According to a study at Harvard, 60 percent of all bankruptcies in the United States are due to medical bills, and of those medical bankruptcies, 78 percent of the people were covered by some form of health insurance!

It takes ten years for a bankruptcy to vanish from your credit report. You'll be paying higher interest rates—if you can even get credit. Protect your health and your financial resources: Get medical insurance! This week, we look at what you can do to cover your assets and safeguard your health.

DISTINGUISHING PPOS FROM HMOS

The two major forms of private health care insurance are *Preferred Provider Organizations (PPOs)* and *Health Maintenance Organizations (HMOs).* The HMO offers all-inclusive health care for a set amount of money. If you pay anything beyond the basic premium—provided you are willing to stay in the network—it will be a modest amount. (Make sure your HMO covers out-of-network emergency care.)

PPOs, in contrast, charge you a monthly premium (a fixed amount each month, regardless of whether or not you use any insurance benefits) as well as deductibles (an amount you need to pay out of pocket before insurance coverage kicks in) and copays (an amount you pay for each service rendered even after your insurance coverage kicks in) that can be substantial. In general, the higher the copays and deductibles, the lower the premiums. Subscribers will typically have a choice of seeing in-network or out-of-network physicians, and the out-of-network choices will cost you more. In general, HMOs are less expensive but offer less flexibility.

If you work for a company with an employee health plan, peruse the medical plan's brochures and booklets from the insurance carrier or your Human Resources rep to make sure you take advantage of all you're entitled to. Do you have immediate

BE CREATIVE

If you are a member of a group of any sort from a union to a large hobby group to an alumni association, see if medical coverage is sponsored for the members. This is an invaluable source if you are not employed by a large company or corporation capable of negotiating special rates or willing to subsidize the premiums for its employees. For example, AARP has several kinds of insurance coverage. All you need to qualify is to be the right age. Speaking of age, if you're sixty-five or about to turn sixty-five, you may want to buy Medigap insurance to supplement Medicare.

Ask family members, friends, and former colleagues what types of medical insurance they have and if they are pleased with it. Investigate what's available for someone your age with your medical history in your home state. It's not a fun search, but it can mean the difference between life and death. Carve out the time to do it.

family members with special medical needs? Will someone in your family fit that description soon? You might want to discuss the possibility of expanding your policy's coverage with a special rider or purchasing supplemental coverage elsewhere. If both you and your partner have medical plans through work (how fortunate you are!) and you have children, take the time this week to compare the two plans in terms of coverage, your needs, deductibles, copays, and so on to find out which plan makes the most sense for the kids. (You'll need to choose one as the children's primary plan.)

ASKING THE RIGHT QUESTIONS

Be a savvy shopper. Be sure you know the answers to the following questions:

- Does your policy cover you for emergency care at the local hospital?
- In the event of a serious illness such as cancer, diabetes, or heart disease, will standard care including surgery be provided? What are the limits in terms of treatment and expense, if any?
- Is there a lifetime monetary cap on benefits?
- What is the deductible?
- How much is the copay for office visits and prescription drugs?
- Are the prescription drugs you regularly take covered? What is the price?
- If you travel—within the United States or abroad—will you be covered?
- Which preventative and diagnostic measures (such as colonoscopies, pap smears, and vaccinations) are covered? Some plans even cover gym memberships.
- Is dental and eye care included? Are there restrictions or limitations?
- If you get your policy through work, how long do you have to wait to be covered?

Conversely, if you lose your job, for how long will you continue to have coverage? Usually COBRA kicks in under these circumstances. You will have the same medical coverage for (traditionally) six to eighteen months, but you have to pay the premium. This is a key piece of information especially if you or someone covered under your policy has a chronic condition.

- Can you get coverage for family members?
- Can you be excluded from coverage for any reason?
- What procedures are not covered?
- What about a choice of primary care physicians and specialists? Can you go outside the network of providers if necessary? What are the consequences? For example, if your insurance will not cover a physician outside the network, will they cover a diagnostic test he or she orders?
- If you need to see a specialist, will you first need a referral from a general practitioner?

Keep your insurance information booklets and brochures in a specific folder in your file cabinet alongside other medical-related information. Recycle the old information when you file the new. If you can, request this information as a PDF instead so you can file the information in a folder on your computer. Be sure you have a few blank claim forms handy should a need arise for a doctor visit. And again, see if these are available online. You can save space in your file cabinet and maybe a tree.

If you have a large family with many young children, chances are you will need a "Pending" folder just for medical claims. You want to stay on top of these so that you aren't out of pocket by any sizable amount or for any longer than is written in your policy.

EXAMINING YOUR CHOICES WHEN YOU HAVE NO COVERAGE

A person might not have coverage for many legitimate reasons, ranging from an inability to afford the premiums to having a preexisting condition. I am a cancer survivor, for example, and unless I receive coverage through a group or marriage, or Congress changes the rules, no legitimate insurance company will give me coverage until ten years after the original diagnosis. As of this writing, I am just past my seven-year anniversary as a survivor. You need to be creative. Here are tips I have learned along the way:

> Everything is negotiable, including your doctor and hospital bills.
> If you live near a large teaching hospital, they should have a lower-cost clinic.
> Don't use an emergency room for an event that is non-life threatening.
> Know the low-cost private clinics in your city.
> If you need a prescription, ask your doctor if a generic brand drug is okay.

Seven years ago I was diagnosed with cancer. At the time, I had no idea how high medical costs truly were. In 2002 a total abdominal hysterectomy with staging for cancer at a first-class medical facility in Los Angeles was $40,000. Hospitals are businesses, and like all business entities, they want to make a profit. That said, every hospital has a financial office you can contact to negotiate the fees quoted. How can you ask for a discount? It's easy. If you have insurance, the hospital and the doctor have to wait weeks and sometimes longer for the insurance company to pay them. If you have no insurance, don't be shy about asking for the "cash discount" (that is, no insurance) price for the procedure or service in question. Understand the gift you are giving the medical entity: They may be making less but the payment is *immediate.* In my case the hospital fee was ultimately reduced from $40,000 to $9,500. My ob/gyn donated his services and my oncologist took $1,000 off his surgical fee.

This particular facility is a teaching hospital. This means that affiliated with the main hospital is a lower-cost clinic. The fees at all such institutions are a fraction of a regular hospital visit. Once again, you need to play by the financial rules. Typically you lay bare your financial life to qualify and save your physical life. Ultimately I had a private room at the hospital for all six of my chemotherapy treatments for a fraction of the cost a person with medical coverage would pay. Chemotherapy drugs alone cost a fortune. My chemotherapy was administered for a little over $900 for each of the six treatments. This may sound like a lot, but it was better than $16,000 each that I would have paid had I not been labeled a clinic patient.

If your need is real and you remain calm, communicative, and unemotional, you should be able to effectively renegotiate any fee or bill. Until there is affordable medical coverage for everyone, we need to be sure that one way or another we get the care we deserve. Don't forego that care because you are ashamed of your situation. Focus on getting well first.

Lower Your Prescription Costs

Pharmaceutical reps ply physicians with sample drugs, so don't hesitate to ask for a handout. For example, after each of my chemo treatments, I had to take an antinausea pill for a day or two. Imagine my surprise when I learned that *each pill* cost $100. My sainted oncologist sent me home each month with just enough samples to get me through. His generosity saved me more than $1,000.

If no samples are available or you've used the quota the doctor allows per patient, ask him if you can use the generic version of the medication. This is nothing more than a version made after the original drug company's patent expires. The maker of the generic version has not incurred research and marketing expenses and can pass the saving on to you.

Under certain specific circumstances, you can purchase a higher dose pill for less money and cut the pill in half. However, be sure to get your doctor's blessing as well as the right equipment. Surf to www.halftablet.com and see if this is a possibility for you. And while we tend to demonize drug companies, you should know that several programs make drugs available to those who can't afford them. You will need to qualify, but it's worth a try. Visit www.pparx.org, which is a clearinghouse for drug companies and consumers. Or call 888-477-2669 EST from 8 a.m. to 8 p.m. No legitimate service will charge you a fee to join or ask for a credit card number or checking account to cover your membership. You will pay only a discounted fee for your drugs if they are available through the program. Sometimes the drugs are free.

Always check with your insurance company to inquire whether it provides prescriptions through an in-house mail-order pharmacy. Many insurance companies, provided you are willing to purchase a three-month supply of a drug, will offer you a price that beats most pharmacies.

Another option is to get your prescription through our friendly neighbors in Canada. One company is Canada Pharmacy, www.canadapharmacy.com. To check out others, surf the Web.

The IRS and Healthcare

Given the out-of-control rise in healthcare costs in America, the folks in Washington—at least some of them—are currently scurrying for change. By the time you are reading this, I suspect that at least a few measures will have passed to help the average American pay for medical care. In the meantime, I wanted to point out two existing plans that can help: the health savings account and the flexible spending account.

Health savings account (HSA). If you are in good health, a health savings account paired with a high-deductible insurance policy will allow you to sock away up to $3,050 a year ($6,150 for a family). That money is tax deductible, and you can use it to pay for insurance premiums, deductibles, copays, and just about anything else related to healthcare (including eyeglasses, weight-loss programs, and over-the-counter meds).

And here's a cool trick, if you can afford it: Open the HSA but don't touch the money. Use other money, such as money in your regular savings account, to pay for your needed medical expenses, and treat your HSA strictly as a retirement account that, just like a Roth-IRA, will allow your money to grow tax-free for as long as you like. Make the maximum contribution every year, invest it wisely, and after twenty years you can take the money out for whatever need. As long as you save all your receipts for medical expenses, the money can be withdrawn without your paying taxes. Many banks and brokerage houses offer HSA accounts. Shop around to find one with low fees and good investment choices.

Flexible spending account (FSA). Unlike the HSA, the money you put into an FSA does not roll over from year to year, and what you can spend the money on is more limited. You set up an FSA and use it to pay for expenses not picked up by your insurance—deductibles, copays, over-the-counter drugs, out-of-network doctor visits, and such. Unlike money in an HSA, FSA money cannot be used to pay for your insurance premiums themselves. The FSA is more for employees of companies that offer health insurance plans. The cap for how much you can contribute varies from employer to employer (the IRS sets no limits). Whatever you put into the FSA is tax-deductible, but if you don't spend it all (money put in during 2010 must be used up, depending on the plan, by March 2011 or possibly sooner), you lose it. That means you have to be careful with this tricky plan. Talk to a Human Resources rep in your company about the FSA.

Medical Tourism

Medical procedures offered here are available in countries around the world for a fraction of the U.S. cost. Brazil is known for plastic surgery and India for heart procedures, for example. If you're considering travel abroad for a medical procedure, be sure to talk it over with your home physician first. A number of both U.S. and foreign-based agencies have sprung up to cater to the growing demand for medical tourism. One is www.indushealth.com, and another is www.MedSolution.com. Do extensive research before making this decision. Here is a checklist to help you get started:

How much less is the surgery in question than it is in the United States?

Does the doctor and his staff speak English? What about the staff in the medical facility itself?

Where did the doctor receive his training?

Is the facility accredited by any medical agencies in the country?

Is the hospital or clinic equipped to handle an emergency?

What legal recourse is available should something go wrong?

Will my insurance provide coverage?

What about the cost of transportation as well as lodging before and after the surgery?

How soon before I can return home?

Where will I stay during the recovery period?

FINDING AN ADVOCATE

I'd like to close this week with a word about the importance of an advocate no matter where you are treated, especially if you have a serious health condition. Some hospitals have advocates on staff, but your best choice is someone who loves you and is available to come with you to doctor's visits and hospital stays. I have a client who is a physician on the staff of a large metropolitan hospital. She never leaves a family member alone in the hospital room. And she's an attending physician there! Things can go wrong and you want to know you have a representative, especially if you are going to be unconscious for a few hours or days.

Studies have shown that a patient with a serious condition hears about 30 percent of the doctor's communication. Diagnoses and case updates can be overwhelming for the brain to process all at once. Your advocate needs to be intelligent, calm, and unemotional. He or she must speak the language fluently. Before your appointments, it's best if you and your advocate come up with a list of pertinent questions to ask the doctor. In addition, don't hesitate to communicate your wishes to your physician. I had an agreement with my oncologists: I wouldn't do online research because it can be misleading. I got all my information from them and we agreed I would be told only what I absolutely needed to know. However, everyone is different. Take the approach to treatment and care that works for you.

Arranging for the presence of an advocate is the best use of your new organizing skills you can imagine. I am grateful to the friends who came with me to my doctor and hospital visits. They brought comfort, support, and often laughter to a terrifying ordeal. I am forever in their debt. To this day they remember things my oncologist said that I have absolutely no memory of. By the way, I am delighted to report that I have been pronounced not only free of cancer but cured.

WEEK TWO

Homeowner's and Renter's Policies

This week, you can

- Check to be sure your homeowner's coverage is adequate
- Create a home inventory
- Decide whether you need renter's insurance

LET'S START AT THE VERY BEGINNING with a question: Do you need homeowner's insurance? The answer is a loud, resounding, unequivocal "Yes!" Your home is probably the largest investment you will make. You don't want to be wiped out in the event of a robbery or an act of vandalism, to name just a few of the bad guys who might come around during your tenure. Not to mention the repair guy with a heart of gold who knocks your Ming vase off its pedestal on the way to the laundry room. The good news is that if you own a home, it's just about impossible to get a mortgage without insurance, so you are probably covered. The next hurdle is finding out if your coverage is adequate.

ASSESSING YOUR HOMEOWNER'S POLICY

Do you faithfully pay your premium every year without a thought to the adjusted value of your home, any contents you have added, or improvements you have made? This week, you might want to go over your policy with your agent.

Your home should be insured for its *replacement cost,* which is what it would cost to build a new, similar home. Local builders are often your best source for the replacement cost. Some people overinsure their homes. Remember that you don't need to insure for the market value of the home, because that market value includes a good chunk for the land itself. Even if your home burns to the ground, the land will still be there.

This is a good time to switch from disposable batteries in your camera to the rechargeable kind. For long-lasting rechargeable batteries, try Sanyo's eneloop (at www.eneloopusa.com). When your regular batteries need to be tossed, check out www.call2recycle.com for a location near you that's set up to dispose of them in a responsible way. Record your holiday memories while saving money and the environment.

You also need to assess your valuables. They might not be covered unless your insurance company knows about them.

By the way, some potential heartbreakers such as floods, earthquakes, and volcano eruptions may not be covered by your regular policy. You'll have to purchase riders to be sure you are adequately insured. Here in the Los Angeles area, as you might expect, earthquake coverage is extremely expensive but worth it in the event of a quake. What natural disasters are common in your area? Be sure you are covered.

Adequate insurance is a key ingredient in your financial life. Shop around for quotes from reliable companies with solid reputations. And finally be sure you know all the perks of your policy. For example, when my clients move from one home to another, they frequently purchase moving insurance from the mover transporting their possessions, unaware that their homeowner's policy already covers them on the road and at the warehouse should that stop be necessary. Read your policy

carefully. You may find some hidden, money-saving treasures.

PERFORMING A HOME INVENTORY

When I started organizing clients more than twenty years ago, one of the most time-consuming tasks was creating a home inventory book. We'd have to painstakingly photograph every area of the home and then document items of high value with individual photos. It could take days to do a large home filled with valuable art, furniture, and jewelry. Today it takes no time at all thanks to technology.

In the event of a loss, you want to be able to prove you owned the item you are claiming. A receipt is the first step. When you also have visual documentation of the item in your home, you'll have the item replaced in no time. By the way, when it comes to jewelry, you can't replace the actual ring grandma left you, but with a detailed image, you can at least have it copied.

With a digital camera or a digital video recorder, you can document the inside of your home, cataloging all your possessions quickly. And it's a snap to make copies. Keep the original memory card in a safe place such as a safety deposit box. Keep copies in your file cabinet and perhaps send one to Aunt Sadie. In the event of an insurance claim, you can literally show your agent exactly what you lost.

For valuable items such as jewelry and art, you'll want to have the purchase receipt, any special documentation such as certificates of authenticity or a provenance, and of course an appraisal. Keep the original documents in your safety deposit box if you have one or in your home safe. (Provided it's fireproof and too heavy for a thief to simply pick up and stash under his arm as he exits your home with that Picasso.) Keep copies in your files. These documents are gold when it comes to dealing with your insurance adjuster. You'll be in an emotional state if items have been stolen. Take the drama of "Where are those documents?" off the table. We think this step is so important, we've made it the tool of the month as well. And you just might have fun making this visual record of the items you have worked so hard to afford.

Following is a list of items to include in a home inventory. For each, include, if possible, the quantity, the purchase date, the place of purchase, the serial or model number, the brand name or manufacturer, the cost, and the current replacement cost.

Furniture
Clothing
Electronics
Jewelry
Art and other collectibles
Computer hardware and software
Fixtures
Heating and cooling equipment
Appliances
Water softener
Dehumidifier or humidifier
Medical equipment
Kitchen tools
Toys
Lamps
Plants
Clocks
Curtains
Sheets, towels
Books, CDs
Hardware, gardening equipment, other items in the garage or shed

GETTING RENTER'S INSURANCE

If you rent an apartment, you might feel that you don't need insurance. Take a moment, however, to examine your situation. What's the replacement cost if that new flat-screen TV gets toasted in a fire? What happens if you are robbed and your new laptop computer or heirloom jewelry is stolen?

What if the kids turn on the bathroom faucet right before you leave for work and forget to tell you? You may not care about your stuff, but old man Smith downstairs may sue you when the flood ruins his new paint job and damages that nice carpet he just installed.

Renter's insurance isn't expensive. In Los Angeles, for example a $25,000 replacement policy for a renter costs just over $100. And if you have a car, a boat, or an RV insured with the same carrier, you will probably get a discount for being a multiple policyholder. Take a few minutes to consider what the right decision is for you and your situation.

Be sure you insure your home goods. I've lived through earthquakes and been witness to the destruction of fire and floods. Insurance is a lifesaver. Don't leave home without it!

WEEK THREE

Disability and Long-Term Care Coverage

This week, you can

- Decide if you need disability insurance and how much coverage is adequate
- Consider the value of long-term care insurance for you and loved ones

WHEN WE'RE HEALTHY, IT'S HARD to fathom being sick, unable to work, or incapacitated. I've had the experience of "life as you know it" changing in a flash. I am here to tell you it's good to cover all your bases.

UNDERSTANDING DISABILITY INSURANCE

So, what exactly is disability insurance? Should you become disabled and unable to work, disability insurance replaces a portion of your income. Assuming that you are not sitting on a huge portfolio nor have rich parents who could help you out, you should have disability insurance that covers roughly two-thirds of your income. (Another portion is generally covered by Social Security.)

Many companies offer the option of disability coverage, and it's worth investigating the details if this policy is available to you. However, you may not want to count on the group policy your company offers because most group policies offer relatively few benefits. Consider a supplemental individual policy. In addition, disability policies carry a certain waiting period before they kick in. The time period is typically three months—that's where your emergency cash reserve of at least three months' income comes in.

A good policy has an adjustment for inflation. Disability insurance premiums vary greatly, depending on the nature of your work (how risky is it?), your income, and your age. In general, a good policy will cost you perhaps 2 to 3 percent of your income. So if you are earning $60,000 a year, the premium costs approximately

$1,200 to $1,800 a year. Disability insurance is always important but is crucial if you have young children.

Realize that if you are already getting, say, your homeowner's and car insurance through one company, you are in a better position to negotiate.

BUYING LONG-TERM CARE INSURANCE

Buying a long-term care (LTC) insurance policy won't keep you from growing old, but it could spare you the indignity of impoverishment should you one day need daily assistance. Here's the catch: LTC insurance is pricey and complicated and—despite the assertions of some insurance brokers—doesn't make sense for everyone. The devil is in the details. Let's take a look.

The costs of nursing homes vary enormously, but the average cost in the United States is $75,000 a year (about $205 a day). Unfortunately, you can't count on Uncle Sam to pick up the tab. Medicare provides very limited long-term care benefits. In most instances, you will be required to fork over substantial copayments. Medicaid will pay for some services, but only if you're broke. It's LTC to the rescue: It can pick up the entire expense, or part of the expense, for nursing home care, an assisted living facility, or home care. But is it worth the expense? Let's run the numbers.

Your Age
The younger you are when you buy LTC insurance, the cheaper the premiums. Of course, the younger you are, the more premiums you'll pay over time. It usually makes the most sense to buy LTC insurance while in your fifties or early sixties. A typical policy purchased by someone at sixty will cost about $2,200 a year in premiums. (There is usually a ninety-day waiting period before you can begin receiving benefits.) With that figure, if the person ended up in a nursing home, he would receive $150 a day in LTC payments for five years. According to government estimates, the chance that someone over sixty-five will enter a nursing home is 40 percent. The higher probability is that you will have a long and healthy retirement, and that should be your first financial priority. LTC insurance comes next.

The Cost in Your Area
Explore the price of long-term care in your area by calling nursing homes and home health care agencies. If you plan to retire in another community or state, be sure you check the fees there. You won't need to use insurance to cover 100 percent of the cost of a nursing home or home health care. If Social Security will provide $20,000 a year and your investments will yield another $20,000 a year, you may need only $25,000 of insurance coverage to pay for a $65,000-a-year nursing home. Consider buying only five or six years of coverage. The average stay in a nursing home, according to insurance industry experts, is less than three years. By the way, if you're like most people and you'd prefer to get care in your home, be sure your insurance will cover that. Not all do.

FINDING AN AGENT YOU TRUST

Don't choose just any insurance agent. Ask for referrals from coworkers, family, and friends. Find an agent you trust, who handles a lot of LTC insurance, and who works with various insurance companies. And finally, because the contract can be long and full of Byzantine insurance-speak, consider having an attorney look it over before you sign. Try your local bar association or the National Academy of Elder Law Attorneys at 502-881-4005 or www.naela.org for a list of attorneys who specialize in reading insurance contracts.

DETERMINING IF YOU NEED LONG-TERM INSURANCE

Long-term care insurance isn't for everyone. If you are blessed, for example, with unlimited funds, why would you bother?

The same is true for disability insurance. Take into consideration your family history and your particular career when considering both long-term care and disability insurance. If your family is dependent on your income, you should seriously consider getting enough disability insurance to cover 65 percent of your income. Social Security should help make up for most of the rest.

When I was growing up in Brooklyn, I knew Italian grandmothers who lived on their own well into their nineties. Every day they were busy helping out with the great-grandkids. They gave long-term care to others. No disabilities there. In the last analysis, barring an unfortunate accident or disease, one of the best insurances you can have is living a life of purpose. But if disabling diseases run in your family, talk to your physician about whether there is a genetic factor, and use that information accordingly.

WEEK FOUR

Planes, Trains, and Automobiles

This week, you can

- Celebrate the kinds of insurance you *don't* need
- Review your automobile coverage and be sure it's adequate

WHEN YOU ADD UP THE PREMIUMS for the various insurance policies you may need, it can be a big chunk of change. I thought you would be relieved to know that there are actually insurance policies you don't need. Let's start this week with this good news!

FINDING OUT ABOUT UNNECESSARY INSURANCES

We've already looked at several forms of insurance: health insurance, long-term care insurance, and homeowner's insurance. In this section I list six kinds of insurance you don't need.

Travel insurance. If you buy travel insurance and die in a plane crash, your family gets a settlement. You've likely seen the vending machines at the airport selling this insurance. Today many travel sites offer such insurance at the end of your trans-

action as well. But it's typically a big rip-off. The odds of dying in a plane crash are miniscule.

Rental car policies. Your normal auto insurance policy will almost always cover you if you have an accident in a rental car. If in doubt, call your agent before your next trip to be sure you are covered.

Extended warranties on small electronics. Don't insure yourself for anything as minor as the cost of fixing a camera or GPS. Most defective electronics identify themselves within ninety days. Instead, put the money you would have spent on an extended warranty into your own portfolio, and if you want, carve out a separate emergency or repair fund.

Credit card protection. You cannot lose your house because someone stole your credit card and took off for Rio. Federal law limits your loss to $50. Don't throw out $200 or so a year on useless credit card protection.

Cancer insurance. You see a lot of policies these days for cancer insurance because insurance companies know that people dread cancer. But you need a good general health insurance policy that covers *all* health perils, not a policy that covers only one disease.

Life insurance from credit card and mortgage companies. Many credit card and mortgage companies offer a guarantee that they will pay a lump sum large enough to at least cover the mortgage to your spouse should you die. If you're worried that your spouse or children might not be able to pay off your mortgage, buy a term life insurance policy directly from an insurance company. You'll wind up spending half as much.

Don't you feel relieved to know that you can save money by not buying any of these policies? Let's turn our attention now to a crucially important insurance that you *do* need: automobile coverage. I've been in an accident with an uninsured motorist. My insurance had to cover the cost of the repair to my vehicle as well as my medical expenses, even though the other person was at fault.

BUYING AUTO INSURANCE

Automobile insurance, a must if you own a car, covers you in case of an accident. It will cover bodily injury to you, your passengers, pedestrians, and other motorists. It will cover property damage you cause others. Depending on whether you opt for collision (a good idea if you own an expensive car but a waste if you own a clunker), it will cover damage to your own vehicle.

Each state sets a minimum dollar figure for required coverage, but that typically isn't enough. In California, for example, the minimum is 15/30/5, meaning that your carrier would pay $15,000 for bodily injury to a single person in a single accident, $30,000 for injury to all people involved in an accident, and $5,000 for property damage. Work with your insurance broker to be sure you are adequately covered. Consider exceeding the minimum requirements, taking your net worth into account—the other party will be sure to do just that if you are ever sued.

Just as teenagers' coverage is routinely more expensive due to their lack of experience, auto insurance companies reward older people with clean driving records. These drivers can get the best rates because they're experienced, often own safer cars, and—if retired—tend to drive less. Be sure you take advantage. If you've had the same auto insurance carrier for a number of years, it may be time for a cost comparison to see if you're getting the best deal. If you take AARP's Driver Safety Program, you may receive an additional discount. Go to www.aarp.org/families/driver_safety or call 800-227-7669. Your insurance carrier may have such a program as well. I'm covered by the Auto Club, which has several ways to reduce your premium at any age.

Your final cost of insurance depends on where you live, your age, the type of car you drive, and your driving record. You may not be able to change your residence, and you certainly can't change your age, but you can drive safely and drive a solid car. Always buckle up—and no text-messaging while driving!

LOOKING AHEAD

As this month comes to an end, I hope you've taken steps to protect your financial life. Celebrating the holidays is next. We're going to rein in expenses for gifts, travel, and parties. And we're going to expand our thinking when it comes to taking advantage of the true meaning of the season. Let's strike a balance. We want to support our local retailers and put some power into our economy, but we don't want to do this at the expense of our own financial security and well-being.

OCTOBER SUMMARY

WEEK ONE

Review your medical insurance coverage, and examine ways to get care if you don't have insurance.

WEEK TWO

Don't lose out just because you wanted to save on premiums.

WEEK THREE

Look at long-term care and disability insurance.

WEEK FOUR

Discover the types of insurance you don't need and the one type you do.

11. NOVEMBER

The Season for Sane Spending

Don't let yesterday use up too much of today.

—WILL ROGERS

IF YOU STARTED ORGANIZING YOUR finances according to the principles of Zen Organizing last January, you've surely made incremental monetary gains. Perhaps you now have an emergency fund or maybe you just purchased insurance to protect your family. You might even have a will for the first time. This month and next you need to safeguard your progress.

The goal is to make fiscally responsible decisions this holiday season that are in keeping with everything you have accomplished to date. I have no doubt you will be amazed how easy it is to save money and celebrate in style. After all, at the heart of all the celebrations in November and December is the desire to spend time and share experiences with family and friends. It isn't necessary to max out a credit card (or two). You want to enter the New Year without the burden of emotionally fueled financial decisions that will put a damper on your progress. If you have children, they will be learning an invaluable lesson in fiscal responsibility just by your example.

This month, we're going to look at all the elements of the holiday season, from the cost of Thanksgiving dinner and gift buying to an examination of practical travel tips. The key to your success will be utilizing the financial tool that's at the heart of all your progress this year: a realistic budget. You'll be making one for entertaining and one for gift giving. These budgets are like a personal business plan for the holidays. You know what they say: Failing to plan is planning to fail. Devote some time to create your budgets and your shopping list. The relatively small amount of time these activities take will yield tremendous rewards, from saving money to raising your self-esteem. Now that's something to celebrate!

HABIT OF THE MONTH: THINK POSITIVELY

Every day we repeat messages to ourselves—and often those thoughts are negative. If worry were a virtue, most of us would be up for sainthood. Destructive thoughts traditionally go something like this: "I can't handle everything that's on my plate. It's too much for one person." We tend to either beat ourselves up or comfort ourselves with stuff. This month let's stop the cycle. The second we hear one of those thoughts in our heads, replace it with a positive affirmation. Here is one, but feel free to write your own.

I am smart, thoughtful, level-headed, and fiscally responsible. All decisions this month regarding extra expenses are made with care. My family and friends love me for who I am rather than for the stuff I can buy. I am enough.

TOOL OF THE MONTH: COUPONS

Starting this month, the newspapers will have coupons for in-store specials just about every day. You might also be receiving e-mail coupons that you can print, or you can go to sites similar to the following to find coupons to fit your particular needs:

www.mybargainbuddy.com
www.fatwallet.com
www.slickdeals.net

Just about everyone I know gets excited about these offers but few remember to save them. Grab an envelope or a small container that fits neatly into your purse or wallet so you can keep coupons with you. If you really want to have fun, keep a running tally of the amount you save. And if you want to go for the gold, at month's end, transfer the amount you saved into a savings account and make the savings concrete.

WEEK ONE

Holiday Budget

This week, you can

- Figure out how much you can spend for the holidays
- Create a plan for a less costly but festive holiday season

EACH HOLIDAY SEASON, EVEN THE most well-intentioned among us can fall off the fiscally responsible bandwagon and indulge in a binge of emotionally driven spending. According to the American Consumer Credit Council, the average American family spends upwards of $935 on gifts, party food, and decorative and holiday items during the holidays. Not only is that a lot of money, it increases as the months go by if you charge those expenses on your credit cards and take months, even years, to pay them off. But this year, you'll be in better shape because you'll have a budget. Grab your financial notebook, your resolve, and your creativity!

DECIDING HOW MUCH TO SPEND

Turn your financial workbook to a blank page. The first step is to decide how much money you can comfortably, sensibly, and sanely spend this holiday season, which runs from Thanksgiving to New Year's Day (or Thanksgiving through the December holidays). Write down that figure in the upper-right corner. Did you have to do some calculating? Is it an educated guess? Or did you pull that figure out of the air? Your holiday spending budget should not rob your emergency savings account. If you are lucky enough to receive a bonus at work, a holiday check from your parents, or some year-end dividends from your stock portfolio, don't allow yourself to spend this windfall profit without a second thought.

Remain conscious about your holiday expenditures. You'd "run the numbers" if you were ready to purchase a home or buy a new car, right? We're going to do just that to create your holiday spending budget. A reasonable holiday budget, provided you're not in debt, might run as high as one week's pay. Anything beyond that, and it's probably time to rein in those reindeer.

GOING BACK TO BASICS

In this section I describe the most common items that require an extra outlay of cash this time of year.

Gifts

Buying gifts is a dangerous area for most of us, especially if we shop at the last minute and (Heaven forbid) without a shopping list. This year you'll be planning your gifts in concert with your budget. And you'll be using store coupons and taking advantage of online offers to save even more. Don't think of these guidelines as constricting; rather see them as releasing your creativity. It's easy to buy a tie for dad at the last minute. It's a lot more fun to consider his hobbies and dreams and find something unexpected and unique that will make him happy. And staying within your budget will no doubt make dad very proud.

Entertaining

These are big months for entertaining, so you'll have to decide what your budget will permit. Did you want to host any of the big traditional holiday meals such as Thanksgiving, Chanukah, Christmas Eve, or Christmas Day? Were you planning on tossing a New Year's Eve party or hosting a New Year's Day Open House? Did you want to have a quiet party just for friends and coworkers? Your budget will dictate how much celebrating you can do.

Consider the elements for each party (food, beverages, decorative items, and so on) and how many people you had intended to invite. Subtract the total from your budget that remains after gift costs are deducted. By the way, do you have time to clean your house or will your remaining budget allow you to have a cleaning person for a day?

Decorations

Holiday decorations add to the merriment of the season. If you are not careful, however, they can rob you of valuable time and cause you to spend money you don't have. Here are some tips to guide you:

- Do you have enough decorations to open a store? Don't make another purchase! If you have any young family members or friends who are just starting out, why not reduce your total and help them save money this year? You'll gain space in your attic or garage.
- If you must have a memento from every season, pick up one new ornament during the after-holiday sales and you'll get your new ornament for half off. Some ornaments go on sale several days before Christmas. If you're going to a party and need a trinket for under the tree, what could be more perfect than a decoration you just got for half price?
- When it comes to lights, keep in mind last year's electric bill. Did you blow your budget but win the local home decorating contest? Let some-

one else have a shot this year. Put up a few lights and invest the money you'll save.

- Are you going to be gone for part of the month? Do you have crazy deadlines at work? Maybe this is the year you need to husband your energies for other pursuits than decorating.

Travel

Are you going to visit your family this month or are you running off to a sun-soaked tropical island? Add the total cost of your trip and deduct it from your newly revised budget. Remember to calculate everything, whether it's a full tank of gas or first-class airfare and a swanky hotel room. When my golden retrievers were alive, for example, I had to remember that the total tab for every trip included the cost of a dog sitter. It all adds up.

LETTING THE NUMBERS BE YOUR GUIDE

As this week comes to a close, you will no doubt have a feeling of control and an increased sense of peace. Numbers don't lie. They tell you without emotion, judgment, or criticism exactly what you can afford. It's not unlike knowing how much rent or mortgage you can handle. You wouldn't move into a mansion if your budget indicated you belong in a starter house. Nor should you purchase extravagant gifts if your finances indicate that a modest celebration is in order. Whatever you can afford, my job over the course of the month is to help you find creative, fun ways to utilize what you have to create the experience you seek.

WEEK TWO

Gift-Giving

This week, you can

- Determine who gets a gift this year
- Get many creative and affordable gift ideas
- Save money when you go out to shop

Johnny, why did you ditch class today? demands his concerned mother. "Because all my friends did, Mom," replies Johnny. "Well, tell me this, young man, would you jump off a bridge if all your friends suggested that?!" We've all heard a version of this exchange as we were growing up. I'd like to suggest that just because you have friends, family members, or coworkers who are spending lavishly and going into debt this holiday season, you don't have to follow suit. Nor do you have to feel guilty or explain yourself. It's never prudent to compromise what is best for your long-term financial health in an attempt to keep the peace or make others happy.

Won't you feel proud over the next two months when your credit card bills reflect your growing fiscal acumen? If you have a card that accrues points or miles, you can pay off in full the purchases you've made and enjoy your perks. You might even have accrued enough points during the past year to acquire some items you can give as gifts or cash. Make your credit card work for you.

CREATING A GIFT-GIVING BUDGET

When creating a holiday gift budget, the first thing you need to do is decide who will be on your gift list this year. Open your financial notebook to a new page and make your list. Start with mom and dad and end with your postal carrier. Put down every possibility. It's easier to go back and eliminate than to realize on December 23 that you left some key people off the list. Using Excel makes this process a snap.

Write the names in a column on the left side. Next to each person make a notation

WALSH'S INITIAL GIFT BUDGET		WALSH'S REVISED GIFT BUDGET	
Recipient	*Gift Amount*	*Recipient*	*Gift Amount*
Don (husband)	$75.00	Karen (adult child)	$45.00
Marsha (wife)	$75.00	Jane (adult child)	$45.00
Karen (adult child)	$50.00	Howard (adult child)	$45.00
Jane (adult child)	$50.00	Mom	$30.00
Howard (adult child)	$50.00	Dad	$30.00
Mom	$35.00	Aunt Marie	$25.00
Dad	$35.00	Uncle Joe	$25.00
Aunt Marie	$25.00	Cousin Jamie	$25.00
Uncle Joe	$25.00	Homeroom teacher	$15.00
Cousin Jamie	$25.00	Mr. Douglas (boss)	$15.00
Homeroom teacher	$35.00	Total	$300.00
Postman	$15.00		
Mr. Douglas (boss)	$40.00		
Total	$535.00		

of the amount of money you would like to spend. You know what's coming, right? Add those figures and see if you can afford having all these good folks on your holiday gift list.

Suppose Don and Marsha Walsh have determined that a comfortable gift budget is $300, and gifts will be purchased for thirteen people. Take a look at their initial gift budget.

For the Walsh's, as in the most common scenario, the total far exceeds the amount in the budget. The first step is to go back over the list and see where you can reduce the amount. This calculation might just bring the wish list in line with the budget.

If you are concerned about your family's expectations, make your plan known. Try something along these lines: "I'm trying to better organize my finances, so this year I've started saving to buy a house (to contribute to my retirement, to eliminate debt, and so on). In keeping with this new goal, this holiday I've had to institute financial boundaries and will be reducing the amount I spend on gifts this year. I hope you will support me in achieving my goal." Don't be surprised if they not only support you but want to join you.

The Walsh's reduced the gift amounts for the children and Mom and Dad by $5 each; their family was all on board with the

WALSH'S GIFT LIST

Recipient	Gift Amount	Gift
Karen (adult child)	$45.00	Book of movie passes and gift certificate for the concession stand
Jane (adult child)	$45.00	Membership at the local museum
Howard (adult child)	$45.00	Video game
Mom	$30.00	Gift certificate for a class at the local community college
Dad	$30.00	Subscription for golf magazine
Aunt Marie	$25.00	Fabric for a new project
Uncle Joe	$25.00	Corncob pipe
Cousin Jamie	$25.00	Passport holder for her trip abroad this summer
Homeroom teacher	$15.00	Scented candle
Mr. Douglas (boss)	$15.00	Donation to a charity such as Habitat for Humanity
Total	$300.00	

new fiscal program. Marsha's boss will receive a card with a certificate inside, indicating that she has made a contribution in his name to charity.

If reducing the amount you plan to spend per gift still doesn't bring your list in line with your budget, it's time to eliminate some folks. You can still send them a beautiful card with a heartfelt note of thanks. In the example, the Walsh's decided to cut the postman from the list. In addition, Don and Marsha decided that they won't buy each other presents. Instead, they will celebrate Valentine's Day with a gift. See the new list, which is now in line with the $300 budget.

Do you already have a gift in mind for anyone on your list? Uncle Charlie, for example, collects hand-carved corncob pipes, so his gift is a no-brainer. As you make these notations in your gift list, like Don and Marsha's, be sure the money you have allotted for this person is the correct amount for the gift you have in mind.

You can also put in a separate list the folks who can receive a simple thank-you note in their holiday card in lieu of a gift. If you're handy with a computer and love to take photos, you might consider making a digital scrapbook of highlights from the year. You can send this to the folks for whom you can't afford a gift. This will be especially appreciated if you have children or perhaps took a special trip this year. Investigate the possibilities at sites like www.snapfish.com, www.shutterfly.com, or www.kodakgallery.com.

BUYING INEXPENSIVE BUT THOUGHTFUL GIFTS

The rest of the people on your list are the ones for whom you need to get creative. I'm going to bet that in years past you stumbled exhausted through the mall on December 24 looking for anything that would be a remote possibility. You were so tired you didn't even look at the price. You just handed over your credit card, crossed the name off your list, and then moved on to the next name. Those days are over. Come December 24 this year, you can sit with a cup of hot chocolate and embrace how good it feels to be the King or Queen of Early Shopping.

Here are some more suggestions to inspire you.

Does the person in question have any hobbies, such as golf or scrapbooking? If you know nothing about the particulars of this hobby, research what a person who pursues this hobby will appreciate. And remember magazines are devoted to all types of hobbies. Does your friend or relative have a subscription? Is there a store devoted to their passion? Give a gift certificate.

Has your friend or loved one been dreaming about a special vacation? Find a coffee table book with beautiful images and lots of useful information about the area in question. Every time they look at it, they will think of you.

Call your local community college and ask for a brochure of spring classes. Find something that would be of interest for one of the people on your list. Give them a surprise enrollment. It's never too late for Aunt Tilly to learn how to dance or for Uncle George to learn the basics of a computer. These classes usually last several weeks and are inexpensive. Your recipient will be thanking you all spring.

Is someone on your list taking a trip soon? Arrange to have some champagne sent to the room. Or perhaps your friend is off on a cruise to Alaska and you both live in Los Angeles. Pick up a warm muffler, hat, or gloves. Odds are that they don't have these items in their wardrobe.

Do any of the recipients support a particular charity? Make a donation in their honor. Some charities will give you a certificate showing the recipient how your donation was used. This is perfect for the friend or family member who has everything. Think outside the gift box.

Are new parents on your list? I bet they'd like a quiet dinner at a local restaurant more than another baby blanket. Give then a gift certificate to their favorite neighborhood haunt. Or get them some tickets to a show. If you kick in your time as the evening's baby sitter, they might write you into their will! What other services could you offer as a gift? If Cousin Izzy is having a hard time paying the bills, perhaps give her the gift of shoveling the snow from her driveway or mowing her lawn for a month. Make a list of the skills and talents you have that could brighten someone's day. Then revisit your list with this in mind.

Anyone who makes scrapbooks knows how sweet this gift is because it equally represents the gifts of time and creativity in addition to the photos. Your gift doesn't have to honor your present. Find an image of a relative from her youth or perhaps one of a late parent, and create a memento that can be framed. Investigate the possibilities at www.creativememories.com or go to one of their retail stores.

Kids today are wired. They want iPods, iTunes selections, video games, Wii games, and such. But you don't have to feed the frenzy. Consider things you played with as a child: a big magnifying glass, a bag of seashells, a fistful of foreign coins, a hunk of clay. None of these should cost more than a few dollars. Think, too, of giving gifts of your time. For example, collect pine cones and paint them green and red and string them together with curly ribbon. Take your child to the local museum; many large cities have museums devoted just to children. Awaken their creativity and show them that there is an interesting life beyond electronic gadgets.

What about investing in Mother Nature to honor someone you love? In many communities and some countries, you can plant a tree in honor of someone. This is good for your friend or relative and equally good for planet earth! Check with your Chamber of Commerce or the mayor's office for guidance in your area.

Record your family history. Very often the story of our families and even those of our friendships goes undocumented. Why not use a digital recorder this holiday and ask your family to tell their story? How did the couples in your family meet? Where were they educated? How did your parents learn about parenting? What do they know now that they wish they had known before you and your siblings arrived on the scene? Wouldn't this be a great gift for your loved ones to have? If you make the recording now, you'll be set when it comes to celebrating this year. We record events, but we rarely record the story behind the festivities.

You can find wonderful charities with online sites that accept your donation and enable you to print a certificate. The amount of the donation is private. Some charities offer special benefits for a specific donation amounts. For example, you can buy a stove for a woman in the Sudan, shoes for an Afghan girl, or feed for a horse for a month. You can match the charity to the interests of the recipient. Begin your research at www.thehungersite.com. In fact, you can sign up to click each day at the site. The vendors who advertise donate money for every click the site receives. While there, you can investigate helping additional sites who assist other groups in need such as breast cancer research and illiteracy.

A word about making homemade gifts. If you are known for your cookies, hand-knit sweaters, or scented candles, you can certainly please people with these treasures. Before you decide to go that route, however, be sure you factor in how many items you need to make, the cost of the supplies, and—this is the big one—how much time it will take you to accomplish your goal. It might make more sense to buy some gifts and use your time to make extra money this holiday season. Run the numbers, and let them direct your energies this holiday season.

It happens to all of us. We receive a gift that has clearly been purchased with great thought and presented with love and all we can think is: "What were you thinking?" What's a person to do? The first order of business is to be gracious. Express your thanks in person and later with a note. It's permissible to pass this gift on to someone who would actually appreciate it, provided she does not know the person who gave you the item in the first place. You don't want Cousin Betty showing up at a family gathering wearing the scarf her mother gave you for Christmas! If re-gifting feels uncomfortable to you, give the gift to a charity. Someone should enjoy it.

SHOPPING SMART

Believe it or not, you have finished the hard part. You have your list and your ideas. Instead of making shopping a chore, why not make it fun? Have hot chocolate to celebrate the purchase of the last gift, ask your best friend to accompany you, or have your photo taken on Santa's lap.

This year, try shopping online to save you time. You might be able to knock off your gift shopping duties in one afternoon without leaving home. Factor in the cost of ribbon, gift wrap, gift tags, cards, gas, or transportation money and the value of your time and see if it doesn't behoove you to have the online retailer gift wrap your item.

Some good ideas come with a caveat. Please don't get caught up in the ease of online shopping and use your credit card with abandon. Be sure you have your budget in mind and are deducting the items as you go along. Remember that you can put items in your online shopping cart and make the purchase later, after a twenty-four-hour cooling-off period to be sure you're making the right decision. If you do go overboard, whittle away at another expense until you're once again in the black.

If you do have to schlep to the mall or elsewhere, be sure you have your shopping list before you leave home. Know which stores are most likely to have the items you want to purchase. Don't backtrack to the same stores on different days. Be geographically intelligent and go to each area just once. You save gas, time, and energy—all of which translate into dollars saved.

Use cash wherever and whenever you can this holiday. It's easy to "cheat" and go over your per-person limit or charge a few extra items. According to columnist Erin Burt at Kiplinger's, using only cash makes your budget a reality. "When you shop with cash, you're more aware of how much you spend and how much you have left because you can touch it. And once the money's gone, it's gone." Keep your holiday budget in an envelope. After each purchase, slip the receipt into the envelope and record the amount spent on the front of the envelope. Keep a running tally; otherwise you will have a rude awakening at some point and have to whip out your credit card. I'd like to see it get dusty in your wallet this season from lack of use!

Watch the newspaper for sales and don't forget to subscribe to the newsletters from your favorite retailers. You'll be receiving coupons and insider info on secret sales all year long. Allow me to offer a caution about sales and coupons. These can be money savers for the things you need, but if you don't need the item and can't use it as a gift, it isn't a deal. It's a space waster in your home and a money thief.

Remember to save your receipts to make returns and exchanges easier. When you receive your purchase receipt, ask the salesperson for a gift receipt. This allows the recipient to return or exchange the gift without knowing the price you paid.

If you have gifts that need to be mailed, get to the post office early. You have to factor in the value of your time when you are de-ciding whether to have the store wrap and send your gift or if you should do it.

Here's another reason to shop online: The vendor can mail your gift for you. Many department stores and some vendors such as Amazon have specials. If you spend a certain amount (at Amazon it's only $25), your shipping is free. You're saving money and time, which are precious commodities all year long.

When the holiday season ends, keep a fresh gift list on Excel or in the back of your financial notebook. Then purchase gifts and collect ideas all year long. Make it a perennial pursuit rather than the exhausting, anxiety-provoking one.

If you need money this season and have extra time, retail stores in your area are very likely looking for temporary help over the holidays, especially on weekends, when most people shop. If you don't work in retail at your regular job, it could be educational and fun to do something different for a few weeks.

IT'S ALWAYS THE SEASON

This week may mark your first adventure in holiday shopping with a plan. If you approach this with an open mind, I think you will find it not only makes economic sense but is fun. I listen a little more carefully to conversations now that I shop with a plan. I'm always looking for gift ideas because birthdays, weddings, and graduations happen throughout the year, and I don't want to blow my budget on anyone's gift! Have fun this week and remember to listen all year long.

WEEK THREE

Family Gatherings

This week, you can

- Plan a holiday gathering within your means
- Save time with meal preparations

THANKSGIVING IS THE MOTHER OF all Dinner Parties. If you can plan and execute this holiday meal, you can do anything in the realm of entertaining! Very often we rely on a dangerous mixture of tradition and emotion to host this holiday (or any of the big family gatherings next month). This year you're going to be like one of the famous chefs on television. No detail will be left to chance. Not only will you be able to afford your celebration, you will enjoy it more without any sticker shock in the days that follow.

PARING EXPECTATIONS, GUEST LISTS, AND MENUS

If you are traditionally a guest, you have an easy role to play and probably don't need to set a great deal of money aside to make the day successful. Do you bring flowers, candy, or dessert? Are you known for a particular dish you contribute to the meal? Will small children in the home expect you to show up with a treat for them? Decide how much money your contribution to the day will cost. At the beginning of the month you figured out the amount you could spend on your holiday season celebration. Once you work out your budget for Thanksgiving, you'll subtract that amount from the total you allotted for the holidays and have your new balance.

If you are the host, the holiday celebration is going to be more complicated. Traditionally when people plan their holiday expenses, they fail to factor in the cost of feeding a large group of people. And the cost can be significant.

How many people will be attending? Cooking for twenty costs more than cooking for two, so the larger your group, the greater the grocery bill.

What will you be responsible for this year: food, decorations, beverages, desserts? Please don't say: "Everything!" Ask your guests to participate and bring something to the table. Thanksgiving is all about everyone sharing in the meal. Why not make it easy on yourself this year and be ready with a list of what you need when guests ask how they can contribute? Take the guesswork out of the equation for you and for them. At the end of the meal, give everyone an opportunity to assist with clean up. We all know the real party is in the kitchen.

Taking food contributions from guests into account, design your menu. When you are ready, you can create your shopping list from this menu. By the way, don't *presume* you have all the ingredients. Check the cupboards and pantry. You want to avoid the supermarket the day before Thanksgiving at all costs. Next decide about decorations (flowers, candles, seasonal items). Once again, check your stock from last year. You would be surprised how much money gets wasted when we unnecessarily buy in duplicate and triplicate.

Once you have these particulars nailed down, you can better estimate the cost of the day. Take this figure and deduct it from the total you felt would handle your holiday celebration. You have your new balance. See if you need to reduce the guest list, the menu, or your expectations.

As we move through the following section, if you realize you need a new tablecloth or turkey roaster, be sure you subtract those expenses from your total holiday budget. Our mind can cast items like these into limbo (as in, charge it on my credit card). If there's one action we want to avoid this holiday season, it's using our credit cards to cover expenses we can't afford. Perhaps one of your guests can loan you the item in question. Everyone can admire Aunt Edith's tablecloth and your friend Charlie will be delighted he loaned you his jumbo turkey roaster. And you will have more money in your pocket for the remaining holiday expenditures.

CREATING A THANKSGIVING BUDGET

In this section, I show you a budget based on the following guest list. Use this as a jumping-off point for your own holiday meal:

Dave and Hanna Watson
Their daughters, Emma and Amy, and
   their spouses
Their grandkids, Carl, Grace, and
   Katie
Mom and Dad
Phyllis and John, their neighbors
Aunt Marie and Aunt Dolores

Now that the guest list is settled at fifteen people, Hanna talked to her guests and created a menu and a shopping list. Because prices vary across the country, we can't include specific prices in the sample budget.

WATSON'S THANKSGIVING BUDGET

Menu Item	Assigned To	Cost
Turkey	Self	XX
Mashed potatoes	Self	XX
Cranberries	Phyllis & John	NA
Stuffing	Self	XX
Gravy	Self	XX
Vegetable side dishes	Aunts Marie & Dolores	NA
Rolls	Mom & Dad	NA
Apple pie	Emma	NA
Pumpkin pie	Emma	NA
Soda	Amy	XX
Bottled water		XX
Wine	Phyllis & John	NA
Candles	Self	NA (use scented candles from last year)
Flowers	Self	(Buy fresh at farmer's mkt.)

UNDERSTANDING THAT TIME IS MONEY

In the spirit of saving time and making Thanksgiving a big hit this year, here are some additional tips to help you get ready.

Take a minute to think about last year's holiday, beyond all those leftovers that clogged the fridge for days on end. Jot down the things you did that saved time and money, especially if you tried some new techniques. Be sure you repeat these steps next year. Likewise jot down the things that didn't work and be sure you don't repeat them.

Do you host the family every year? If you enjoy this tradition, continue it. But if you are tired of having the entire family over, why not pass the baton? Who else could handle this meal in your family or circle of friends? Don't assume no one is interested. Assume rather that someone wants to try but doesn't know how to tell you. Start making phone calls. And be sure your attitude is one of the Helpful Mentor rather than the Exhausted Family Saint. Decide if you want to pass the baton forever or just this year. Be open to sharing recipes, your turkey roaster, and the family china.

Scan the newspaper for coupons and sales in the weeks leading up to the holiday. And use them! If you go to a store such as Costco where the quantities are large, shop with a friend and split some of the items. But make sure this is a better deal than your local supermarket.

Visit your local farmer's market. You'll have better tasting food if you use the freshest ingredients. You will save money at these markets and support local farmers. It's win/win for everyone.

If you have a freezer, shop early in the month for your turkey and any ingredients that you can purchase frozen. Prices will rise during the month and you don't want to pay the premium rate if you can avoid it. If you can, shop alone, on a full stomach, when you're in a good mood—you'll be more likely to buy only what you need.

When you plan your menu, in addition to making food assignments, pare the dishes to the essentials. Make mashed potatoes or sweet but not both. It's a big meal, so no one needs bread and salad. And figure one pound of turkey for every guest unless they're a vegetarian. We just need the side dishes! Pare the dessert list as well. No one needs three desserts after a huge meal.

Plan your guest list. Don't be afraid to whittle it if you need to. When it's complete, how will you let everyone know the details for the day? Will you send an e-mail, make phone calls, text them, or use formal invitations? Decide the method of communication and then schedule the day that you will extend the invitations.

If a store carries holiday decorations you'd like to have but can't work into your budget, see if you can snag them at half price the day after Thanksgiving. The turkey tureen will look just as beautiful next year.

TEACHING AN OLD DOG NEW TRICKS

Whether you're an old hand at entertaining or a newbie, you can always learn something new from a careful budget and a plan for the festivities. Very often just seeing things in black and white allows us to have a new insight. The willingness to plan is your foundation. If you are a charter member of the fly-by-the-seat-of-your-pants holiday entertaining clan, try the exercises offered this week. You will be amazed at the discoveries you will make— and the money you will save!

WEEK FOUR

Holiday Travel

This week, you can

- Discover some ways to save on holiday season travel
- Consider vacationing at home

THIS IS THE BUSIEST TRAVEL TIME of the year. If you have to drive a long distance, be sure the car gets serviced a week or two before Turkey Day. At the very least, check the oil and water levels and fill up the gas tank a few days before the holiday. Are you a member of the Auto Club or some other organization that provides roadside assistance? Have your membership card with you and a fully-charged cell phone. If you have children in the car, provide them with snacks and entertainment. The happier they are, the less likely you are to be serenaded with a chorus of "Are we there yet?"

Travel on trains and planes should be booked well in advance. If you travel for business and have accumulated airline miles or hotel points, see if you can't cash in some of these. You might have enough for a few nights at a local hotel.

CREATING A TRAVEL BUDGET

Don't forget to deduct your travel expenses from your total budget. These are exactly the kinds of expenditures that explode our credit balances. "Oh! But I had to see mom and dad for the holiday!" Yes, but you also have to pay for the trip.

Following are some items to keep in mind when creating your holiday travel budget:

Airline or train tickets
Parking at the airport or train station
Transportation when you get to your destination (rental car, taxis)
Hotel
Meals out
Sightseeing
Pet sitter

Be sure to check your luggage well in advance to be sure you're covered. What about entertainment for the kids? Do you have a portable DVD player, for example? You might get them a new movie or game for the trip to be sure they are occupied. Be sure to wrap it as an official stocking stuffer!

FINDING TRAVEL DEALS

The travel industry has been offering some incredible perks lately. If you don't subscribe to your local paper, pick it up next Sunday. You'll find food coupons for the week along with great travel ideas. You can also do some research online. A few of my favorite Web sites are www.bing.com, www.travelzoo.com, and www.farealert.com. Plus, go to the Web site for your favorite airline and sign up for free e-mail alerts.

Every major airline offers a mileage club. See if your credit card company has an affiliation. I have clients who charge all their monthly expenses on their credit card so they can accrue air miles. This is a great idea provided you pay off the card each month. Otherwise, your interest is the price you're paying for those miles or other perks.

Large hotel chains also offer point programs. If you travel for business, be sure to take advantage. You might score a free hotel room in your own city and have a mini vacation provided by your work. (The same advice holds true for rental car companies.) I worked in New York City for three days and secured enough hotel points for a free night at a luxury hotel in San Francisco. Some hotel memberships allow you to transfer lodging points into air miles. Sign up (it's free) and investigate your perks.

Airlines offer e-mail alerts about specials. Don't hesitate to sign up. Many also offer newsletters. You might find out about a sale before it's announced to the general public. Be sure you know the baggage requirements for your airline. Here's a trick I use: I have a small suitcase that it fits in the overhead. I carry an overnight bag as my second piece of luggage and call it my purse. Inside that bag is my real purse! I don't have to check a bag and I have all my belongings with me. This won't work for a ski trip or a large family, but if you're winging your way home alone for the holidays, take the easy route.

You can subscribe to travel newsletters that alert you to industry sales and specials. I have some of the more popular ones listed in the "Resources" section. My favorite is www.travelzoo.com.

Research a city you'd like to visit and book your trip for the off season. You'll save on hotel and car rentals. And if you can fly on a Tuesday, Wednesday, or Saturday you will save on your airfare as well. You're likely to save also if can fly on the holiday itself. For a short trip with no change of planes, this can work like a charm. Just catch the first flight out and you'll be home in time for the big family meal. If you have an area earmarked for a trip, start saving articles in a cyber folder or your literal file cabinet. Check out www.Digital-City.com and see if the city is listed. You'll have access to the activities planned for the time of your visit. If you are interested in several areas, create a "Travel" section and then have files for each city or area.

Investigate local options. A little over two years ago, I decided I wanted to go to China. Trips at the time were running close to $3,000. I visited Shanghai, Beijing, and Xian. I was gone for twelve days. The tour included everything: flights, meals, hotel, even entry at all tourist attractions. My friends all assumed I was spending a fortune. The entire package was $1,500, half the price. How did I do it? I purchased a Chinese newspaper published in America. The travel agencies advertising there catered to the Chinese American community. I saved a bundle and, yes, the tour was in English as well as Mandarin. Price breaks are always available. All you have to do is some investigating.

Terminal food, whether it's at an airport, a train station, or a bus station, costs a fortune and is not nutritious. Pack snacks such as trail mix, string cheese, and bread.

Do you subscribe to magazines and never have time to read? Take a few with you and discard them as you finish. If you have a portable reading device such as a Kindle, you can get caught up on books you've wanted to read. Not a reader? Travel with an iPod, a portable DVD player, or a portable video game device.

STAYING HOME

When you take your holiday vacation time this year, consider using it not to travel but to stay close to home. Spend a day at home or go out and get to know your city better. If you choose the former, it shouldn't be a day of painting the house, pulling weeds, or mending the fence. It needs to be a day of rest and relaxation.

What are some inexpensive things you could do at home that you would find relaxing? How about a hot bath with a scented candle burning and your favorite music playing in the background? What about sleeping in till noon like you did when you were a teenager? Call someone you love who lives far away and get caught up on all the news. (Most cell phone plans have free weekend minutes—take advantage.)

If you live in a large city such as New York or Chicago, you have a world of activities waiting for you. When was the last time you went to a museum? Often these are free. Get out there and explore! Even if you live in a tiny town, I'm going to bet there are places not that far away that you could enjoy. Did something historical happen in your area? Take a tour of the site. What matters is that you relax and do something outside the norm.

If you want to avoid the drama and expense of travel at this time of year but you want to be with your family, invite them to come to your city. Having a house filled with family and friends can make the holidays come alive. Figure out how much a trip out of town costs versus having guests. Remember that they will need to be fed and in most cases housed. Are you putting them up at a hotel or spreading them out over guest rooms and couches in your home? How many days will they stay? How will the number of people and the number of meals you need to provide affect your budget? Don't forget that more people means more laundry, more paper products (toilet paper anyone?), more water and electricity, and the like.

THE PAUSE THAT REFRESHES

November sets off a time of family togetherness that's priceless. But it requires planning if you don't want to remember it as the month that created a hole in your careful financial plans. Crafting a holiday guide doesn't have to rob the season of its joy and spontaneity. In fact, such a plan creates a springboard for exactly that experience.

NOVEMBER SUMMARY

WEEK ONE

Create a realistic holiday budget.

WEEK TWO

Be creative rather than extravagant with holiday gifts.

WEEK THREE

See how great meals don't have to cost a fortune.

WEEK FOUR

Make use of budget-minded tips for holiday travel.

12. DECEMBER

Year-End Money Moves

With money in your pocket,

you are wise and you are handsome.

. . . and you sing well too!

—YIDDISH PROVERB

BEING FISCALLY RESPONSIBLE DOESN'T mean you have to turn into Scrooge. But you can change the way you live, make other choices, and celebrate this month's holidays differently. You can be an example to friends, family, and coworkers. It's okay to spend *and* celebrate, but do it sanely. Last month you laid the groundwork for your celebrations. December means the year is coming to an end and a new one is on the horizon. You need to tend to some financial housekeeping.

HABIT OF THE MONTH: GIVE OF YOURSELF

This month, open your heart more often than you open your wallet. Remember that having money can certainly make life more comfortable, but true joy comes from relationships. Who is giving thanks that they crossed your path this day? Relinquish a parking spot at the mall to someone who looks more frazzled than you; wave someone into your lane of traffic; open a door for someone burdened with bundles; take a minute to express gratitude to a service employee; or rescue a stray dog. Kindness is free.

TOOL OF THE MONTH: A FISCAL NEW YEAR'S RESOLUTION

How easy it is to make New Year's resolutions. And how easy it is to forget them! This month, make a realistic financial resolution for the coming year. Reveal your resolution to a handful of trusted friends, because we're more apt to stick to our resolutions when we share them. Looking for a good financial resolution for the upcoming year? Here are a few possibilities: Get out of debt. Find a higher-paying job. Read at least four financial guidebooks. Improve your credit rating. Contribute the maximum to your 401(k). You get the idea!

WEEK ONE

Tasks for Every December

This week, you can

- Take care of end-of-the-year financial business
- Look for additional tax deductions

ONCE A YEAR, EVERY YEAR, A FEW financial tasks demand your attention. Many of these tasks are discussed elsewhere in the book, but this week we go over them again because the end of the year is fast upon us.

REVIEWING YOUR TAXES AND DEDUCTIONS

Here are a few examples of deductions that are easy to overlook. Even though each might result in only a small savings, the total might be significant. Uncle Sam offers you these opportunities to save. Be sure you take advantage!

Review your investment portfolio to make certain that everything is in balance. (See details on rebalancing your portfolio in week two of July.) If you have taken any losses on any investments, consider doing

some tax-loss harvesting, a topic I discuss next week.

Make all charitable contributions for the year by December thirty-first. I have much more on charitable giving in week three of this month.

Did you remember to add the miles you logged doing volunteer work for charity? What about receipts for the cookies you made for the bake sale that raised money for the local chapter of your favorite charity?

Spend down your flexible spending account if you have one. (See October, week one.) You have to spend what you have in your account by the end of December or the end of March, depending on your plan administrator (the same outfit that signs your paycheck). Find out by which date you use it or lose it.

Pay all your medical expenses for the year. If you think that your total medical expenses for the calendar year may surpass 7.5 percent of your income, they may be deductible. Did you remember to keep track of miles you logged traveling to doctors' appointments? If you have a chronic illness, this can add up. If you think you're going to surpass 7.5 percent of your income this year, but not next, pay now for any drugs or medical supplies that you may need in January and February.

Pay your investment advisor or tax guru.

Contribute to your kids' college fund. Each parent can give up to $13,000 a year to each child per calendar year without paying a gift tax. Have you contributed as much as you can to your child's 529 college plan this year?

Make sure you've paid tax-deductible career and investment expenses. Union fees, dues to professional organizations, subscriptions to publications you need for your career, and payments for upcoming work-related seminars or travel can be prepaid by December thirty-first to get a tax deduction for the current year.

Pay your December mortgage (and possibly January's, too). If you want, you can pay your next year's state and local taxes and very likely deduct those from your IRS payments as well.

Contribute to your retirement plans. You usually have until the time you file your taxes to make contributions to your IRA or Roth-IRA, but now is the time to think ahead and make sure you have the funds set aside.

If you are over $70^1/_2$, make *sure* you take the minimum distribution from your traditional IRA account. If you don't, you'll get hit with one of the nastiest tax penalties on the books: A full 50 percent of the required distribution!

This is a great time to scour the newspaper and listen to radio and TV tips about tax deductions. You might want to make a quick call to your tax guru just to be sure you take advantage of any end-of-year deductions.

KEEPING YOUR EYE ON THE BOTTOM LINE

This past year you've been on a steep learning curve when it comes to being financially savvy. I know this is a tough week to find a free hour to spend going over your finances. But I promise the time is well worth it. You've got your financial engine revved up. Let's not lose any momentum because the holidays are here!

WEEK TWO

Tax-Loss Harvesting

This week, you can

- Be sure you don't overpay your taxes
- Learn the benefits of selling losing investments

REGARDLESS OF HOW PATRIOTIC YOU may be, I doubt that you are eager to *overpay* your taxes. One of the simplest tax-avoidance maneuvers—tax-loss harvesting—is often ignored. *Tax-loss harvesting* refers to selling investments you've lost money on and asking Uncle Sam to essentially share the pain. Tax-loss harvesting isn't difficult to do—really!—and it just might save you a bundle.

FOLLOWING THE STEPS FOR TAX-LOSS HARVESTING

In this section are four easy steps to getting the government to help share the pain of your investment losses. Be aware, however, that you must act by December 31 for this maneuver to work.

If you haven't yet invested in the market, peruse this week's material so that when you are in the market, you'll be a wise investor. You can use this time also to get caught up.

This is a tough time of year for scheduling extra time, but don't let celebrations interfere with your fiscal health.

Step 1: Peruse Your Portfolio

To reap the benefits of tax-loss harvesting, you must have lost value in a taxable (non-tax-deferred) account. IRAs and 401(k) plan losses don't count. In most cases, you're looking for a stock or a stock fund that has fallen in price since you purchased it. The price you paid for a security (stock, bond, or mutual fund) is the *cost basis,* so you are looking for a cost basis less than today's market price. If your investment papers do not list the cost basis, you'll need to contact a representative at your brokerage firm or mutual fund.

Step 2: Sell Your Losers

Many people find it difficult to sell securities that have lost value. They feel like they are locking in their losses. That's true, in a sense. But (as you're about to see in the next step) losses aren't always such a bad thing.

Step 3: Seal Your Nest Egg

By selling a loser, you have experienced a *capital loss,* and capital losses are generally tax-deductible. So far, so good. Now you have to watch out for just two main things: the wash rule and sealing your portfolio.

First the *wash rule:* The IRS disallows any tax deduction if you repurchase the same security within thirty-one days, so don't. But being out of the market for a month presents you with a second potential problem if the market heats up, because you'll be left out in the cold. The solution is to *seal* your portfolio by buying a similar but not identical security, called a *proxy.* You can then keep your proxy, or sell it after thirty-one days and repurchase your old security. And selling your depressed security should not be seen as anything horrible because your proxy will be similarly depressed and poised for a similar price pop if the market starts to boil.

Step 4: Garner Your Profits

Suppose you bought a stock or a stock fund for $10,000 several years ago, and the market value has since dropped to $6,000. If you sell, you will have a capital loss of $4,000. You can use that $4,000 in one of two ways. First, you can apply the entire amount to offset any capital gains (gains from selling a security at more than you bought it for). But even if you have no capital gains this year, you can still deduct up to $3,000 from taxes owed on your regular income. That's a substantial saving for minimal effort. The remaining $1,000 of your capital loss can be written off next year's taxes. And if you pay state income taxes, you likely can write off some of those, too.

If you are unfamiliar with tax-loss harvesting, you might want the assistance of a financial professional, at least until you feel more comfortable with the process.

FINE-TUNING THE PROCESS

When buying and selling mutual funds, make sure that there isn't a load (commission) or short-term redemption fee. Also be aware of the commissions you pay for trading individual stocks or exchange-traded funds. And finally, know that the IRS rules can be tricky when it comes to what constitutes a "similar but not identical" security.

Taking advantage of tax-loss harvesting requires a learning curve, but the potential savings are great enough that it is well worth putting in the effort.

WEEK THREE

Charitable Giving

This week, you can

- Decide how to choose a charity
- Learn the ins and outs of charitable giving

IF YOU HAVE MORE THAN ENOUGH TO get by, why not share with those less fortunate? As if giving to charity weren't a reward in itself, philanthropy often offers sweet tax deductions. If you know the ins and outs of charitable giving, the government will kick in plenty to help you support your favorite cause.

CHOOSING A CHARITY

Here are a few pointers for choosing a charity, as well as a few tricks to getting the most out of Uncle Sam.

Examine your values. Ask yourself what kind of charity you want to support. Then get a list of legitimate charities as well as charities that do the most good. Two invaluable Web sites for this type of research are www.charitynavigator.org and www.charitywatch.org. You can search for charities of all kinds, as well as find out impor-

tant information about what they do, how they do it, and what percentage of your contributions go to the work itself and what percentage go to overhead and salaries. (I have a hard time giving to any charitable organization that pays their CEO more than a corporate CEO would make.)

Instead of cash, donate stock that's appreciated in value. Donate stock and you won't have to pay capital gains tax on the profits, and the full value of the stock can be deducted as a charitable donation. Here's an example: You bought stock in the XYZ Corporation in 1990 for $1,000. That stock is now worth $5,000. If you sold the stock, you would owe the IRS capital gains tax on $4,000, which is $600 at the current capital gains tax of 15 percent. But suppose you give that appreciated stock to a charity instead of selling it. You can take a deduction for the full value of the stock. If you're in the 36 percent tax bracket, you just got a deduction worth

$1,800 (15 percent of $5,000). And you've spared yourself from having to pay the capital gains tax of $600. In the end, the charity gets a full $5,000 and it cost you only $2,600 ($5,000 minus $1,800 minus $6,000). Amazing, huh?

Transfer your insurance policies. You may not need your insurance policies anymore anyway. Perhaps your kids are now grown, and both are successful in their careers. Money isn't a problem. Why not let charity reap the final rewards, while you reap a big tax deduction?

Create a charitable remainder trust. You give your assets, or a certain proportion of your assets, to charity. The charity pays you a steady stream of income (way, way above what you'll get from CDs or bonds) until the day you die. Most major charities have remainder trusts. Just call the front desk and ask.

Contribute to a charitable gift fund. If you aren't sure what charity you want to give to, no problem. Consider opening a charitable gift fund, such as the one available through the financial supermarket Fidelity Investments. Go to www.charitable gift.org. Anything you contribute to the fund this year can be deducted from your Federal income tax for this year, up to 50 percent of your adjusted gross income. After the money is deposited, dole it out whenever you like to (just about) whatever charities you like. Fidelity will charge you 0.60 percent a year for this service, which is well worth it given the potential tax benefit.

Know your limits. Depending on whether you contribute cash or property, the amount of your deduction may be limited to 20, 30, or most often 50 percent of your adjusted gross income.

Prequalify your charities. Not all nonprofits and charitable organizations are created equal, either in how well they spend your money or how much you can deduct for giving to them. The Web sites www.charitynavigator.org and www.charitywatch.org can help you know the size of the deduction you can potentially get by giving to a particular group. If you're really generous and give lots of cash, some charities, such as churches and research groups, can earn you up to a 50 percent deduction on your taxes. Other potential charities, such as a fraternity, may only give you as much as a 30 percent overall deduction. Beware that contributions to certain nonprofits will get you no deduction. Groups that lobby, for example, are not going to get you anything off your taxes.

Know how to deduct for tickets to charitable events. Pay $100 for a charity dinner, and you can usually deduct $80, which represents the price of the ticket minus the cost of the meal.

Your time and sweat cannot be deducted. While volunteering can be a great way to give, it won't get you any deductions at tax time. You can, however, deduct mileage, tolls, hotel expenses, and other costs associated with your volunteer efforts.

'Tis the season to give! Why not do so in a way that benefits both a cause you support and your tax liability? The good feeling you'll have deep in your soul is a side benefit without measure. I once had a client who was worth millions. One day when we were chatting about money she said: "I have a ridiculous relationship with money. I can't stop it from coming to me. Do you know why, Regina?" I assured her I had no idea. "It's because I'm always giving it away. You have to give in order to receive. It's the law of circulation." Indeed it is.

WEEK FOUR

Move Smoothly into the Future

This week, you can

- Clean out your financial files
- Make an inventory of your financial accomplishments this past year
- Look to the future by setting new financial goals

THIS IS THE WEEK THAT THE LAST OF the parties will come to an end. Most of us will be grateful to get back to our routines. This is the perfect time to gaze into the bright New Year on the horizon and make some specific plans for it. Have you ever noticed that every achievement, every action, indeed every system in life has to be maintained? You lose weight but still have to work to keep those extra pounds from creeping back. Fido doesn't stop shedding. Clean your house in the morning and by the afternoon a fine patina of dust will have once again taken up residence. The list is endless. Your finances also need attention to stay healthy and organized. Let's get our "savings pigs in a row" this month so that the New Year begins on a fiscal strong note.

TUNING YOUR FINANCIAL FILES

Dedicate an afternoon to getting your files ready to start absorbing receipts for the New Year. Let me give you an example. Let's say you support a number of charities during the year. You'd have a folder called "Donations." As the year ends, take out those receipts and place them in a large envelope. On the front of the envelope, write "Donations" and the year.

In a separate section of a file drawer or file box, collect envelopes for all tax-deductible items. The original file folder is now once again empty. When January first dawns, you're ready to file current receipts.

Tax time will be here before you know it, and with your envelopes clearly marked, you'll be ready to add your deductions.

Once you file your taxes, these envelopes need to go into a box dedicated solely to storing tax backup materials. The oldest records and envelopes will be tossed. (Don't forget to shred any documents with account numbers or your social security number.) If you keep an ongoing record of expenses in a program such as Quick-Books, you can file these envelopes immediately. Your deductions are entered in your computer and all you have to do is add your total expenses with a few mouse clicks.

Now is the perfect time to look through your files and remove any projects that have been completed. If Junior went off to college this fall, for example, you won't need to save all the research materials you collected for colleges, scholarships, and other related material. You can probably toss or shred most of it. Place any material you want to keep in the archival area you have set up. If you have a minimal amount of material, consider scanning it into a computer file.

Go through every section of your files and see what can be tossed, shredded, or archived. You want your files to be lean storehouses of active information. Popular areas where material tends to stagnate include medical claims/reports; property and investments that have been sold; and school materials for your kids from the previous year. After you eliminate or simply whittle every file, don't forget to see whether you have new files to add.

This process shouldn't be too time-consuming or overwhelming provided

SHOP HOLIDAY SALES

Yes, I know that throughout the past twelve months I have been saying to reduce your spending. But the week after Christmas is a great time to stock up on holiday cards, gift wrap, and decorations. They are even more beautiful when you don't pay full retail price! Just make sure you don't buy more than you need.

you followed the instructions set forth when you created your system in January. Initially it takes both time and attention to set up a working file system. However, after that is accomplished, doing a periodic purge and tune-up shouldn't take you too long. And the time you save over the course of the year makes it all worthwhile.

ACKNOWLEDGING YOUR ACCOMPLISHMENTS

Now that the year has come to an end, be sure and take some time to pat yourself on the back. What did you face head-on this past year and master? Did you acquire renter's insurance for the first time in your life? Or have you created a realistic budget that allows you to live within your means? Perhaps you met with a financial planner and felt on track for your future. Whether it was a big step or you just put your toe in the financial waters, acknowledge what you achieved.

Following is a handy checklist for you to help monitor your progress. How many of these did you accomplish this year?

Did you create your budget? Have you been able to stick with it?

Do you know your FICO score? Did you boost it this year?

Are your files and briefcase organized?

Is your emergency fund in place?

Do you pay your bills on time?

Is everything and everyone properly insured?

What's the state of your retirement account?

Have you been able to reduce or eliminate debt?

How are the kid's college funds doing?

Do you have an investment portfolio?

Is tax time less stressful for you?

Do you handle monetary windfalls such as bonus checks or tax refunds with more skill?

Have you discovered creative ways to boost your earnings?

What cost-cutting tips did you embrace?

Do you save regularly? Into what type of account do you put the savings?

Did you decide to work with a financial planner?

Do you have a will?

Did you decide to buy or lease a car?

Do you have the right type of mortgage?

Did you decide to downsize and save?

Did you have a fiscally sane holiday season?

Perhaps the most important thing to remember about this list is that few readers have accomplished every single item. You don't need to be an overachiever. Be like the tortoise. He moved at a slow but steady pace and reached the finish line. You will too. Whatever you accomplished this year is a victory and a turning point in your life. Don't compare yourself or your progress to anyone else; just keep moving forward.

PREPARING FOR WHAT'S ON THE HORIZON

Life is about change. It is ever evolving and so are your finances. Successful money management is not a static affair. For example, are there new faces at the table due to a move, a marriage, or a birth? Were there unexpected financial changes this year such as losing a job or downsizing from the family home to a condo? Or did you score a big pay raise or bonus? All of these changes can alter the financial backdrop of your life and warrant the adjustment of long-term goals.

Do you have a plan to handle changes on the horizon? What if, for example, your children graduate from college in June? How will you manage the extra money you no longer have to divert to support them at school? What if you finally saved your emergency fund money? Do you have a plan to invest the extra cash coming in? Your financial life, like your organizing efforts, is always expanding, growing, and changing. Sound financial management, like life itself, is more a journey than a destination. Take the time this week to examine your goals for the new year.

GOING FROM RAGS TO RICHES

One day I was organizing an affluent client, whom I'll call John. He's a kind, gracious, fabulously wealthy investment banker. He had been on a business trip with a famous billionaire and was offered a ride back to L.A. in the billionaire's private jet. During the flight, the man asked John if he was wealthy. My client's response floored me. John said: "Well, I'm okay. I don't ever have to work another day in my life and I can take care of my family." I put up my hand and stopped John. I said: "Can I be the one to tell you that you are wealthy?" He laughed and gave me this advice: "Regina, when you start to make a lot of money, don't let it make you crazy. There will always be someone with a bigger house, more money in the bank . . . or a private jet."

And then John shared more with me. He had come from a middle-class background. He got married, made a fortune—and walked away from it all and started over. He said he wasn't fulfilled by what he did for a living at that time and wasn't happy in his marriage. The money he had now came later in life from a second career. And in between he struggled. "I know what it's like to have money," he said. "And I know what it's like to be poor. I can tell you that what matters in life are your health, your family and friends, and the strength of your spiritual beliefs. Those things get you through."

I couldn't agree more. I hope you make a fortune and live a financially secure, long life. But never forget what's really important.

And when the tough times come, remember these words:

In order for God to take you to another place,
He must first move you from where you are.
The moving often seems like disaster but
It's only the creaking and groaning
of a reluctant door.
—ANONYMOUS

DECEMBER SUMMARY

WEEK ONE

Perform timely financial tasks that reap rewards.

WEEK TWO

Find out about the benefits of tax-loss harvesting.

WEEK THREE

Discover the many faces of charitable giving.

WEEK FOUR

Monitor your progress and set new financial goals.

ACKNOWLEDGMENTS

One Year to an Organized Financial Life has been both an amazing journey and a gift. You know what they say: "When the student is willing, the teacher appears." The teacher was brought to me by two of the most gifted women working in publishing today. Thank you to my editor, Katie McHugh. I can't do a book without you! Literary agent Marilyn Allen has believed in me and understood Zen Organizing from the start. It's a gift to be represented by such an elegant, intelligent, and skillful woman.

Russell Wild is the ultimate collaborator. He is respectful, kind, gracious, hilarious, and a walking encyclopedia of all things financial.

We both want to thank all the generous professionals who gave of their time for interviews. Their expertise blesses the pages of this book. And we extend kudos to Christine Marra and her incredible team: copy editor Susan Pink, who never sacrifices a writer's voice for correct punctuation, and Donna Riggs, who turns an index into a work of art. This is our third book together. I can't imagine making it through the difficult final days before launch without these gifted ladies.

Wendie Carr and Lindsey Triebel have my gratitude forever for the tireless PR work they do on behalf of all of my books. If they are ever bored, annoyed, or irritated by my endless requests and ideas, they never let on. Thank you, ladies.

Jon Resh had my heart when he came up with the ducks in a row design for the first two books in this series. I couldn't wait to see what his brilliant mind would imagine for Financial Life. What can I say? Pigs have never been lovelier! Thank you, John. The wonderful Jane Raese once again designed the interior. When the material threatens to overwhelm, a little piggie is there to make you smile.

The day before Russ and I began our collaboration, I learned that my sweet old golden retriever, Spirit, had to be put to sleep. My cousin Jamie Ann De Stefano came to my rescue. Thank you, Jamie. This book is for you.

And, last but not least, I say "Woof! Woof!" to Norman, the Wonder Poodle, and to little Hurley, the mighty miniature Schnauzer. I've never written a book without a golden retriever at my feet. Norman and Hurley told me to keep the faith.

RESOURCES

BANKS, ONLINE

HSBC Direct
www.HSBCDirect.com

ING Direct
www.INGdirect.com

Emigrant Direct
www.Emigrantdirect.com

ONLINE CALCULATORS

Credit Card Calculator
Bankrate.com
http://www.bankrate.com/calculators/
managing-debt/minimum-payment-
calculator.aspx

Mortgage Calculator
Bankrate.com
www.bankrate.com

Moneychimp
www.moneychimp.com

Mortgage-calc.com
www.Mortgage-calc.com

Reverse Mortgage Calculators
AARP
www.AARP.org

Golden Gateway
www.GoldenGateway.com

CARS

Car Pricing Guide
Kelley Blue Book
kbb.com

Edmunds
www.Edmunds.com

Swapalease
www.swapalease.com

Gas Prices
GasBuddy
www.gasbuddy.com

GasPriceWatch
www.gaspricewatch.com

Insurance, Driving
AARP Driver Safety Program
www.aarp.org/families/driver_safety

CHARITABLE GIVING AND VOLUNTEER SERVICE OPPORTUNITIES

American Institute of Philanthrophy
www.charitywatch.org

AmeriCorps
www.americorps.gov

Charity Navigator
www.charitynavigator.org

Peace Corps
www.peacecorps.gov

American Red Cross
www.redcross.org

Fidelity Charitable Gift Fund
www.charitablegift.org

Heifer International
www.heifer.org

Mercy Corps
www.mercycorps.org

National Search and Rescue Dog Foundation
www.searchdogfoundation.org

Oxfam
www.oxfam.com

Six Degrees
www.sixdegrees.org

The Hunger Site
www.thehungersite.com
(This site will also link you to other charity sites for breast cancer, literacy, animals, and more.)

Volunteer Match
www.volunteermatch.org

COLLEGE

Canadian Universities
http://www.aucc.ca/_pdf/english/
publications/canada_universities_e.pdf

Saving for College
www.savingforcollege.com

U.S. Department of Education
www.studentaid.ed.gov

Scholarships
College Board, a nonprofit
www.collegeboard.com

U.S. Department of Education
www.studentaid.ed.gov

Student Financial Aid
U.S. Department of Education
www.ed.gov/programs/fpg

Student Loans
Stafford Loan program
http://www.staffordloan.com

CREDIT REPORTS AND IDENTITY THEFT

FREE ANNUAL CREDIT REPORT
www.annualcreditreport.com
or call 1-877-322-8228
Created by the three nationwide consumer credit reporting agencies (Equifax, Experian, and Transunion), this centralized service allows consumers to request free annual credit reports.

Equifax
www.equifax.com or call 1-877-576-5734

Experian
www.experian.com/fraud
or call 1-888-397-3742

Transunion
www.transunion.com or call 1-800-680-7289

Identity theft
Report identity theft by contacting the Federal Trade Commission at ftc.gov/idtheft.

DONATIONS

Goodwill Industries International
www.goodwill.org
Sells clothing and household goods.

Salvation Army
www.salvationarmy.com
Sells clothing and household goods.

Give the Gift of Sight
www.givethegiftofsight.com
Provides free prescription eyewear to individuals in North America and developing countries around the world. Drop off eyeglasses or sunglasses at LensCrafters, Pearle Vision, Sears Optical, Target Optical, BJ's Optical, Sunglass Hut, or Lions Club.

Hungry for Music
www.hungryformusic.org
Distributes used musical instruments to underprivileged children.

Luggage
www.suitcasesforkids.org
Provides luggage for foster children who move from home to home.

Reader to Reader
www.readertoreader.org
Accepts books for children and teens and distributes to school libraries nationwide.

INVESTING

Socially Responsible
Socialinvest.org
www.socialinvest.org

Basic Investment Advice
Investopedia.com
www.investopedia.com/university/beginner

The Little Book of Common Sense Investing, by John C. Bogle (Wiley, 2007)

Save Your Retirement, by Frank Armstrong III and Paul B. Brown (FT Press, 2009)

Intermediate Investment Advice
Securities and Exchange Commission
http://www.sec.gov/investor/pubs/assetallocation.htm

Index Investing for Dummies, by Russell Wild (Wiley, 2009)

Bond Investing for Dummies, by Russell Wild (Wiley, 2008)

Financial Supermarkets
Fidelity
www.fidelity.com

Charles Schwab
www.schwab.com

TIAA-CREF
www.tiaacref.com

T. Rowe Price
www.troweprice.com

Vanguard
www.vanguard.com

LEGAL

LawDepot
www.Lawdepot.com

Legalzoom
www.legalzoom.com

MANAGING YOUR MONEY DAY-TO-DAY

Dinkytown
www.dinkytown.com

Expensr
www.expensr.com

Mint
www.mint.com

Quicken
www.quicken.com

wesabe
www.wesabe.com

Best Rates on CDs, Savings Accounts, Money Markets, and Mortgages

Bankrate.com
www.bankrate.com

Moneyaisle.com
www.moneyaisle.com

Vanguard
www.Vanguard.com

Children, Money lessons in comics form

www.centsables.com

Finding a Financial Professional

The Certified Financial Planning Board of Standards
www.cfp.net

CFA Institute
www.cfainstitute.org

Financial Planning Association
www.fpanet.org

National Association of Personal Financial Advisors
www.napfa.org

Loans, Arranging, from Family and Friends

Virgin Money
www.virginmoneyus.com

Up-to-date Information on Financial Everything

Yahoo finance
http://finance.yahoo.com

Bloomberg
www.bloomberg.com

CNN Financial News
www.cnnfn.com

Morningstar
www.morningstar.com

Moneychimp
www.moneychimp.com

MEDICAL

Medical Tourism

IndUShealth
www.indushealth.com

MedSolution
www.MedSolution.com

Prescriptions

Partnership for Prescription Assistance
www.pparx.org
Program for affordable drugs.

Canada pharmacy
www.canadapharmacy.com

MISCELLANEOUS

www.hulu.com

www.networksolutions.com

Small Business Administration
www.sba.com

www.wonderwebusa.com

www.yellowpages.com

OFFICE AND FILING SUPPLIES

DAY RUNNER
www.DayRunner.com

Exposures
www.exposuresonline.com
Offers binders, magazine holders, et al.

Fitter
www.fitter1.com
Fitter Active Sitting Disc transforms your
chair. Check out other ergonomically correct
products.

iPrint
www.iprint.com
Business cards.

Levenger
www.Levenger.com
Binders, calendars, magazine holders, and
more.

Office Depot
www.officedepot.com

OfficeMax
www.officemax.com

Relax the Back
www.Relaxtheback.com
Ergonomically correct office furniture.

See Jane Work
www.seejanework.com

Staples
www.staples.com

The Geek Squad
www.geeksquad.com
Computer and IT help.

Vistaprint
www.vistaprint.com
Business cards.

ONLINE AUCTION AND SALE SITES

Craig's List
www.craigslist.com

eBay
www.ebay.com

PHONE SERVICE THROUGH
THE INTERNET

Skype
Skype.com

Tracphone
www.tracphone.com

Vonage
Vonage.com

PROFESSIONAL ASSOCIATIONS

Clutterers Anonymous
www.clutterersanonymous.net

Codependents Anonymous
www.codependents.org

Messies Anonymous
www.messies.com

National Association of Professional
Organizers (NAPO)
www.napo.net
856-380-6828

RECYCLE

1-800-GOT-JUNK?
www.1800gotjunk.com
or call 1-800-468-5865
Removes just about anything (furniture, appliances, electronics, yard waste, and renovation debris) and makes every effort to recycle or donate items.

Rechargeable Battery Recycling Corporation (RBRC)
www.call2recycle.org or call 1-877-273-2925
Recycles used portable rechargeable batteries and old cell phones.

Worldwatch Institute
worldwatch.org/resources/go_green_save_green

REDUCE AND STOP UNWANTED MAIL

Direct Marking Association (DMA)
www.the-dma.org
Reduces your total volume of mail when you register for the Direct Marketing Association's Mail Preference Service (MPS).

Opt-Out of Preapproved Credit Card and Insurance Offers
www.optoutprescreen.com
or call 1-888-567-8688
Official Web site of the Credit Reporting Industry to accept and process consumer requests to opt-in or opt-out of prescreened credit card and insurance offers.

RETIREMENT

Insurance, Long-Term
National Academy of Elder Law Attorneys
www.naela.org

How Much Will You Need to Retire?
Firecalc.com
www.firecalc.com

T. Rowe Price Retirement income Calculator
http://www3.troweprice.com/ric/ric/public/ric.do

Social Security
www.ssa.gov
Estimate of your Social Security payments when you retire.

SMART SAVING AND SPENDING

The 1-2-3 Money Plan, by Gregory Karp, FT Press, 2009

AARP, American Association of Retired People
www.AARP.org

Auto Club
www.autoclub.com

Consumerist.com
www.consumerist.com

Suddenly Frugal
www.suddenlyfrugal.com

Union Plus
www.unionplus.org

www.PaperBackSwap.com
An online service for swapping books with others.

Priceprotect.com
www.priceprotectr.com

Shopper.com
www.shopper.com

Green Saving

Environmental Defense Fund's online quiz to calculate your personal energy impact
http://www.fightglobalwarming.com/carboncalculator.cfm
Online quiz to calculate your personal energy impact.

Environmental Protection Agency
www.Energystar.gov
Click the "Federal Tax Credits" icon and find out what energy-saving upgrades to your home might earn you a refund at tax time.

Reusable plastic bag
www.reusablebags.com

SEARCH ENGINES

Bing
www.bing.com

Google
www.google.com

SHOP

Digital Gifts
Creative Memories
www.creativememories.com

Kodak Gallery
www.kodakgallery.com

Shutterfly
www.shutterfly.com

Snapfish
www.snapfish.com

Coupons
Coupons for DVD kiosks
www.InsideRedbox.com

MyBargainBuddy
www.mybargainbuddy.com

FatWallet
www.fatwallet.com

Slickdeals
www.slickdeals.net

Mystery Shoppers
www.mysteryshoppersamerica.com

www.secretshopper.com

Stores
Bed, Bath, and Beyond
www.bedbathandbeyond.com

Costco
www.costco.com

Michaels Arts & Crafts
www.michaels.com

Target
www.target.com

The Container Store
www.thecontainerstore.com

TAX FORMS AND TAX HELP

1040 or 1040EZ
www.irs.gov

AARP tax help
https://locator.aarp.org/vmis/sites/tax_aide_
locator.jsp

IRS free tax preparation software
www.irs.gov/efile

TRAVEL

Flight, Hotel, and Car Reservations
www.bing.com

www.cheaptickets.com

www.DigitalCity.com

www.expedia.com

www.farealert.com

www.hotwire.com

www.kayak.com

www.orbitz.com

www.sidestep.com

www.travelocity.com

www.travelzoo.com

General Travel Information
Automobile Association of America
www.aaa.com

Centers for Disease Control
www.cdc.com/travel
Provides travel health information.

Department of Homeland Security
www.travel.state.gov/passport
Apply for a passport or get information on
traveling abroad.

National Weather Service
www.nws.noaa.gov
Weather reports on destinations in the United
States.

Transportation Security Administration
www.tsa.gov/travelers
Updated information on items a traveler is
permitted to bring on an airplane.

Weather Channel
www.weather.com
Weather reports on destinations in the United
States.

Weather Underground
www.wunderground.com
Weather forecasts for destinations in the
United States and abroad.

THE AUTHORS

Regina Leeds
www.reginaleeds.com

Russell Wild
www.globalportfolios.net

INDEX